MEXICAN POL...

THE DYNAMICS OF CHANGE

HOWARD HANDELMAN
University of Wisconsin–Milwaukee

St. Martin's Press   New York

Sponsoring editor: Beth A. Gillett
Development editor: Meg Spilleth
Editorial assistant: Kimberly Wurtzel
Manager, Publishing services: Emily Berleth
Publishing services associate: Meryl Perrin
Project management: Graphic Composition, Inc.
Production supervisor: Scott Lavelle
Cover design: Evelyn Horovicz
Cover photo: Cliff Hollenbeck / International Stock

Library of Congress Catalog Card Number: 95-73203

Manufactured in the United States of America.

10 9 8 7
f e d c b

For information, write:
St. Martin's Press, Inc.
175 Fifth Avenue
New York, NY 10010

ISBN: 0-312-10154-6

Contents

Preface

Mexican Politics: The Dynamics of Change analyzes the transformation of Mexico's political and economic systems, discussing the most critical challenges confronting that nation today. The text is designed for undergraduate courses on Latin American politics and is also appropriate for wider comparative politics courses. Following a historical chapter that traces the antecedents of modern Mexico, the book focuses on contemporary political institutions and policy.

The opening chapter introduces the reader to the series of dramatic events that have shaken Mexico since the closing years of the Salinas administration. It focuses particularly on the Zapatista uprising in Chiapas, using it as a vehicle for examining the text's central questions:

1. Can Mexico's political leaders transform government institutions, the political party system, and the representation of group interests sufficiently to allow a relatively smooth transition from authoritarianism to democracy?
2. Can the Mexican economy resume steady growth while also moving toward a more equitable distribution of wealth, income, and services?

Within this framework other important issues are discussed: the challenge of decentralizing the state and establishing a better balance between the branches of government; court reform; electoral fraud; campaign financing; possibilities for political participation; protection of human rights; political corruption; corporatist group representation and potential alternatives; narcotrafficking; privatization of the economy; the renewed economic crisis since 1994; restraining inflation and the foreign debt.

Chapter 2 offers an overview of Mexico's historical development and discusses how that legacy continues to influence the country's contemporary political and economic systems. Chapters 3–5 respectively examine the branches of national government, the changing role of political parties and elections, and the nature of interest group representation and popular protest. In particular, *Mexican Politics* analyzes electoral competition more extensively than have prior texts, reflecting the growing importance and competitiveness of national and state elections. Chapter 6 discusses Mexico's political economy, focusing on the current neoliberal development model and the ongoing challenge of restoring economic growth and improving socioeconomic equity.

Chapter 7 explores Mexico's relations with the United States in a historical context and then focuses on contemporary issues, particularly trade and the NAFTA accord, immigration, and the narcotics trade. Given Mexico's growing economic and political importance to the United States, these issues may be of particular interest to many American readers. Finally, the book throughout analyzes recent dramatic political and economic developments: the Chiapas uprising, the assassinations of Luis Donaldo Colosio and José Francisco Ruiz Massieu, the startling decline of Carlos Salinas, the financial crisis of 1994–95, and the inauspicious start of the Zedillo administration. Chapter 8 analyzes important recent trends and looks to the future. A list of acronyms follows chapter 8.

Mexican Politics focuses on the relationship between Mexico's socioeconomic modernization (expanded literacy, urbanization, the growth of the middle class) and growing pressures for more political pluralism. It places greater stress on political institutions than have other texts, as the country begins to move away from extreme presidential dominance. Finally, the book speculates on the likelihood that Mexico will soon join the current, worldwide wave of democratization.

I would like to thank Don Reisman, formerly at St. Martin's, for conceiving of this book and asking me to write it. I owe a special thanks to Herzonia and Arminda Yañez for being such wonderful friends and hosts over the years in my visits to Mexico. Thanks also to Francisco Zapata (El Colegio de México) for sharing with me his knowledge of Mexican labor and to Ricardo Pascoe of the PRD for his insights into Mexican politics particularly as it relates to his political party. The generous support of the University of Wisconsin–Milwaukee's Center for Latin America and a UWM sabbatical made the research for this book possible.

Finally, my thanks to those Mexico scholars who read various portions of this book and offered helpful comments: Joseph Klesner, Kenyon College; Eduardo Magalhaes III, Simpson College; Peter Snow, University of Iowa (retired); Dale Story, University of Texas, Arlington; Keith Yanner, Central College; and Michelle Zebich-Knos, Kennesaw State College. Needless to say, all errors of fact or interpretation are my own.

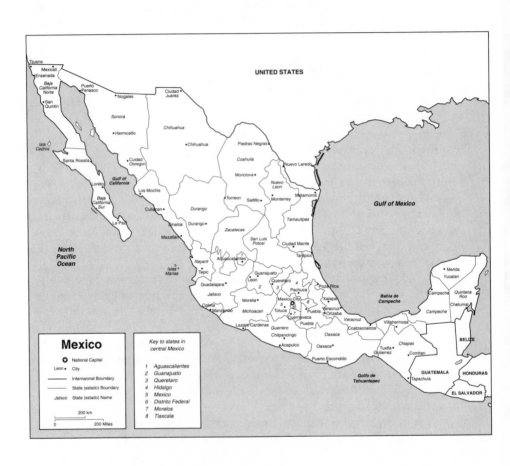

UNITED STATES

Tijuana
Mexicali
Ensenada
Baja
California
Norte
Puerto
Penasco
San
Quintin

Nogales
Ciudad
Juarez

Sonora
Chihuahua

Hermosillo
Chihuahua
Piedras Negras

Isla
Cedros

Santa Rosalia
Ciudad
Obregon
Coahuila
Nuevo Laredo

Gulf of
California
Los Mochis
Monclova

Loreto
Nuevo
Leon
Matamoros

Baja
California
Sur
La Paz
Culiacan
Torreon
Saltillo
Monterrey

Durango
Tamaulipas

North
Pacific
Ocean
Sinaloa
Durango
Zacatecas
San Luis
Potosi
Ciudad Mante

Mazatlan

Islas
Marias
Nayarit
Tepic
Aguascalientes

Gulf of Mexico

Guanajuato
Queretaro
Pachuca
Poza Rica
Bahia de
Campeche

Guadalajara
Leon
2
3
4
Xalapa
Campeche
Merida
Yucatan

Jalisco
Morelia
Mexico City
8
Veracruz
Orizaba
Quintana
Roo
Chetumal

Colima
Manzanillo
Michoacan
Toluca
5
6
1
7
Puebla
Veracruz
Villahermosa
Campeche

Lazaro Cardenas
Cuernavaca
Puebla
Oaxaca
Coatzacoalcos
BELIZE

Guerrero
Chilpancingo
Oaxaca
Tuxtla
Gutierrez
Chiapas
Comitan
GUATEMALA
HONDURAS

Acapulco
Puerto Escondido
Golfo de
Tehuantepec
Tapachula
EL SALVADOR

Mexico

⊗ National Capital
Leon ● City
——— Internaional Boundary
——— State (estado) Boundary
Jalisco State (estado) Name

200 km
0   200 Miles

Key to states in
central Mexico

1 Aguascalientes
2 Guanajuato
3 Queretaro
4 Hidalgo
5 Mexico
6 Distrito Federal
7 Morelos
8 Tlaxcala

1

Mexico: The Ongoing Crisis

As New Year's Day 1994 approached, Mexico stood poised to savor a major diplomatic achievement. On that day, the North American Free Trade Agreement (NAFTA) would take effect, joining the economies of Mexico, the United States, and Canada into the world's largest free trade zone. While NAFTA has subsequently altered economic relations less than either its proponents or critics predicted, its symbolic importance should not be underestimated (see chapter 7).

From the time that it was initially proposed by President Carlos Salinas de Gortari in 1990,* NAFTA had been principally a Mexican initiative, impacting that country far more than it did either of its two trading partners. The accord was designed to enshrine Mexico's transition toward an open economy and to solidify its ever-increasing economic links with the United States. But NAFTA was supposed to be far more than a trade agreement. It also was intended to symbolize Mexico's ascent from the Third World toward the First. The George Bush administration understood this full well. Indeed, U.S. support for the treaty was motivated, in part, by Washington's desire to reinforce the Mexican political system and give President Salinas and the PRI, Mexico's official party, an international stamp of approval.

As Carlos Salinas entered the last year of his presidency, he could look back with satisfaction at a record of unexpected success. Brought to office in 1988 in an election severely tainted by fraud, he had assumed the presidency with questionable legitimacy and a reputation for being an intellectual and a technocrat (a professionally trained government administrator) with no demonstrable political skills. Once inaugurated, however, he proved to be a most astute national leader. His administration reduced inflation, began a gradual economic recovery (after years of decline), privatized much of the vast state economic sector, reduced trade protectionism, and introduced a major public works and social services program for the poor. In the process, Salinas became a popular president at home and a respected leader abroad.**

* Many Latin American men use their father's surname followed by their mother's, particularly in official contexts. In everyday usage, however, they generally drop their mother's family name. When appropriate I will employ the double surname in the first usage (Salinas de Gortari), particularly for contemporary figures, and subsequently employ the more commonly used single surname (Salinas). Some important political figures, however, use only their father's surname, while others always use both names (Ruiz Massieu).
** As we will see, however, his popularity and favorable reputation totally collapsed soon after he left office. Most Mexicans now blame his economic policies for the current financial crisis. Soon

1

Only weeks before NAFTA's inauguration, Salinas, like all modern Mexican presidents, had handpicked his expected successor. Constitutionally barred from seeking a second term, he had considered a short list of "precandidates" (potential candidates), consulted with key political and interest group leaders, and finally revealed the individual whom the PRI (Institutional Revolutionary Party) would enthusiastically nominate as its next presidential candidate, Luis Donaldo Colosio Murrieta, the nation's secretary of social development. Because no official-party presidential candidate had been defeated since the party's founding in 1929, Colosio could reasonably have expected victory in the August 1994 election.

To be sure, the previous presidential contest had exposed the PRI's vulnerability. The country's economic decline under President Miguel de la Madrid (1982–88), falling living standards, and public disenchantment with government performance had opened up new opportunities for the political opposition. Even the highly suspect official vote count had awarded Salinas only 50.7 percent of the total valid votes, down 20 percentage points from the PRI's 1982 performance (though still a comfortable 18 percent ahead of his nearest rival). There is no way of knowing what result an honest tally would have yielded. But one comprehensive postelectoral survey indicated that Salinas's true total was about 35 percent, giving him a narrow 3–4 percent margin of victory in a tight, three-way race.[1] Yet, despite his inauspicious start, Carlos Salinas's effective presidency, coupled with the opposition's organizational weaknesses, had seemingly restored the PRI to its preeminent position in the 1991 state and federal elections.[2]

In selecting Colosio as the PRI's next presidential candidate, Salinas once again turned to the group of young, highly educated, technocrats who have led Mexico for some two decades. Like all Salinas's precandidates, as well as the past two presidents, Colosio had earned an advanced degree from a top-ranked American university. Though he was not the most popular or charismatic candidate Salinas could have named, Colosio's record as director of PRONASOL (the government's popular program for welfare, social services, and infrastructure in low-income areas) had created an important base of political support for him. His long association with the outgoing president (whose campaign he managed in 1988) also assured Salinas that the next administration would maintain policy continuity.

In astonishingly short order, however, Salinas's plans for choreographing NAFTA and the impending presidential race unraveled. Rather than projecting an image of a confident, modernizing, but stable country, as President Salinas and his advisors had hoped, Mexico soon appeared underdeveloped and somewhat chaotic. On the very day that NAFTA took effect, approximately 600 to

---

after government investigators arrested his brother, Raúl, for organizing a major political assassination, the former president left the country in disgrace. Subsequently it was discovered that Raúl Salinas had nearly $100 million hidden in a Swiss bank and probably several hundred million dollars elsewhere. Not surprisingly, Carlos Salinas is now the object of widespread scorn.

1,000 peasant soldiers of the Zapatista Army of National Liberation (EZLN) captured four towns in the impoverished southern state of Chiapas and held them for several days.[3] During the weeks that followed, foreign network television, newspapers, and magazines focused, not on NAFTA or on the modern, high-tech sectors of Mexican life, but on the bandanna-covered faces of the EZLN's Mayan rebels and their charismatic and eminently quotable spokesperson, "Subcomandante Marcos" (Subcommander Marcos, a military pseudonym).

Chiapas was but the first of two blows inflicted on the Mexican body politic during the early months of 1994. On 23 March, the PRI's presidential candidate, Luis Donaldo Colosio, was assassinated in the city of Tijuana. The Mexican public reeled in disbelief as their country's image was further tarnished. During the course of the Mexican Revolution and its aftermath (1910–29), political violence and assassination had been all too common. Since that time, however, the nation had enjoyed an unprecedented era of political stability and continuity. To be sure, the deaths of several public figures over the years had aroused widespread suspicion of deeper political intrigue, most recently the 1993 murder of Cardinal Juan Jesús Posadas Ocampo (allegedly the work of drug dealers in a case of mistaken identity). But no political leader of Colosio's rank had been murdered since 1928. Consequently, the candidate's death traumatized the nation and profoundly undermined its self-confidence.

Only six months later another leading PRI figure, party secretary general José Francisco Ruiz Massieu, was also shot dead. Many Mexicans suspected either the conservative wing of the PRI or drug traffickers (or possibly both) of being behind the two murders. These events, coupled with a rash of high-profile kidnappings of Mexican businessmen and continuing public suspicions about the cause of Cardinal Posadas Ocampo's death, encouraged a spate of conspiracy theories and a sense of national malaise.

The Chiapas rebellion and the assassinations raised fundamental questions about Mexico's stability and the viability of its political and economic institutions. When Mexico entered a deep recession shortly after Salinas left office, the political regime suffered a further loss of legitimacy. Is the country on the verge of a major upheaval, as Subcomandante Marcos and his Zapatista supporters would have us believe? Or is Mexico still the maturing incipient democracy that government officials affirm? There is no simple answer.

In many respects Mexico has been a bastion of political stability for more than sixty years, particularly when compared with other Latin American nations. Indeed, since the fall of the Soviet Communist Party, the PRI has been the world's most long-lived ruling party. All of Mexico's presidents since the 1930s have peacefully completed their term of office and turned power over to their elected successor. Thus, the country has avoided the coups so common to the region, while containing, though not entirely eliminating, the military's political influence.[4] And, although Mexico has experienced several guerrilla insurgencies in recent decades, none of them (including the Zapatistas) have posed a fundamental threat to national stability comparable to that of their counterparts in Central America, Peru, Colombia, Uruguay, and Argentina. Still, there can be no doubt that Mexico is once again in crisis, the latest in a series since the 1960s. Continuing political intrigue and a steep economic decline since early 1994 have greatly increased popular apprehension.

CYCLES OF CRISES

For nearly three decades analysts of Mexican politics have depicted the country as repeatedly being in a state of crisis or major transition, "on the brink" or "at a crossroads."[5] The nation has faced a series of challenges, each seemingly imperiling the political order: the 1968 massacre of several hundred young protestors at Mexico City's Plaza of the Three Cultures (Tlatelolco) demonstrated the government's potential for repression; President Luis Echeverría Alvarez's clashes with Mexican business leaders and the ensuing financial crisis in the mid-1970s provoked rumors of a military coup; the 1982 external debt crisis and the country's resultant economic decline ended its "economic miracle" and undermined the regime's legitimacy; the government's inept response to Mexico City's massive earthquake in 1985 further exposed the state's inefficiency and corruption; the 1988 presidential election, which many Mexicans still believe was really won by opposition candidate Cuauhtémoc Cárdenas, demonstrated the limits of Mexican democracy. In 1994, the Chiapas rebellion and the Colosio and Ruiz Massieu assassinations again raised doubts about the political system's stability. Most recently, the 1995 economic crisis has brought the government's current development model into question.

Each crisis has seemingly placed the country at a crossroads, facing a choice between meaningful reform or dangerous decay. But throughout these challenges the nation's political elite has demonstrated tremendous resiliency and an amazing capacity to adjust, while still resisting fundamental change in the political order, no matter how advisable.[6] In the years following the Tlatelolco massacre, the government opened up the electoral system by lowering the voting age and allowing opposition parties greater congressional representation. In time, many of that era's student activists were coopted into government posts. The 1982 debt crisis led Presidents de la Madrid and Salinas to abandon Mexico's failed industrial development model and restructure the state sector. Unlike other Latin American leaders who have implemented harsh neoliberal reforms,* however, Salinas created a popular, grassroots welfare and public works program to ameliorate the pain that restructuring invariably inflicts on the poor. And, following the Chiapas uprising, the government introduced limited socioeconomic changes in the state and substantial electoral reforms at the national level, making the next presidential election the clean-

---

* Neoliberal policies, contrary to what the name may suggest to American readers, feature reduced state economic activity and the granting of greater free rein to free market forces (see chapter 6 for further discussion of neoliberalism and its meaning outside the United States).

est ever.[7] So even though the EZLN rebellion and the Colosio murder staggered the PRI leadership, the party regrouped within months and swept the 1994 elections, this time without recourse to major fraud.

Like Carlos Salinas, the current president, Ernesto Zedillo Ponce de León, also began his term inauspiciously. Because Mexico's growing trade deficit had left the nation's currency substantially overvalued, his administration was soon forced to let the peso depreciate. The inevitable consequence has been inflation and unemployment. At the same time, the government has been haunted by deepening public suspicions regarding the recent political assassinations, as the authorities constantly change their theories and explanations. The rebellion in Chiapas remains contained, but when President Zedillo launched a military offensive against the Zapatistas early in his term it fizzled.

Once again dealing with a crisis through conciliation, the government brokered a far-reaching electoral reform agreement with the major opposition parties. Announced at the close of 1995, the proposed electoral law will likely move Mexico closer toward fair national and state elections. Should President Zedillo also restore economic growth and control inflation, and should the country's latest electoral reforms lead to relatively fair electoral contests and honest vote counts, Mexico's ruling elite may once again keep the wolf from the door. That is to say, such success might yet put off the fundamental restructuring of political power. Regardless of who controls the government, however, the next generation of political leaders will have to address two fundamental challenges. Until they do, those flaws will continue to wear away at the nation's political and social fabric, guaranteeing future crises.

The first challenge is Mexico's poor distribution of income and resources, which first resisted decades of rapid economic expansion (1940–80) and then intensified during the economic crisis of the 1980s. Thus, the richest 20 percent of the population enjoys a disproportionately large share of the national income (as high as 64 percent in some years), while the poorest half receives correspondingly little (as low as 15 percent).[8] The rural population in particular still lacks adequate access to social services and receives a paltry share of national income. To be sure, Mexico's income concentration is less severe than Honduras's, Brazil's, and Jamaica's. But it is more extreme than in El Salvador, Chile, Costa Rica, India, Pakistan, and a range of other Third World nations.[9] It is such socioeconomic injustice, along with political repression and corruption, that motivated the Zapatista rebellion and gave it such resonance throughout the nation.

Mexico's second underlying weakness is its authoritarian tradition and the state's unwillingness so far to allow full democracy. Over the years scholars have debated the nature of the political system:

> In the optimistic spirit of the 1950s some analysts depicted the regime as "one-party democracy" in the process of . . . evolution toward "true" . . . democracy. During the disenchantment of the 1970s, most observers described the system as "authoritarian," but even this characterization was subject to qualification.[10]

Today, most analysts characterize Mexican politics as semiauthoritarian. Although the country has active opposition parties, competitive elections, a relatively free press, free speech, and other important aspects of democracy, it also still has single-party rule, unequal election competition, political corruption, manipulation of the press, and periodic state repression of dissent. At the same time, while the Mexican state is not yet democratic, it is also not fully authoritarian. That is, it is not as repressive as Cuba's government or as the right-wing military regimes that have ruled Brazil, Chile, and Uruguay in recent decades. Nor does the government systematically brutalize the population as have recent governments in Haiti, El Salvador, Guatemala, and Peru.

In the past quarter century, Mexico's political system has opened up considerably. That political liberalization has affected the electoral system so that many opposition candidates now have a real chance of winning local and state elections. Although the PRI has yet to lose a presidential race, the opposition parties' official share of the vote in the 1988 and 1994 elections finally reached 50 percent (with the real total in 1988 undoubtedly higher). Though the PRI's campaign resources still far outstrip the opposition's, recent reforms in election procedures are producing more honest vote counts. Although no non-PRI governor ever held office prior to 1988, the National Action Party (PAN) now holds that post in four states.

Still, for every sign of democratic transition there are lingering signs of authoritarian resistance. Since the 1970s the government has enacted a series of electoral reforms that have substantially augmented opposition representation in Congress, though never threatening the PRI majority. More recent reforms have produced fairly honest election counts for the presidency, but fraud remains a problem at the local and state levels. President Salinas overturned several PRI gubernatorial victories that appeared to be fraudulent, but the leading opposition candidate for governor of Chiapas in the 1994 election was nearly killed in a suspicious hit-and-run traffic accident. There and in several other states the Party of the Democratic Revolution (PRD) alleged that it had been denied gubernatorial victories through fraud and intimidation. Thus, the observer of Mexican politics today is reminded of Zeno's paradox. That ancient Greek philosopher posed the following question: if the distance between two objects is repeatedly cut in half, how long will it take until the two come together? The answer, of course, is never.

Similarly, as Mexico's political leaders constantly "halve the distance" between their semiauthoritarian regime and authentic democracy, one must wonder if they will ever reach the end point. Lorenzo Meyer, a noted Mexican intellectual, has compared his country's wait for democracy to events in Samuel Beckett's famed play *Waiting for Godot*. Two characters alternate between hope and despair, expecting the arrival of the mysterious Godot, with whom they have an appointment. As the play ends, Godot has not arrived but the protagonists still have not abandoned hope.[11] In Mexico, increased urbanization, literacy, and education have intensified public pressures for democracy and social justice. But the PRI's latest presidential victory suggests that, whatever the electorate's discontent with the status quo, it may still be more fearful of change.

MEXICO'S IMPORTANCE TO THE UNITED STATES

With some eighty-five million people, Mexico has the world's eleventh largest population and thirteenth biggest economy. It also contains the world's fourth largest proven oil reserves, and as of 1990 produced more manufactured goods than either South Korea or Taiwan, East Asia's emerging industrial powers.[12] Since the start of the 1980s, Mexico has been the United States's third largest trading partner, trailing only Canada and Japan. Yet, despite its tremendous importance to the United States, Americans have surprisingly little familiarity with Mexico's political system, economy, or culture.

Although American media coverage of Mexico has increased in recent years, particularly during the NAFTA debate, more press space and air time is still devoted to Britain, Japan, Russia, and Germany.[13] And while millions of Americans vacation in Mexico City, Cancún, and Acapulco, few realize that Mexico experienced the twentieth century's first mass revolution or that the country has enjoyed Latin America's longest period of civilian rule.

Mexico's political system is in many ways quite impenetrable, lending itself to the type of speculation that characterized kremlinology during the Cold War. Political scientists often differ sharply in their interpretations of the most fundamental aspects of the country's political system. But it would be erroneous to view Mexican politics as incomprehensible or as totally distinct from politics in the United States. For example, the conspiracy theories surrounding Colosio's and Ruiz Massieu's murder and the public's cynicism regarding government inquiries are reminiscent of the aftermath of President John F. Kennedy's assassination. Similarly, anyone familiar with the ballot-box manipulations carried out by Chicago's political machine during its heyday can better appreciate the PRI's sophisticated electoral techniques.

Some American analysts have focused on the many differences between Mexico and the United States. For example, more than a decade ago Alan Riding observed in his book *Distant Neighbors:*

> Probably nowhere in the world do two countries as different as Mexico and the United States live side by side. . . . Probably nowhere in the world do two neighbors understand each other so little. More than by levels of development, the two countries are separated by language, religion, race, philosophy and history.[14]

But while Riding quite properly noted the anomalies of a Third World country sharing an extensive border with an advanced industrial democracy, in some respects he overstated the cultural gap between the two countries, a gap that has narrowed further since his book was published. In fact, the two cultures often blend along their border. In the *barrios* of Los Angeles, San Diego, San Antonio, Tucson, and Albuquerque, where Spanish is the dominant language, one can eat the food, hear the music, and view the *fiestas* of Mexico. Approximately 5 percent of all Americans, far more in the border states, primarily speak Spanish at home, making it the United States's second language. On the other side of the frontier, *maquiladoras* assemble manufactured goods for the

American market, as vast quantities of American consumer goods, movies, and music regularly penetrate Mexican popular culture.

Observing this phenomenon, one scholar has coined the term "MexAmerica" to describe the cultural blend and economic bonds that have developed on both sides of the Mexican-U.S. border.[15] Lest one underestimate the importance of this phenomenon, the border is over two thousand miles long, and "by [the year] 2000, it is estimated that the *real* border between these two countries—which extends for 100 miles on either side of the legal demarcation—will be the most populated area in North America."[16]

Of course each society's influence extends far beyond the border region. Mexican American music (played by groups such as Los Lobos and the Texas Tornados) and Mexican food (often in its perverted, mass-market forms) are now an integral part of American popular culture. Salsa has replaced ketchup as America's most widely consumed condiment. Similarly, in Mexico's cities, Denny's restaurants, hamburgers, American rock, and a host of U.S. commercial products are all-pervasive. Some two-thirds of Mexican foreign trade is transacted with the United States.[17] Manufactured products have replaced petroleum and agricultural products as Mexico's principal export to the United States. Even before NAFTA, Mexico was the leading exporter of color televisions, computer keyboards, and refrigerators to the U.S. market. Each year it also sends north automobiles, engines, and auto parts valued at over $4 billion.[18]

Not only commercial trade but a substantial number of people cross the frontier. Each day about three-quarters of a million people, some 270 million annually, cross the border legally between Mexico and the United States. Between 1960 and 1990, nearly one-fifth of all legal immigrants to the United States, some 2.75 million people, came from Mexico. In addition, close to 1 million undocumented Mexican workers are apprehended annually.[19] While Americans are becoming increasingly apprehensive about that immigration, many experts argue that these legal and illegal immigrants have filled important gaps in the U.S. labor market, accepting jobs that Americans are unwilling to take (chapter 7).

Because Mexico's economic and cultural ties to the United States will certainly increase in the coming decades, Americans need to better understand the important political and economic transformations currently taking place in their southern neighbor.

THE REVOLUTIONARY TRADITION

Mexicans do not call their own war of independence a revolution. As in the rest of Latin America, the overthrow of Spanish colonial rule did not precipitate fundamental changes in the social and economic order. Society remained highly stratified by class and race, with wealth and power still highly concentrated. Indians and Mestizos, who constituted most of the population, had few political and economic resources. Foreign intervention and internal struggles between regional strongmen produced chronic political instability and enfeebled government for much of the nineteenth century. Finally, in 1876 General Porfirio Díaz imposed a thirty-five-year dictatorship that brought the country political stability and economic growth, though at a considerable cost. In time, his regime's economic injustices and political repression unleashed a tide of discontent.[20]

Mexico's revolution was the twentieth century's first mass insurrection, preceding Russia's by seven years. During the next decade, "the wind that swept Mexico" changed the course of that nation's history—uprooting villages, destroying cities, and costing over one million lives.[21] By the time the fighting ended, the country had a new constitution and the start of substantial changes in the political and socioeconomic order.[22] But it would be more than another decade before political stability was fully restored.

Unlike other twentieth-century revolutions, Mexico's insurgency lacked both a dominant leader and a unifying party. No revolutionary figure had the stature or authority of Lenin, Mao Zedong, or Fidel Castro. And many of the most important participants—Francisco Madero, Emiliano Zapata, Pancho Villa, Venustiano Carranza—failed to survive the upheaval. The many revolutionary armies were a heterogeneous lot without a unified command like that of Nicaragua's Sandinistas or China's Communist Party. Mexico's own revolutionary party was not established until a dozen years after the struggle had concluded. Thus, the construction of a new order was more gradual and moderate. Over time, however, a new ruling elite emerged, consisting of "generals who . . . were not career soldiers, but victorious revolutionaries, politicians on horseback."[23]

The Mexican Revolution also was not as radical as many other twentieth-century insurrections. But the changes it wrought were far from inconsequential. Mexico was the first Latin American nation to topple its traditional, oligarchical power structure. Though the masses remained marginalized in many ways, a political class emerged apart from the economic elite. Over the years the ruling class's composition has changed periodically. The early "politicians on horseback," largely from the country's northwest, gradually gave way to civilian politicians primarily born in the central states. They, in turn, have been supplanted by highly educated technocrats, usually from Mexico City's middle class.[24] But whatever their origins the political elite has repeatedly demonstrated tremendous acumen and agility over the years.[25] In the name of revolutionary change, they have protected much of the status quo, skillfully deflected challenges to the political system, but changed when change was unavoidable.

CORPORATISM, REPRESENTATION, AND STABILITY

How to facilitate change while restoring political stability: this was the daunting challenge facing Mexico's new political elite as the country emerged from the revolutionary upheaval. The years prior to the *Porfiriato* (the long reign of Porfirio Díaz) had been marked by civil conflict, constant government turnover, and chronic instability. By establishing centralized control over regional *caciques* (strongmen), Díaz provided both stability and the framework for economic growth. But like most dictatorships the *Porfiriato* could not accommodate social change or permit a peaceful transfer of power. In 1910 its repressive order gave way to nearly two decades of violence and political chaos.

To achieve the delicate balance between stability and orderly change, the country's revolutionary statesmen fashioned two critical institutions. First, they restored a powerful presidency, but limited the chief executive to a single, six-year term. Since the 1920s, then, Mexico's presidents have exercised enormous power, restricted by few checks and balances. In that respect, the nation has maintained a centralized, authoritarian tradition dating to the Spanish colonial viceroy. However, the modern single-term limit has offered two important advantages: first, it has prevented the resurgence of a prolonged personal dictatorship such as the *Porfiriato;* second, since each new president brings in a new administrative team, every six years there is a rotation of high-ranking talent and a regeneration of ideas and perspectives.

The second critical postinsurrectionary innovation was the creation of a ruling party. The National Revolutionary Party (PNR) was designed to bring the country's major political bosses and the plethora of small political parties under a single umbrella.* As the official party evolved, it took on a broader function, the representation and cooptation of mass interests. President Lázaro Cárdenas (1934–40) reorganized the party and gave it a corporatist structure.

> Corporatism . . . rejects the notion of open competition and the principle of government neutrality in favor of a more deliberate effort to organize and regulate public-private sector relations. The government assumes responsibility for directing the society, and private economic and social groups become its instruments for doing so. Instead of competing with each other to influence officials, interest groups deal with them directly and on the latter's terms.[26]

Under these arrangements, the state recognizes specific organizations, such as labor unions or business groups, as the sole legitimate interest group representing their sector of society. While alien to most Americans, corporatism is quite common in Latin America and in many European nations. Depending on whether it operates in a democratic or an authoritarian setting, corporatism subjects interest groups to varying degrees of state control. In Scandinavian and British corporatism, for example, loose links to a democratic state still allow interest groups considerable autonomy. On the other hand, in earlier fascist regimes such as Italy's and Spain's, state-dominated corporatism was an important source of social control.[27]

Presidents Plutarco Elías Calles (1924–28) and Lázaro Cárdenas, principal architects of modern Mexican politics, understood that the Revolution had altered the country's political landscape forever. Millions of people had been

---

* First established in 1929, the PNR changed its name to the Party of the Mexican Revolution (PRM) in 1938 and then to its current title, the Institutional Revolutionary Party (PRI), in 1946.

uprooted from their villages to fight and often die in the struggle. Following such intense mobilization, elite accommodation alone could not restore social peace. Mexico's leaders could scarcely exclude the masses from the new political order. Consequently, Calles established an official political party and Cárdenas created its peasant and labor sectors in order to promote simultaneously mass representation and state control. Villages throughout the country were organized into a national peasant confederation. Blue-collar workers were encouraged to unionize and join the party's labor sector. A third party sector was established for government employees, small business, and other segments of the middle class.

All of these groups have been afforded greater access to the state. In return, however, they have been forced to sacrifice their political autonomy. While corporatism has given some labor leaders considerable influence and has sometimes benefited the rank and file of powerful unions, it also has left peasants, unorganized workers, and even members of weaker unions with little voice. At the same time, the incorporated labor unions, peasant federations, and "popular" (middle-class) organizations have been governed from the top down with little grassroots input. In short, the PRI has offered Mexicans only limited and well-controlled political representation. During the 1960s, one of the country's leading political scientists estimated that 50 to 70 percent of the population was "effectively barred from making any type of demand upon the political system."[28] While that proportion has declined since that time, a sizable segment of the nation's population continues to have little or no influence over the political process.

Just as mass representation has been more apparent than real, so too have democratic elections. Unlike revolutionary elites in Cuba, China, and the old Soviet bloc, Mexico's leaders created a space for opposition political parties. They recognized that the appearance of competitive elections would add to the regime's legitimacy. Consequently, every six years, the PRI presidential candidate has traveled the length and breadth of the country "pressing the flesh," while party workers have saturated the landscape with PRI signs and posters. But lacking a democratic tradition or confidence in democratic institutions, the political elite has generally shown little interest in fair electoral contests. Their triumph, and Mexico's tragedy, has been their capacity to create the illusion of democracy without the reality. As a prominent Mexican scholar has noted, they "created a dominant party system that resulted in a new authoritarianism, which was very careful to preserve the democratic forms while emptying them of content."[29]

A CHANGING SOCIETY AND POLITICAL CULTURE

When the Mexican Revolution began, the country was overwhelmingly rural and approximately 90 percent illiterate. Consequently, opportunities for political participation were quite limited for most of the population. Two decades later, when the official party was founded and the new political system began to take shape, two-thirds of the people were still illiterate. Even as recently as the 1960s, Gabriel Almond and Sidney Verba's celebrated cross-national study of political attitudes indicated that most Mexicans belonged to either "parochial" or "subject" political cultures. Members of the first group, living primarily in more isolated, rural areas, failed to appreciate fully the ways in which government policies impacted upon their lives and, consequently, rarely participated in the national political system. Those in the "subject political culture" typically had some education and political experience, though not a great deal. They understood the importance of state policies and were aware of major political issues, but still did not feel confident of their ability to influence government.[30] Only through the growth of a larger "participant political culture," argued Almond and Verba, composed of citizens actively interested in politics (typically more educated and urbanized people), would a country such as Mexico be able to establish effective democracy.

While aspects of Almond and Verba's Mexican study have been challenged, many of their findings are supported by political modernization research.[31] Political awareness and participation tend to correlate with literacy, urbanization, and exposure to the mass media. In recent decades, Mexico has been transformed from a primarily rural nation to a largely urban one. The literacy rate now exceeds 90 percent (though most of the population still hasn't advanced beyond a primary school education) and most people have access to radio and television.[32] Thus, Mexicans are far more politically aware today than they were when single-party dominance was introduced in 1929 or even when the student massacre took place in 1968.

Increasingly skeptical about their country's political and economic systems, Mexicans still appreciate their past achievements and remain uncertain about the proper path to change. Raised in a society whose school system and mass media constantly contrast the country's current accomplishments with the tyranny and chaos of the prerevolutionary era,

> Mexicans are highly supportive of the [broad] political institutions that evolved from the Mexican Revolution and . . . the democratic principles embodied in the constitution of 1917. However, they are [also] critical of [contemporary] government performance.[33]

Thus, a 1990 survey found only 18 percent of the Mexican population expressing confidence in their government, about half the level found in the United States or Canada at that time.[34] In light of their country's extensive history of electoral fraud, Mexicans, not surprisingly, distrust their own electoral process, yet many feel powerless to change it. In a national survey conducted one year after the controversial 1988 presidential election, over half of the respondents indicated that they could "do nothing about electoral fraud."[35]

As Mexicans have become more educated and better informed over the years, they have grown more critical of their political system and increasingly committed to democratic reform. But many remain unsure where to turn. Though dissatisfied with government and the PRI, they often have less confidence in the political opposition. For example, 61 percent of the people polled shortly before the 1988 presidential election doubted that an opposition party victory would lift the country out of its deep recession.[36] The opposition parties' disappointing showing in the 1991 and 1994 national elections further indicated the electorate's hesitancy to turn away from the PRI.

In time the combination of socioeconomic change at home and pressures from abroad will likely accelerate Mexico's movement toward democracy. Cross-national research indicates that higher national educational levels are conducive to the emergence of democratic government.[37] For example, in recent years the expanding urban middle classes in Taiwan and South Korea have pressured their authoritarian regimes to democratize. While conditions in Mexico are not fully analogous, we may still expect that as the country's skilled working class and middle class continue to grow and as the urban and rural poor acquire new opportunities to organize, pressures for democracy will mount.

At the same time, the Mexican government has become increasingly hard-pressed to defend its record in the court of international public opinion. For example, official corruption and political repression became issues in the debate over NAFTA in the United States. Since the 1980s a wave of democratic reform has transformed Eastern Europe, Latin America, and parts of Asia and Africa.[38] As nation after nation has moved from authoritarian to more democratic government, their experiences have often had a demonstration effect in neighboring countries. For example, South Korean television coverage of prodemocracy demonstrations in the Philippines motivated viewers toward parallel action in their own country. The more that democracy takes hold in Latin America and other parts of the Third World, the greater its influence will likely be in Mexico. Even the leftist, Zapatista rebels have endorsed pluralist democracy.

THE MEANING OF CHIAPAS

Considering how few rebels were involved in the Chiapas uprising and how poorly armed most of them were, it is noteworthy that the revolt attracted so much attention. In part, this can be attributed to the EZLN's ability, particularly Subcomandante Marcos's, to orchestrate the mass media at home and abroad. Scarcely had the revolt started when journalists from throughout the Western world arrived to cover it (many were already in Mexico to report on the start of NAFTA). Equally promptly, the Zapatistas were waiting with Spanish- and English-language communiqués, accompanied by pithy sound bites. But more than good public relations was involved. The Chiapas rebels sent shock waves throughout Mexico because their demands so articulately addressed the country's failures.

In many ways, Chiapas's economic and political conditions highlight the deficiencies of the Mexican Revolution.[39] While the state possesses considerable oil and natural gas wealth, its population is among the poorest in the country. In fact, its socioeconomic conditions resemble those of Guatemala, Mexico's impoverished neighbor to the south. Its poor rural population (heavily Indian) is dominated by the state's landed elite, and its state and local governments are among the country's most corrupt and repressive. Yet until recently Chiapas was a bastion of electoral support for the government. Like other political machines, the PRI garners the most votes from those who benefit the least from the established order, that is, the poor, many of whom depend on the government or ruling party for survival. Thus in the 1988 presidential election, Carlos Salinas officially won 90 percent of the vote in the state, by far his largest margin anywhere in the nation.[40] Yet, ironically, it was in this same state six years later that the failures of Mexico's political and economic systems were exposed at the most inopportune moment for the Salinas administration.

The timing of the Zapatista uprising, designed to discredit NAFTA and embarrass the government, was quite unexpected, just as the revolt's style was unprecedented.* The EZLN leadership was extremely adept at handling, even manipulating, the news media. Mexican intellectuals and professionals poured over the latest issues of the progressive news weekly *Proceso,* which devoted most of its pages to the Zapatistas. Journalists labeled Subcomandante Marcos, the highly articulate and engaging rebel spokesperson, the world's first postmodern revolutionary. Shrewdly analytical, constantly showing flashes of humor not often associated with guerrilla leaders, Marcos regaled reporters with his self-parody and his extended critiques of Mexican society.[41]

Not since Fidel Castro's famed interviews in the Sierra Maestra mountains with the American journalist Herbert Matthews had a guerrilla leader so captivated the world's imagination. Moreover, Marcos had an added air of mystery that Castro and Nicaragua's Daniel Ortega lacked. Hidden behind his woolen ski mask, he kept his real identity a secret. His green eyes and obvious university polish made clear that he was not a Mayan peasant. He described himself as an urban leftist in his late thirties. But the best efforts of Mexico's national security apparatus failed to identify him for over a year. Eventually, authorities revealed that he was Rafael Sebastián Guillén Vicente, a thirty-eight-year-old, middle-class graduate of the national university (UNAM) with prior experience in Central America's revolutionary movements.

A Different Kind of Rebellion.   Marcos's cosmopolitan style contrasted with the apparent innocence of the Tzeltal and Tzotzil Indian peasants who make up most of the EZLN's foot soldiers. These recruits were not the battle-hardened guerrilla soldiers that the world had come to know in Vietnam, El

---

* The government had generally ignored reports from its military and even the press of incipient guerrilla activity in the area. Likely it was afraid that reports of early rebel activity in Chiapas would hurt NAFTA's chances of passage in the U.S. Congress.

Salvador, and Guatemala. Compared with other revolutionary movements, the EZLN was extremely sparing in its use of violence. Few police or local political officials were harmed during the Zapatista seizures of towns in Chiapas. A hotel owner in heavily touristed San Cristóbal de las Casas reported that foreigners had been advised to leave town in advance of the rebel occupation so that they would not be exposed to danger. After their capture of San Cristóbal and four other towns, many of the Zapatistas laid down their rifles or machetes, took their bandannas from their faces, and returned home to tend their small fields. One American journalist who interviewed a peasant soldier during the first days of the uprising had to caution him not to reveal his full name to the media.[42]

The Zapatistas' message was as unique as their operating style. In the wake of communism's collapse in Eastern Europe and the Sandinistas' electoral defeat in Nicaragua, EZLN communiqués avoided traditional marxist rhetoric. Rather than promising a worker-peasant state led by a vanguard party, they called for pluralist democracy and honest elections.[43] Little was said of socialism. Instead, the Zapatistas insisted that the Mexican political system reform itself by living up to its own rhetoric. That would require greater social justice for the poor and truly democratic elections.

In Mexico City, some hundred thousand people rallied in support of the rebels' demands. A few EZLN proposals attracted support from opposition parties across the political spectrum, from the Party of the Democratic Revolution (PRD) on the left to the National Action Party (PAN) on the right. Thus, several weeks after the uprising a national opinion poll revealed that while most Mexicans disapproved of the Zapatistas' methods, 75 percent approved of their goals.[44] Many Mexicans viewed the rebels as folk heroes with a place in the nation's pop culture. Street vendors, kiosks, and shops throughout the country sported Zapatista paraphernalia—shirts, dolls, even inflated condoms with a tiny ski mask over the end.

Ultimately, the rebels' influence did not come from their military might or their numbers. Few believed that their relatively small, regional movement could topple the government.* Rather, their strength lay in their capacity to expose the flaws of the political and economic order. The EZLN questioned Mexico's official image, that of a vibrant, modernizing country moving confidently toward democracy. On the contrary, they noted, the country still suffers from social injustices, deep economic inequalities, rigged elections, and extensive political corruption. Even if most Mexicans didn't approve of the Zapatistas' methods or even their final objectives, they accepted much of that critique. Their symbolism and their appeal were rooted less in marxism than in the mythology of the Mexican Revolution itself. In choosing to call themselves Zapatistas, they assumed the mantle of Emiliano Zapata, an Indian villager

---

* At the time of the uprising there was some speculation that supporting movements would emerge elsewhere in Mexico. Parallel mobilization would have threatened the country's political stability, but it never developed.

whose integrity and commitment to social justice have made him the most revered hero of the Revolution.

The Government's Reaction.   Initially badly shaken by the Chiapas uprising, President Salinas and his advisors soon responded more decisively. In so doing, they rejected the assessments of conservative intellectuals such as Enrique Krauze who had dismissed the Zapatistas as relatively inconsequential.[45] After first sending twelve thousand troops to restore government authority in the state and drive the Zapatistas from the captured towns, Salinas turned to conciliation. Within days he offered the Chiapas rebels amnesty.* He quickly removed the cabinet minister responsible for maintaining internal security, Secretary of Government Patrocinio González Garrido. Himself a former governor of Chiapas with close ties to the state's large landlords, González came from the PRI's most conservative and intransigent old guard, the very type of politician that the uprising sought to dislodge. In his place, the president appointed Jorge Carpizo McGregor. A highly respected human rights advocate with no political party affiliation, Carpizo was considered the most incorruptible member of Salinas's government. In selecting him, Salinas chose the first person in modern times outside the ranks of the PRI to head the very powerful Ministry of Government.

In addition Salinas agreed to hold direct negotiations with the rebels and named his popular foreign minister, Manuel Camacho Solís, as the government's negotiating representative ("peace commissioner"). Camacho, a friend of Salinas's since their university days, had been a leading contender for the PRI presidential nomination and enjoyed a substantial national following. Because of his commitment to democratic reform and his insistence on getting broad negotiating power, his appointment was welcomed by progressives within the administration and by the Zapatistas themselves. Shortly thereafter, the government announced a unilateral cease-fire. In turn, those Zapatista guerrillas who had not already returned to their villages retreated to the Lacandon rain forest.

Subsequent negotiations, however, did not proceed smoothly. The talks dragged on as the two sides were hard-pressed to agree even on an agenda. While the government tried to keep discussions narrowly focused on conditions in Chiapas, the EZLN pushed for a wider range of issues including democracy.

From the outset, Manuel Camacho, whose popularity had grown considerably in his new position, was more sympathetic to the rebels' demands than the administration was. Indeed, he seemed to have his own agenda for democratizing Mexico that went further than Salinas and the PRI leadership were willing to go. Pushed forward by Camacho, the government quickly declared a tentative pact on 2 March incorporating many of the Zapatistas' criticisms

---

* Ironically, however, in his televised speech offering that amnesty Salinas stood in the presidential palace under a portrait of former president Carranza, the man who had arranged Zapata's assassination.

of Mexican society. "Item by item," noted one observer, "it read like an extraordinary admission [by the government] of shortcomings in the program of rapid economic transformation that only [the previous] fall seemed to crown Mr. Salinas as the envy of modernizing leaders throughout Latin America."[46] The proposed accord also expressed the government's unanticipated willingness to undertake broad social reforms in Chiapas.

It called for a variety of government development and social welfare programs, including agrarian reform, creation of new industries, job retraining, support for farmers facing new competition from abroad, low-cost rural housing, roads, hospitals, and clinics. Villagers, it declared, should have "the advantages of the city like television, stoves, refrigerators, and washing machines [sic]." Ironically if implemented these changes would require the kind of intense government economic intervention that the Salinas administration had worked so hard to eliminate.

Even though it was the rebels' original demand for greater democracy that had resonated most strongly with the Mexican people, the proposed agreement hardly addressed the issue of political reform. But as negotiations continued in Chiapas, a multiparty congressional group produced an electoral reform law. The bill greatly strengthened procedures for protecting the integrity of the vote and insuring an honest electoral count (see chapter 4). Although both the EZLN and a portion of the PRD called the reform inadequate, it did produce a fairly honest vote tally in the 1994 presidential election.

Despite the public enthusiasm that greeted Manuel Camacho's announcement of a provisional peace accord, a final settlement was not reached. Subcomandante Marcos, who had never appeared enthusiastic about the proposed settlement, announced that it would have to be submitted to peasants throughout Chiapas in a referendum that would take months to complete.[47] As the ratification process slowly proceeded, the political atmosphere in Chiapas soured. The government blamed the Zapatistas for instigating new peasant land seizures, while the EZLN accused the military of harassing villagers.[48] After four months, the Zapatista leadership announced that 97.88 percent of Chiapas's peasants had rejected the accord.[49]

Subcomandante Marcos maintained that the 2 March agreement had been inadequate because it didn't guarantee a transition to democracy. The government responded, however, that it would discuss major political reforms only with the legally recognized political parties, not with a rebel movement. With the peace process in disarray and the new PRI presidential candidate, Ernesto Zedillo, publicly criticizing his efforts, Manuel Camacho resigned as government negotiator and lashed out at Zedillo. Like the Zapatistas, Camacho seemed to doubt the administration's commitment to democracy.

As the country moved toward the August presidential elections, however, the impact of the Chiapas uprising seemed to fade. The administration did its best to remove the entire issue from the public eye. Despite rejecting the initial accord, the rebels expressed their willingness to reopen talks and pledged to honor the cease-fire as long as they were not attacked. By then, many Mexicans were becoming disenchanted with the Zapatistas' intransigent negotiating style and losing interest in the process. But the basic questions that the EZLN had raised about the weakness of Mexican democracy and the absence of social justice remain a major challenge to the new administration of Ernesto Zedillo.

FROM LUIS DONALDO COLOSIO TO ERNESTO ZEDILLO

Less than three months after the Chiapas uprising, Mexicans were again traumatized, this time by Luis Donaldo Colosio's murder. His death evoked memories of the chaotic decades that followed the Mexican Revolution, when Presidents Francisco Madero and Venustiano Carranza, ex-president (and incumbent) Alvaro Obregón, and revolutionary leaders Pancho Villa and Emiliano Zapata all were murdered. Most people believed that Colosio's assassination was tied to some larger, yet-unknown conspiracy, very possibly involving the ruling party.

During the following months, government investigators fueled public suspicions by alternately declaring either that the murder had been the work of a lone assassin in their custody or that it had been part of a larger plot. Three members of the security contingent that guarded Colosio in Tijuana and the local PRI official who had hired them were jailed and then released.[50] Because Tijuana is a major narcotics center whose police are linked to the drug cartels, early speculation focused on a possible drug connection to the candidate's death. Others suggested that his murder had been ordered by PRI hard-liners who found him too receptive to democratic reform. Still not satisfactorily resolved, Colosio's death remains a source of intense speculation.

As Americans have learned from the ongoing conjecture surrounding John F. Kennedy's assassination, it is frequently difficult to unravel such events. Any irregularity in the apprehension of the assassin or in the ongoing probe only fuels further misgivings. As we shall see, Mexico's sense of intrigue deepened subsequently, following the murder of PRI Secretary General José Francisco Ruiz Massieu.

Following Colosio's death, many Mexicans hoped President Salinas would tap Manuel Camacho, still the government negotiator in Chiapas at that time, as the party candidate. But his very popularity and his public criticisms of the administration had made him anathema to the PRI machine. Instead, the president turned to Ernesto Zedillo, a former education minister and federal budget director who had been Colosio's campaign manager at the time of his death. A leading economic policy maker with a Yale Ph.D., Zedillo fit the mold of Mexico's new technocratic leaders. Having served as an architect of Salinas's economic policies, he symbolized continuity in public policy rather than innovation. But unlike Colosio he had never previously run for public office and was not considered an effective politician. He proved to be a rather uncharis-

Table 1-1. Results of the 1988 and 1994 Presidential Elections

Party	1988	1994
PRI	50.7%	53.4%
PAN	16.8	28.6
FDN/PRD*	32.5	18.0

* In 1988 Cuauhtémoc Cárdenas was the candidate of the National Democratic Front (FDN). By 1994 that had been replaced by the Party of the Democratic Revolution (PRD).
Source: Federal Electoral Institute (IFE).

matic candidate who performed so poorly in the country's first presidential debate that he briefly fell behind Diego Fernández de Cevallos, the PAN candidate, in the opinion polls.

Ultimately, however, the PRI candidate emerged victorious at the ballot box once again, this time without the taint of fraud. The days when the party's presidential candidate could easily win over 75 percent of the vote appear to have passed. For the second time consecutively the PRI officially won about half the valid vote, an outcome that had been considered unthinkable before 1988. But with the opposition vote split between left and right (PRD and PAN), Zedillo's total was enough to give him a sizable lead over his nearest competitor.

Within months after Zedillo took office, however, the nation entered into yet another round of crises. Early in 1995 government investigators launched a political bombshell when they announced the arrest of Carlos Salinas's brother, Raúl, on charges of masterminding the murder of José Francisco Ruiz Massieu. Reputedly a political reformer, Ruiz Massieu had been expected to exert substantial influence in the Zedillo administration. From the outset some government investigators had suspected that the murder was orchestrated by members of the party's so-called dinosaur wing—the conservative old guard, opposed to political reform. But no explanation has been offered as to why Raúl Salinas (or, for that matter, his brother, the president) would want Ruiz Massieu (the Salinases' longtime associate and former brother-in-law) dead.

The authorities also charged Ruiz Massieu's brother, Mario, who had originally headed the Salinas administration's assassination probe, with covering up Raúl's role. After an unprecedented, angry exchange between Carlos Salinas and President Zedillo (it had been an unwritten rule of Mexican politics that former and sitting presidents do not criticize each other publicly), Salinas left the country, apparently on Zedillo's request. Mario Ruiz Massieu fled Mexico and was arrested by U.S. authorities after he had allegedly deposited millions of dollars in American banks, money believed to have come from the drug cartels. These developments further undermined the government's legitimacy. So too did a sharp drop in the value of the peso and the return to deep economic recession at the start of 1995 (see chapter 6).

CONCLUSIONS

Several years ago, historian Alan Knight declared:

Mexico is in crisis. . . . However, it is hardly a new one. . . . Since 1982 the alarm bells have hardly stopped ringing. But, as we enter the 1990s and the period of recent crisis approaches double digits, we might pause to consider how long a crisis must endure before it ceases to be a crisis . . . before, that is, people become deaf to the alarm bells and learn to live amid crisis.[51]

Ernesto Zedillo's victory and the PRI's strong showing in the 1994 congressional contests indicate that the Chiapas rebellion and the Colosio murder, serious as they were, had not yet undermined the party's long-standing political control. If anything, public concerns about disorder and instability strengthened Zedillo's electoral support since the PRI remained a symbol of stability and many voters feared change more than they disliked the status quo. Moreover, at the time of the 1994 election (though clearly no longer), voters endorsed Salinas's economic policies. Exit polls revealed that 53 percent of them felt that the economy had improved during his administration, while only 21 percent believed it had deteriorated. Zedillo's weakness as a candidate or, indeed, the entire electoral campaign mattered little for most voters. Nearly two-thirds of them had made up their minds by the time the candidates were selected, and over half of the electorate indicated that they always vote for the same party. These "early deciders" were particularly likely to vote for the PRI.[52]

Still, Mexico's renewed economic crisis, the ongoing and expanding series of political scandals and apparent conspiracies, revelations of enormous corruption and intrigue by President Salinas's brother, and the unprecedented mutual attacks by Carlos Salinas and his successor all suggest that the Mexico's once-monolithic ruling party is beginning to fracture and hemorrhage. The PAN's unprecedented victory in three gubernatorial races in 1995 further indicates that the PRI's grip on power is weakening.

Notes

1. Wayne A. Cornelius, Judith Gentleman, and Peter H. Smith, "Overview: The Dynamics of Political Change in Mexico," in *Mexico's Alternative Political Futures*, ed. Cornelius, Gentleman, and Smith (La Jolla: University of California–San Diego Center for U.S.-Mexican Studies, 1989), 20. If the several hundred thousand annulled ballots and votes cast for unregistered candidates are included in the count, Salinas's share of the total vote falls to under 49 percent, making him the first minority president in Mexican history.

2. Alberto Aziz Nassif and Jacqueline Peschard, eds., *Las elecciones federales de 1991* (México: Centro de Investigaciones Interdisciplinarias en Humanidades-UNAM, 1992); Arturo Sánchez Gutiérrez, ed., *Las elecciones de Salinas: un balance crítico da 1991* (México: Plaza y Valdes, 1992).

3. The Mexican journal *Proceso* is the best Spanish-language source on the Zapatista movement and on contemporary Mexican politics generally. Estimates of the number of EZLN soldiers

vary widely, with some sources claiming several thousand. The lower estimate cited here comes from *Latin America Weekly Report,* 13 January 1994, 2. Issues of the *Weekly Report* (henceforth referred to as *LAWR*) for the first few months of 1994 also are an excellent source of information on these events, as is the *Mexico and NAFTA Report;* see also Philip L. Russell, *The Chiapas Rebellion* (Austin, Tex.: Mexico Resource Center, 1995).

4. David Ronfeldt, ed., *The Modern Mexican Military: A Reassessment* (La Jolla: University of California–San Diego Center for U.S.-Mexican Studies, 1984); Roderic Ai Camp, *Generals in the Palacio: The Military in Modern Mexico* (New York: Oxford University Press, 1992). Some experts argue that the political influence of the armed forces has grown since the late 1960s, particularly in the last decade or so. But it is still fairly limited compared with that of most Latin American militaries.

5. Examples include Miguel Basáñez, *El pulso de los sexenios: 20 años de crisis en México* (México: Siglo XXI, 1990); Jorge G. Castañeda, "Mexico at the Brink," *Foreign Affairs* 64 (Winter 1985–86): 278–96; Judith Adler Hellman, *Mexico in Crisis,* 2d ed. (New York: Holmes and Meier, 1983); Judith Gentleman, ed., *Mexican Politics in Transition* (Boulder, Colo.: Westview Press, 1987).

6. For an earlier critical analysis of scholarly writings that viewed Mexico as repeatedly being in crisis, see Martin Needler, "Recent Events," in *Mexican Politics in Transition.* Needler even looked back skeptically at his own 1971 article placing the Mexican political system at a crossroads.

7. On new government aid to the state, see *Excelsior,* 14 March 1994, 12.

8. Daniel Levy and Gabriel Székely, *Mexico: Paradoxes of Stability and Change* (Boulder, Colo.: Westview Press, 1983), 144.

9. United Nations Development Program (UNDP), *Human Development Report, 1993* (New York: Oxford University Press, 1993), 170–71. These countries are compared in terms of their Gini coefficient, a statistical measure of inequality.

10. Cornelius, Gentleman, and Smith, "Overview," 10.

11. Lorenzo Meyer, "México o los límites de la democratización neoliberal," paper delivered at the University of California–San Diego Center for U.S.-Mexican Studies, 15 May 1991, 2; Meyer, *La segunda muerte de la Revolución Mexicana* (México: Cal y Arena, 1992), 45–62.

12. Lester D. Langley, *Mexico and the United States* (Boston: Twayne, 1991), xiv.

13. On increased coverage, see Robert A. Pastor, "The American Mind," in Robert A. Pastor and Jorge C. Castañeda, *Limits to Friendship: The United States and Mexico* (New York: Alfred A. Knopf, 1988), 47.

14. Alan Riding, *Distant Neighbors: A Portrait of the Mexicans* (New York: Vintage, 1984), ix.

15. Lester D. Langley, *MexAmerica: Two Countries, One Future* (New York: Crown, 1988).

16. Langley, *Mexico and the United States,* xiii.

17. Roberto Bouzas, "U.S.-Latin American Trade Relations," in *The United States and Latin America in the 1990s,* ed. Jonathan Hartlyn, Lars Schoultz, and Augusto Varas (Chapel Hill: University of North Carolina Press, 1992), 157. Bouzas draws the data from the International Monetary Fund (IMF), *Direction of Trade Statistics Yearbook.*

18. Gabriel Székely, "Forging a North American Economy: Issues for Mexico in the 1990s," in *Mexico's External Relations in the 1990s,* ed. Riordan Roett (Boulder, Colo.: Lynne Rienner Publishers, 1991), 217.

19. Robert A. Pastor, *Integration with Mexico* (New York: Twentieth Century Fund, 1993), 11. The data cited are from the early 1990s.

20. Among the many excellent English-language books on Mexican history are Leslie Bethell, ed., *Mexico since Independence* (New York: Cambridge University Press, 1991); Michael C. Meyer and William Sherman, *The Course of Mexican History,* 3d ed. (New York: Oxford University Press, 1987).

21. For a fascinating photographic account of the Revolution, see Anita Brenner, *The Wind That Swept Mexico: The History of the Mexican Revolution, 1910–1942* (New York: Harper and Bros., 1943).

22. There is considerable debate as to how much fundamental change the Revolution brought. Certainly the most important changes did not come until the late 1930s under President Lázaro Cárdenas.

23. Jean Meyer, "Revolution and Reconstruction in the 1920s," in *Mexico since Independence*, 205.

24. See Roderic A. Camp, *Politics in Mexico* (New York: Oxford University Press, 1993), chap. 5; Camp, *Entrepreneurs and Politics in Twentieth Century Mexico* (New York: Oxford University Press, 1989).

25. Martin Needler, *Mexican Politics*, 2d ed. (New York: Praeger, 1990), chap. 10.

26. Gary Wynia, *The Politics of Latin American Development*, 3d. ed. (New York: Cambridge University Press, 1990), 43.

27. For a discussion of the difference between corporatism and state corporatism, see Philippe Schmitter, "Still the Century of Corporatism," in *The New Corporatism: Social-Political Structures in the Iberian World*, ed. Frederick Pike (Notre Dame, Ind.: Notre Dame University Press, 1974); on Mexican corporatism, see Meyer, *La segunda muerte de la Revolución Mexicana*, 107–18.

28. Pablo González Casanova, *La democracia en México* (México: Ediciones ERA, 1965), 121.

29. Lorenzo Meyer, "La democracia política: Esperando a Godot," *Nexos* (1987): 40.

30. Gabriel A. Almond and Sidney Verba, *The Civic Culture* (Boston: Little Brown, 1963); on the concept of political culture, see Gabriel A. Almond and G. Bingham Powell, *Comparative Politics: A Developmental Approach* (Boston: Little Brown, 1966), 27–30, and Gabriel A. Almond, "The Intellectual History of the Civic Culture Concept," in *The Civic Culture Revisited*, ed. Gabriel A. Almond and Sidney Verba (Boston: Little Brown, 1980).

31. For criticisms, see Ann L. Craig and Wayne A. Cornelius, "Political Culture in Mexico: Continuities and Revisionist Interpretations," in *Civic Culture Revisited*.

32. UNDP, *Human Development Report, 1993*, 135.

33. Wayne A. Cornelius and Ann L. Craig, "Politics in Mexico," in *Comparative Politics Today*, ed. Gabriel A. Almond and G. Bingham Powell, 5th ed. (New York: Harper Collins, 1992), 501.

34. *World Value Survey*, 1990, cited in Camp, *Politics in Mexico*, 59.

35. *Los Angeles Times* poll cited in Camp, *Politics in Mexico*, 62.

36. *Los Angeles Times* poll cited in Cornelius and Craig, "Politics in Mexico," 502.

37. Axel Hadenius, *Democracy and Development* (New York: Cambridge University Press, 1992). This work analyzes statistics from over a hundred nations to determine which socioeconomic factors correlate most strongly with democracy.

38. Samuel Huntington, *The Third Wave* (Norman: University of Oklahoma Press, 1991). To be sure, in some of these countries democracy has had more form than substance.

39. On the causes of the uprising, see José Luis Pineyro, "Los por qué de la corta guerra en Chiapas," *El Cotidiano* 63 (July–August 1994): 3–7.

40. Federal Election Commission data cited in Jaime González Graf, ed., *Las elecciones de 1988 y la crisis del sistema político* (México: Editorial Diana, 1989), appendix 21. The second highest state total for Salinas was a distant 74 percent.

41. Ana Guillermoprieto, "Zapata's Heirs," *New Yorker* 70 (16 May 1994): 61.

42. These observations are based on National Public Radio and BBC reports the week after the uprising.

43. *Perfil de la Jornada*, 18 January 1994, iii–iv.

44. *New York Times*, 26 February 1994.

45. Enrique Krauze, "Zapped: The Doomed Romanticism of Mexico's Chiapas Revolt," *New Republic*, 31 January 1994, 9.

46. *New York Times*, 3 March 1994.

47. *LAWR*, 10 March 1994, 98; 17 March 1994, 110.

48. *New York Times*, 14 March 1994.

49. *New York Times*, 13 June 1994; *LAWR*, 23 June 1994, 265.

50. *LAWR,* 21 April 1994, 158.

51. Alan Knight, "State Power and Political Stability in Mexico," in *Mexico: Dilemmas of Transition,* ed. Neil Harvey (London: Institute of Latin American Studies, University of London, and British Academic Press, 1993), 29.

52. Poll data are taken from the *New York Times,* 23 and 24 August 1994.

2

The Origins of Modern Mexico

While it would be overstated to claim that nations are captives of their past, surely they are shaped by their histories. As the heir to several pre-Colombian civilizations and a colonial heritage, more recently influenced by its powerful neighbor to the north, Mexico enjoys a rich cultural heritage. Unfortunately, however, its historical legacy has not always been propitious for developing a strong nation-state or a democratic political system. This chapter offers an overview of Mexican history from the Spanish colonial era through modern times, stressing the factors that have most directly influenced the contemporary political order.

THE COLONIAL LEGACY

Even a cursory tour of Mexico City's magnificent Museum of Anthropology impresses visitors with the vitality of the country's pre-Colombian civilizations. In all of Latin America, perhaps only Peru has enjoyed a comparably rich indigenous (Indian) tradition. The Aztecs and Maya (whose empire stretched into Central America) were among the hemisphere's most advanced Indian cultures. Other dynamic Mexican civilizations included the Olmec, Toltec, Tarascan, Zapotec, and Mixtec. Today, the Mayan and Toltec temples at Palenque and Chinchén Itzá, the remains of the ancient city of Teotihuacán, and the Zapotec ruins at Monte Albán all eloquently demonstrate the sophistication of those societies.[1]

Within precolonial America, Mexico had one of the largest Indian populations. On the eve of the Spanish conquest, it contained some thirty million people, more than any country in Western Europe at that time.* By comparison, France, Europe's most populous nation, had only twenty million people, while Spain conquered most of Latin America with a population of only eight million.[2] Tragically, however, the arrival of the Spanish conquistadors in 1519 triggered the decimation of the population at a horrific rate. Smallpox, typhoid, typhus, measles, influenza, and other diseases took the greatest toll, as

---

* Of course, population estimates for that period are speculative and inexact.

Indians lacked natural immunities to these imported illnesses. In 1576, for example, a plague believed to be a virulent strain of typhus or influenza killed approximately two million people.[3] By 1650, the combined effects of epidemics, war, malnutrition, and physical mistreatment had reduced the number of indigenous people to about one million, a mere 3–4 percent of what it had been at the time of the Spanish conquest.

Yet even with their ranks greatly reduced, Indians still outnumbered whites by more than eight to one.[4] Thus, unlike North America's British settlers, Spanish colonists remained a small minority. Consequently, like many other conquering cultures that have been surrounded by a far larger, imperialized majority, they created a strongly hierarchical society replete with injustices.* At the top of the social pyramid, controlling political, military, and church institutions, were the *peninsulares,* settlers who had migrated to Mexico from the Spanish peninsula. By the middle of the seventeenth century those immigrants were far outnumbered by *criollos,* whites born in the colony. And at the start of the nineteenth century, *criollos* constituted over 98 percent of Mexico's whites. Although many of them were more affluent than the peninsular government administrators and church officials, they lacked comparable social status or political influence. In the long term, their resentment against the *peninsulares* and the Spanish crown was a major impetus for Mexico's independence movement, as it was throughout Latin America.[5]

At the bottom of the social pyramid stood the Indian majority. They provided the backbreaking labor for two pillars of the colonial economy, agricultural estates and mines. Early in the colonial era, the Spanish crown attempted to provide Indians some protection. During the sixteenth century, for example, Madrid legally restricted the size of colonial landholdings and supported Indian rights to their ancestral land. But so many exceptions were allowed and so many violations of the rules were ignored that these guarantees ultimately meant little.

In the countryside, Spanish settlers were often granted control over the Indians living in a designated area (*encomienda*), allowing them to exploit indigenous labor and extract tributes. The crown's attempts to regulate forced-labor relations and the church's efforts to protect the Indians were not very effective.[6] Rural Mexico was transformed into a semifeudal society with Indian peons owing labor to white *hacienda* owners. Large estates (*latifundia*) controlled the most fertile agricultural property, while adjoining Indian communities were relegated to lower-quality land.

The mines and textile mills (*obrajes*) also extracted forced labor from the Indians, compelling them to toil under extremely difficult and unhealthy conditions. For example, many textile mills locked in their workers during the day, or even at night, and allowed them out only on Sunday. Poor working and living conditions increased the Indians' susceptibility to diseases and drove up their mortality rate. Observing Spanish behavior toward Indians during the early years of colonialism, a Franciscan priest, Toribio de Motolinía, declared:

---

* South Africa's whites acted similarly until majority rule was achieved in 1994.

They do nothing but make demands and no matter how much is done for them they are never satisfied. . . . They make no effort to do anything but command. They are the drones which consume the honey which is worked by the poor bees, the Indians. What the poor people are able to give them does not satisfy them.[7]

Because there were few white women in Spain's New World colonies, male settlers often took Indian concubines, mistresses, or, less frequently, wives. Some of the women consented to these relationships voluntarily, but many did not. Out of the unions grew a considerable Mestizo population, representing a blend of Indian and European cultures. While some offspring were well integrated into Spanish society, many more were rejected by their fathers and raised as Indians by their mothers. Mestizos occupied a broad range of social classes, with a status generally below whites and above Indians. Over time, race became defined more culturally than biologically. According to one estimate, in 1793 slightly over half of the population were Indian, one-fourth were Mestizo, and one-fifth were white.[8] Thus, two of the colonial era's most important legacies were a hierarchical society based on class and race, and an economy featuring highly unequal distribution of land and wealth. To be sure, class lines were not impenetrable, and there have always been limited opportunities for upward mobility. In the twentieth century, the Revolution reduced *criollo* elitism and elevated the status of Indians and Mestizos. Since that time Mexico has respected its indigenous heritage more dutifully than most Latin American nations do. For example, Mexicans like to point out that while their capital has public statues honoring the Aztec leader Cuauhtémoc, it has none for his Spanish conqueror, Hernán Cortés.

In the capital's famed Plaza of the Three Cultures, a Spanish church faces the pre-Colombian pyramid of Tlatelolco. The inscription on a nearby plaque conveys the country's multiracial image of itself: "On August 13, 1521, heroically defended by Cuauhtémoc, Tlatelolco fell into the hands of Hernán Cortés. It was neither a triumph nor a defeat: it was the painful birth of the Mestizo nation that is Mexico today."[9]

Since the Revolution there has been an acceleration of *mestizaje*—the assimilation of indigenous people into Mestizo culture—reducing the proportion of Indians from 45 percent of the national population at the start of the century to between 10 and 15 percent currently.[10] Today most Mexicans are considered Mestizos. But, as the recent Chiapas rebellion clearly reveals, the Indian peasantry that remains has not been successfully integrated into the mainstream of national life. According to the National Indigenous Institute (INI), Mexico currently has between 8.7 and 12 million indigenous people. Speaking sixty-eight languages, they live in over forty-four thousand communities located primarily in the states of Chiapas, Oaxaca, Veracruz, Puebla, Yucatán, Quintana Roo, and Sonora. For the most part, indigenous villagers make up the poorest sector of society. Thus, although the national adult literacy rate is currently over 90 percent, among Indians it is less than 60 percent. Over 40 percent of Mexican adults have at least six years of education, but only 12 percent of the indigenous population reach that level. And, the proportion of Indian households lacking potable water (48 percent) or sewers (72 percent) is twice the national average.[11]

Other legacies of the colonial period (as well as the early independence era discussed below) that prevailed at least until the Mexican Revolution included a powerful political role for the Catholic Church, an active military presence in politics, an authoritarian political system, a heterogeneous political culture, and a dependent economy. Indeed a number of these legacies still endure.

THE AFTERMATH OF INDEPENDENCE

Napoleon Bonaparte's invasion of Spain in 1808 and the capture of its monarch, Charles IV, created a power vacuum in that country's New World empire. In 1810, a *criollo* priest, Miguel Hidalgo y Costilla, led an uprising of Indian and Mestizo volunteers, beginning Mexico's long war of independence. His call to arms, *El Grito de Dolores,* still celebrated as a national holiday, began one of Latin America's few efforts to integrate the Indian masses into the independence struggle. From a small band, Hidalgo's army swelled to eighty thousand men who nearly conquered Mexico City. But tactical errors and desertion by their *criollo* supporters eventually led to their defeat.

After Father Hidalgo's capture and execution, another priest, José María Morelos y Pavón, assumed the leadership of the independence struggle. More militarily skilled than his predecessor, Morelos waged a formidable guerrilla war for four years (1811–15). Though a Mestizo himself, he was committed to Indian rights and liberal reforms. Speaking of his movement, two contemporary historians have noted:

> If the Conquest of Mexico by Cortés represented a negation of Indian values by the Spanish, the Wars of Independence [were to] represent a negation of Spanish values by the Indians. Morelos invoked the names of the ancient emperors, Moctezuma and Cuauhtémoc.[12]

He also called for universal male suffrage, abolition of slavery, an end to the caste system, and the termination of torture. But his progressive agenda was rejected by the *criollo* elite, whose support was necessary for the overthrow of the peninsular government. Like Hidalgo, he was captured and executed by a firing squad. Morelos's struggle was the last effort to achieve independence in a manner that would benefit the Indian and Mestizo masses rather than just the *criollo* elite. Sporadic fighting continued during the five years following his death, but when independence was finally achieved in 1820–21 it was under an elitist leadership with a very different vision for Mexico.

The turning point in the struggle came when a royalist brigadier, Augustín de Iturbide, decided to change sides after a decade of fighting on behalf of the Spanish crown. On 24 February 1821 he issued the Plan of Iguala, calling for Mexican independence and the creation of a constitutional monarchy. With the support of General Vicente Guerrero, a nationalist guerrilla leader, Iturbide gained control over most of the country and achieved national independence. Obviously, Iturbide's monarchist plan differed greatly from Hidalgo's and Morelos's vision. As historian Jan Bazant has noted:

> Independence in 1821 did not bring any immediate revolutionary change in the social or economic structure of the country. The first and principal effect was that the political power formerly exercised by the royalist bureaucracy was transferred to the army . . . a coalition of Iturbide's royalist and Guerrero's republican armies. The second pillar of the new nation was the Roman Catholic Church.[13]

Indeed, allied with the church and the conservative government bureaucracy, the military had greater political authority after independence than it had enjoyed under the crown's control.[14] Between 1821 and 1845, the armed forces' budget exceeded the government's total annual income fourteen times.[15] General Iturbide was crowned emperor, but his reign lasted only two years, and in 1823 the country became a republic. In the absence of centralized authority or government legitimacy, however, political life remained chaotic over the next half century. During its first forty years of independence, Mexico had fifty-five different presidents, with some, most notably Antonio López de Santa Anna, holding the office multiple times.*

The political system was weakened by a range of internal conflicts. For decades Conservatives—supporting strong, centralized government—battled Liberals advocating a decentralized, federalist system. As in the rest of Latin America, Conservatives—led by the landed elite, the military, the Catholic hierarchy, and sectors of the business community—favored an authoritarian political order, the defense of church interests, and a hierarchical class system. Liberals favored a more secular society, separation of church and state, increased opportunities for social mobility, and expanded political freedom (though not necessarily for the Indian majority).[16] Although the Liberals, led by Benito Juárez, emerged victorious in the War of the Reform (1858–61), rival Conservative and Liberal governments still challenged each other until 1864. In addition to these ideological divisions, several other internal conflicts contributed to the ongoing turmoil. Military coups, rebellions by local strongmen, peasant revolts, uprisings by frontier Indian tribes, and social banditry all added to political instability. The country was racked by constant clashes between regional *caciques* (political bosses) battling for personal wealth and power.[17]

Mexico's weak national government often was unable to perform one of its most fundamental tasks, defending national sovereignty. In 1839 Yucatán seceded from the nation for four years. Texas declared its independence as well, and when the United States subsequently annexed it, the ensuing war (1845–48) deprived Mexico of half its national territory. Finally, in 1862

---

* Santa Anna was instrumental in overthrowing Iturbe's empire and later held the presidency repeatedly. He is better known in the United States, of course, for his leadership of the Mexican forces that fought Texan secession at the Battle of the Alamo.

terward, the French—invited and supported by Mexico's monarchist faction—occupied Mexico City and installed an Austrian archduke, Maximilian von Hapsburg, as emperor. It took three years for Juárez's Liberal army to drive Maximilian from the throne.

The Liberal governments that preceded and followed Maximilian (1855–64, 1867–76) introduced a new constitution and modernized the political system. The major losers in the Liberal transformation were the church and the Conservative-dominated military. The new reformers separated church and state, banned monastic orders, permitted civil marriages, placed the clergy under the jurisdiction of civil courts, and sold church property that was not directly related to religious purposes. At the same time, the military lost considerable power and privilege. Juárez was the first nonmilitary president since independence (other than interim chief executives), and, contrary to the norm, his cabinet was composed primarily of civilians.

Central to the Liberals' agenda were economic modernization and educational reform. To encourage capitalist development and stimulate agricultural production, they commercialized much of the church's vast rural property holdings. In addition, they cultivated foreign investment particularly for railroads and other infrastructure. Primary school education was declared free and obligatory. Though Mexico did not come close to achieving universal primary education, it did increase the number of schools by approximately 800 percent between 1844 and 1874, while raising student enrollment by nearly 600 percent.[18]

At the same time, the government "reduced the national debt to a fifth of its postwar figure, revised tax and tariff structures, spurred revitalization and modernization of the mining industry and promoted expanded planting of the chief agricultural exports."[19] Perhaps the Liberals' most important economic project was the completion of a railroad link between Mexico City and Veracruz. Major political reforms included greater freedom of speech and freedom of the press. But while these changes benefited commercial farmers, emerging capitalists, and professionals, they were of little value to the Indian masses and often disadvantaged them. This was ironic since the great Liberal leader Benito Juárez was a Zapotec Indian, one of the country's few political leaders of indigenous origin. Yet Juárez's rural reforms were very injurious to the Indian peasantry. Legislation designed to promote agrarian capitalism not only mandated the sale of church land, but undermined communal land ownership by Indian villages as well.

The law restricted farm ownership to individuals, private partnerships, and companies. To be sure, individual peasants were allowed to buy and sell agricultural land, and the Liberals hoped to advance the Jeffersonian ideal of promoting rural yeoman-citizens supporting democracy and rural modernization.[20] But, in practice, land affected by the reform was generally purchased by wealthy landowners, since capital-poor peasants could not afford it. Rural tax and debt peonage policies also further impoverished the rural peasantry.

As a consequence, the rural poor periodically rose up in rebellion. During

Yucatán's War of the Castes (1847–55), Mayan Indians drove the central government from the state and established virtual independence briefly and then local autonomy until the end of the century. Elsewhere in the south, Augustina Gómez Chechep, a messianic young peasant woman, led an uprising of Chamula Indians (1869–70). Finally, Apache warriors, having fled American settlers north of the border, crossed into Mexico and attacked farmers in the frontier region. The most powerful band, led by the legendary warrior Cochise, killed an estimated fifteen thousand people.[21]

THE PORFIRIAN ERA (1876–1880, 1884–1911)

In 1876, when President Sebastián Lerdo de Tejada tried to secure a second term, General Porfirio Díaz toppled him in defense of the Liberal Party principle of "no [presidential] reelection." Díaz was elected to a single term, following which he turned over the presidency to his handpicked successor, Manuel González (1880–84).[22] But the general returned to office in 1884. Abandoning his earlier commitment to nonreelection, Díaz governed the country for twenty-seven years. During that time he brought Mexico a degree of centralized control and stability that it had not previously enjoyed, but at the cost of severe repression.

The *Porfiriato* (Díaz dictatorship) transformed the country in several important ways. Having endured frequent government turnovers and constant political turmoil since independence, Mexico experienced an extended period of stability under his iron fist. The federal government strengthened the nation-state by establishing dominance over local and provincial strongmen. Toward that end, President Díaz removed regional *caciques* from office and replaced them with administrators loyal to him. He also appointed regional military commanders who had no prior ties to their jurisdictions, thereby making it difficult for them to develop a local following. For the same purpose, he removed district *jefes políticos* (political chiefs) from the provincial governors' authority and placed them directly under his control. Thus, after decades of political disorder, the country finally had a powerful national government.

Economic growth kept pace with political change. The president's civilian advisors, known as *científicos,* believed that national "salvation lay in transforming Mexico into a white man's country oriented by European values and customs."[23] The government created a "favorable climate" for investment by repressing labor unions and banning strikes. Foreign capital poured in, lured by increased political stability and supportive economic policies. In fact, by the end of Díaz's reign, two-thirds of the country's investment came from abroad, particularly the United States.[24] Mines, railroads, electric power, petroleum, and sugar mills, among other things, all attracted foreign capital. As a consequence of that investment, the nation's infrastructure and productive capacities grew enormously.

Mining output rose 239 percent between 1891 and 1910. . . . Industrial production rose at the annual rate of 3.6 percent between 1878 and 1911. . . . Between 1876 and 1910 . . . [the length of] railroad tracks laid increased from 666 to 19,280 kilometers.[25]

During the early decades of the Díaz dictatorship, political tranquillity and economic development were mutually reinforcing. As political stability attracted investment, so did economic growth provide resources for maintaining order. For example, rapid expansion of the nation's railroads not only stimulated economic development, but also enabled the government to dispatch troops more quickly to outlying areas in order to put down any challenges to central authority.[26] In order to placate the provincial *caciques* whom he was replacing, Díaz often offered them opportunities for enrichment. For many years the regime also coopted segments of the middle and upper classes by allowing them to benefit from the nation's growing economy. Economic growth brought about the expansion of the state bureaucracy, thereby providing employment for the burgeoning middle class. In fact, by 1910 approximately three-fourths of the middle class was employed by the state.[27]

The great losers under the *Porfiriato*, however, were the rural poor, the largest segment of the population. Díaz continued the government's policy of selling Indian communal property (*ejidos*) to rural capitalists. In addition, new legislation promoted the sale of public lands to private companies. As a result, agricultural resources became increasingly concentrated in the hands of large landowners, while many peasants were pushed off their plots, often to be forced to work for the large estates. By 1910, "some 5 million [rural] Mexicans were dispossessed and condemned to debt peonage and slavery."[28] Indeed, over half of the rural inhabitants were working on *haciendas*.[29]

New innovations in production techniques coupled with the expansion of the railroads stimulated the commercialization of agriculture and further whetted the landlords' appetite for land. In the state of Morelos, as capital-intensive sugar mills were introduced, plantation owners felt pressured to increase their cane production so as to pay off their investment costs and avail themselves of the mills' greater capacity. In states such as Morelos, growers, backed by the local authorities, evicted neighboring peasants from their farms. Describing this phenomenon, John Womack compares the influence of pre-capitalist *haciendas* over neighboring peasant villages with the more pernicious control of highly capitalized plantations:

> The social difference between the old and the new oppression was as profound as the difference between a manor and a factory. Before, various [peasant] communities and economic enterprises had co-existed. . . . Sugar plantations, traditional villages, small-farm settlements, single independent farms. . . . Not all these different kinds of societies flourished, but they were all grudgingly able to survive. . . . After 1880 this assumption crumbled rapidly. . . . Plantations in Morelos became company towns.[30]

In time the purchasing power of Mexico's rural workers fell below colonial levels.[31] For years, peasant resistance was crushed by the army and the *rurales,* Díaz's rural police. In the northern state of Sonora, for example, the military launched a four-year campaign (1903–7) against a Yaqui Indian uprising. Following their defeat, many of the Yaquis were deported to the Yucatán's henequen plantations, where they worked in virtual slavery.

While conditions for the peasantry deteriorated, *hacendados* with government connections enriched themselves. In the state of Chihuahua, one of the dictator's old army colleagues, Luis Terrazas, became the country's largest landowner. His fifty *haciendas* covered seven million acres, eight times the area of the vast King Ranch in Texas. In addition, Terrazas's family had extensive industrial and banking holdings.[32]

Throughout the *Porfiriato,* not surprisingly, there were localized revolts and other forms of rural resistance. By themselves, however, isolated and poorly armed peasants posed no threat to the regime. While revolutions are always started by mass discontent, they never succeed without more broadly based resistance to the old order, spread across the class structure. Mass movements require the leadership of men (such as Fidel Castro or Mao Zedong) who emerge from the middle and upper class. By the start of the twentieth century, multiclass opposition to the Díaz regime had begun to develop.

Much of the resistance was centered in the north, the region that had experienced the most economic modernization. Although extensive foreign investment had stimulated growth, it often had also threatened the interests of local elites. In Coahuila, for example, the state's richest family, the Madero clan, led the opposition to foreign investment. At the same time, members of the skilled working class and middle class resented new enterprises that frequently reserved their best jobs for foreigners. As with many twentieth-century revolutions, nationalism became the glue that bound diverse social classes in a broad opposition coalition.

Mexicans of all classes were alienated by the Díaz dictatorship's repressive behavior. Peasants who resisted the landlords' encroachment on village lands were brutally put down. The emerging working class was denied the right to unionize or strike. And the middle class took exception to Díaz's suppression of opposition political organizations and newspapers.

THE MEXICAN REVOLUTION (1910–1920)

The Revolution of 1910 was the defining event in modern Mexican history. Critics on the left charge that it did not change enough, that its early socioeconomic reforms were soon frozen. Critics on the right argue that it sent the Mexican economy down an excessively statist path. What is certain is that the Revolution shaped what Mexico was to become for the remainder of the century. Like major revolutions elsewhere—such as France's, Russia's, and China's—Mexico's insurrection was begun by moderate reformers who were soon swept aside by more radical leadership.[33] Unlike many of the twentieth-century revolutions that would follow it, however, Mexico's insurgency never followed a marxist path.

The Revolution's precipitating event was the 1910 presidential election. Porfirio Díaz's opponent was Francisco Madero, a liberal reformer and member of one of Mexico's wealthiest families. Madero led the "antireelectionist" movement seeking to reestablish single-term limits on the presidency, an ideal that Díaz himself had once espoused. Concerned more with political change than socioeconomic reform, Madero focused his campaign on the issues of fair elections and term limits.

Shortly before the election, however, he was arrested, and Díaz soon swept to an overwhelming, but highly suspect, victory. Released on bail, Madero escaped to the United States where his calls for revolt sparked a series of uprisings in Mexico. Peasants in two states formed the heart of the rural revolt. In the north (Chihuahua), Pascual Orozco, a mule skinner, and Francisco (Pancho) Villa, a muleteer and social bandit, became the rebels' most outstanding military leaders. Villa's following consisted of cowboys, small ranchers, miners, blue-collar workers, cattle rustlers, and bandits, all of them threatened in some way by Díaz's economic modernization. Eventually, the División del Norte, Villa's ragtag but reasonably effective army, came to number some forty thousand men, women, and children.[34] In the southern state of Morelos, Emiliano Zapata, a respected horse trainer and village leader, led the Indian peasants' struggle to regain their land. A man of great integrity, Zapata eventually became the Revolution's most venerated leader. Smaller insurrectionary movements also emerged in Baja California, Sonora, and several other states.

On 25 May 1911, following the rebel capture of Ciudad Juárez, President Díaz submitted his resignation. Shortly thereafter Francisco Madero was elected president. But although Porfirio Díaz had been toppled, the army, bureaucracy, and economic institutions he helped fashion—in short, much of the old order—remained largely intact. At the same time, Francisco Madero's vision of change was rather limited, as he had little understanding of the social and economic grievances that had motivated the peasants and workers to revolt. "The people, he [erroneously] declared . . . , were not asking for bread, they were asking for freedom."[35] His administration also suffered from his poor administrative skills. It was not long before the disillusioned Emiliano Zapata, Pancho Villa, and Pascual Orozco resumed their struggle for the land.

As we have noted, the Mexican Revolution was unusual in that it lacked a dominant leader or a guiding party. The assorted revolutionary armies often represented different social classes, with distinct goals. The peasantry, themselves divided according to region, wanted land. Blue-collar workers in the cities, mines, and railroads demanded better wages, improved working conditions, and the right to unionize and to strike. The middle class wanted limits on foreign investment, more opportunities for upward mobility, and more democratic political institutions. At times, these goals came into conflict. Consequently, no sooner had Díaz's army been defeated when the contending revolutionary armies turned against each other, with fighting continuing until the end of the decade.

After only fifteen months in office, Francisco Madero was ousted by General Victoriano Huerta and subsequently shot. Huerta, an opportunist who had served both Díaz and Madero, then encountered resistance from the peasant armies of Pancho Villa and Emiliano Zapata as well as the centrist, Constitutionalist armies headed by Governor Venustiano Carranza of Coahuila and commanded by General Alvaro Obregón. In 1914, fighting a losing battle with the Constitutionalists at home and facing external pressure from U.S. President Woodrow Wilson, Huerta resigned from office. But with their common enemy removed, Carranza's forces turned against Villa and Zapata.

These confrontations reflected the conflicting class interests of the Revolution's different wings. Thus, when the country's most powerful peasant leaders met in 1914,

> They poured out in a torrent of volubility their mutual hatred for [Venustiano Carranza, himself a wealthy landlord]. Villa pronounced his opinion of the middle class revolutionaries who followed Carranza: "Those are men who have always slept on soft pillows. How could they ever be friends of the people, who have spent their whole lives in nothing but suffering?" Zapata concurred: "On the contrary, they have always been the scourge of the people. . . . As soon as they see a little chance, well, they want to take advantage of it and line their own pockets!"[36]

While Villa's Northern Division was one and one-half times the size of the Constitutionalist army, "it was less an army than a 'folk migration' of men, women and children."[37] Ultimately, neither Villa nor Zapata had the weaponry, organization, or political skills needed to govern Mexico. Indeed, neither aspired to the presidency; both harbored much more limited, regional aspirations. By 1917, Carranza's forces had gained control over most of the country. His supporters, meeting in Querétero, issued a new constitution and subsequently elected him president.

The 1917 Constitution contained a number of progressive provisions designed to win peasant and worker support. Thus, Article 123 granted labor a number of rights and protections, some not yet granted in many Western democracies. These included the right to organize unions and to strike; an eight-hour workday and six-day workweek; limits on child labor; the right to share in company profits; and social security insurance covering life, disability, unemployment, and health. Article 27 established Mexico's control over all its mineral deposits. It also called for the breakup of large agricultural estates and the return of communal landholdings that had been illegally seized from the peasantry.

Had Venustiano Carranza implemented many of those provisions, he would have radically changed Mexico's social and economic structures. But as the Revolution's most conservative leader, he had little interest in pursuing such measures. Therefore, Emiliano Zapata continued the struggle for land and justice. In the end, he was assassinated in 1919 in an ambush arranged by Carranza. With his death and a peace settlement with Pancho Villa in the following year, there was no longer great pressure on the government to effect serious reform in the countryside. Ultimately, then, the principal victors in the Revolution were neither the peasants nor the workers, but rather the middle class, businessmen, and modernizing landowners. The country's new leaders were soldier-politicians, drawn particularly from the states of Coahuila, Sonora, and other parts of the Mexican north.

Subsequently, presidents such as Alvaro Obregón (1920–24) and, especially, Lázaro Cárdenas (1934–40) enacted many of the labor reforms, the land redistribution, and the economic nationalism called for by the Constitution. But their administrations were exceptions in what otherwise became a distinctly centrist Revolution. Indeed, some historians argue that the Mexican Revolution was not a mass insurgency from below, but rather a civil war between factions of the middle and upper classes in which the masses were secondary players.[38]

CREATING A NEW POLITICAL ORDER (1920–1940)

The Revolution took a shocking toll in lives and suffering. Among a population of sixteen to seventeen million people, between one and two million died.[39] Millions more were wounded or uprooted from their homes. Hundreds of villages disappeared from the face of the earth. Many Mexicans died while struggling for their vision of social justice: land for the peasantry, better conditions for workers. Eventually, Mexico's leaders would be forced to address these goals in some fashion. But major socioeconomic reforms and redistributive programs were first deferred for more than a decade. The revolutionary elite's initial goal was restoring stability to a society that had been in turmoil for more than a decade.

Violence had extended to the highest reaches of government, with one revolutionary leader after another being killed. As we have seen, Francisco Madero and Emiliano Zapata were both murdered. When Carranza tried to name his successor in 1920, his former military chief, Alvaro Obregón, revolted and had himself elected president. Carranza was assassinated while fleeing Mexico City. Although Obregón's military revolt was Mexico's last successful coup, there were failed attempts in 1923, 1927, 1929, and, briefly, in 1938. Political assassinations also continued. Three years after Carranza's death, Francisco (Pancho) Villa was murdered, and in 1928 Obregón was assassinated after being elected to a second presidential term.

At the same time, broader social violence raged throughout the 1920s. Sonora's Yaqui Indians, ever resistant to centralized control, again waged war against the national government. Bitter labor conflicts pitted workers against employers, labor unions against the state, and competing unions against each other. Although the number of unionized workers at that time was relatively small (some 100,000), their strikes could be quite damaging to the economy because they were more concentrated in crucial industries such as petroleum.

Finally, the decade's most protracted and violent struggle was waged by

conservative Catholics who resisted President Plutarco Elías Calles's anticlerical policies. Known as the *cristeros* (from their rallying cry, "*Viva Cristo Rey!*"
"Long Live Christ the King!"), they waged a peasant-based guerrilla war for
three years (1926–29) at a tremendous cost in human life.

The prolonged turmoil, loss of life, and political instability that followed
Díaz's overthrow caused many Mexicans to look positively on their authoritarian political traditions. So the 1917 Constitution had vested considerable
power in the federal government, particularly the presidency. But to prevent a
reoccurrence of a prolonged dictatorship such as the *Porfiriato* it also prohibited presidential reelection.* By 1934, the country had achieved sufficient stability to begin a cycle of *sexenios* (six-year presidential terms), which has continued unabated until today. Besides preventing an extended dictatorship, the
presidential term limit has facilitated the infusion of new talent and ideas every
six years.

Although the restoration of an all-powerful presidency and the reconsti-
tution of a ruling elite indicate the limits of Mexico's revolutionary change,
these developments did not signify a return to prerevolutionary politics as
usual. Even had the new governing class wanted that, the mobilization of millions of peasants, workers, and members of the middle class during the insurrection precluded that option. It was partly to coopt those sectors that
Presidents Calles and Cárdenas created and developed an official party, which
ever since has allowed those social classes some access to the political system.
Now known as the PRI (after several name changes), the official party has for
nearly seven decades been synonymous with the government and has often
merged with the state (see chapter 4). While creating new channels for mass
mobilization, the official party's corporatist structure has also permitted the
political elite to weaken and exclude any contending labor union, peasant
group, or middle-class organization that could challenge the party's dominant
position.

A second, critical political achievement of the revolutionary elite was dis-
lodging the military from the center of political power. With only infrequent
exception, Mexico had been ruled by military men throughout its history. The
career officers who had governed for most of the nineteenth century were replaced after the Revolution by citizen soldiers who had taken up arms in the
insurrection. From 1917 through the 1930s, all of the nation's presidents had
started their political careers by serving as officers in the revolutionary army.
Bowing to the military's long-standing involvement in politics, Lázaro Cárdenas had assigned one of the ruling party's four sectors to the military.

Still, Cárdenas and his predecessors, Obregón and Calles, had gradually
reduced the army's political influence. Consequently, when Manuel Avila Camacho assumed the presidency in 1940, he was in a position to terminate the

---

* Alvaro Obregón's supporters later amended the Constitution to allow him to be elected to a second nonconsecutive term. However, he was assassinated before he could take office, and subsequently the Constitution was again amended to establish a single-term presidency lasting six years.

military's corporate representation in the party. Avila Camacho was also to be the last Mexican president with a military background.

CÁRDENAS AND SOCIAL REFORM (1934–1940)

In 1934, former president Calles selected Lázaro Cárdenas, a dark horse from the left wing of the ruling National Revolutionary Party (PNR), as the governing party's presidential candidate. Once in office Cárdenas displayed a degree of independence that Calles had never anticipated and made himself Mexico's most influential president in the twentieth century. With a measure of political stability finally restored, Cárdenas believed it was time to address the Revolution's unfulfilled socioeconomic promises. During his administration, the state for the first time enacted substantial redistributive programs benefiting the peasantry and working class.

To be sure, earlier presidents had introduced some progressive economic programs. Obregón, for example, had distributed over one million hectares (2.47 million acres) of farmland to the peasantry, hoping to pacify the countryside after the revolutionary upheaval. Between 1929 and 1934, the government enacted additional agrarian reform.[40] At the same time, Presidents Carranza, Obregón, and Calles had also introduced economic reforms designed to benefit organized labor. But the reach of these policies had been limited. From 1917 through 1934, only about 10 percent of the country's cultivated land was redistributed, and only a like proportion of the peasantry had benefited.[41] Government labor policy generally was designed more to establish state control over labor unions than to benefit the working class.

By contrast, Cárdenas addressed the needs of the poor far more aggressively than any twentieth-century Mexican president. One of his most important legacies was a great expansion of agrarian reform. His administration distributed forty-five million acres of farmland to over eight hundred thousand peasant families, more than double the area disbursed by all other administrations combined since the Revolution. In order to strengthen the beneficiaries' control over their property, the agrarian reform had placed affected land in communal holdings called *ejidos,* whose plots could not be sold or otherwise transferred outside the community. In 1930, these *ejidos* controlled about 15 percent of the country's cultivated land. By 1940, that proportion had tripled to 47 percent, mostly as a result of Cárdenas's policies. During that same period, the number of landless peasants in Mexico fell from 2.5 million to 1.9 million.[42] Because most peasant beneficiaries lacked adequate financial resources, the government offered them technical assistance, agriculture schools, and credit from the National Ejidal Credit Bank. Cárdenas also invested twice as much funding in rural education as the combined total spent by all of his predecessors since 1917.[43] The net result of his reforms was an appreciable improvement in rural living standards.[44]

At the same time, the government mobilized and organized the working class, as labor unions became a central component of Cárdenas's political base. Petroleum workers, railroad employees, miners, metalworkers, teachers, and other important segments of the workforce organized into unions with significant state support.[45] In 1936, the Confederation of Mexican Workers (CTM) was founded, uniting most of the country's industrial and trade unions. By the time the CTM was incorporated into the ruling party two years later, it represented seven hundred thousand members.[46] As the size and strength of the labor movement increased, so did the rate of strikes. The Cárdenas administration intervened in many of those disputes, often resolving them in favor of labor.[47] The real income of Mexican workers improved along with benefits and working conditions.[48]

Heightened labor militancy also promoted economic nationalism, another of Cárdenas's objectives. The president warned employers that if they could not maintain labor peace, the state might be forced to step in. On that basis, the government later nationalized a number of important enterprises that were mired in destabilizing labor conflicts. The most significant instance was the nationalization of the petroleum industry.

> On March 18, 1938, Cárdenas broadcast to the nation, rehearsing the sins of the [foreign oil] companies and announcing their outright expropriation. Workers were already moving in to take control of the plants. . . . In terms of political drama and presidential prestige, the oil expropriation was the high point of the Cárdenas years. . . . From the bishops to the students . . . , Mexicans rallied to the national course. . . . Perhaps a quarter of a million paraded through the streets of the capital [supporting the president's move]. . . . Never before, or after, did the nation display such solidarity.[49]

In all, the Cárdenas era represented the most radical phase of the Mexican Revolution. More than any president in the nation's history, Lázaro Cárdenas championed the cause of social justice, redressed many of his country's glaring economic inequalities, and promoted national self-determination. His expropriation of petroleum (Mexico's most valuable natural resource), the railroads, and other vital industries transformed the state into the country's most powerful economic actor. But although he considered himself a socialist, Cárdenas only implemented more moderate, Keynesian economic policies not unlike those being introduced at the time by Franklin D. Roosevelt and reformers elsewhere.

As he advanced the economic well-being of the poor, Cárdenas also brought them under state political control. When the PNR was reorganized in 1938 and renamed the Party of the Mexican Revolution (PRM), its newly created corporatist structure included peasant and labor sectors. Since then the peasant sector has been dominated by the National Peasant Confederation (CNC), representing the nation's *ejidatarios* (beneficiaries of the agrarian reform). The labor sector has revolved around the Confederation of Mexican Workers (CTM). (See chapters 4 and 5 for discussion of these two groups as well as the middle-class CNOP.)

Under Cárdenas there was a symbiotic relationship between the state and the mass-based sectors of the official party: the government received greater public support, and the lower classes benefited from the government's economic reforms. But the state's control over mass organizations allowed succeeding administrations to manipulate labor unions and peasant organizations in order to withstand democratic, mass participation. Eventually, the very corporatist structures that Cárdenas had created to improve conditions for the masses permitted the state to impose regressive economic policies during succeeding decades. As Nora Hamilton notes:

> What is significant in explaining eventual state control of the popular sectors [especially workers and peasants] is not simply the intent or actions of the Cárdenas government but the apparent failure of the affected sectors to recognize the implicit contradiction of their alliance with the state and the importance of maintaining their independence. The development or reinforcement of authoritarian structures within the peasant and labor movements meant a loss of control of those movements by their membership.[50]

Today, Lázaro Cárdenas remains the country's most revered and beloved president, lionized for his contributions to socioeconomic equality and Mexican nationalism. For more than half a century, the Cardenistas remained the primary voice of social justice within the PRI. In the mid-1980s, they created the Democratic Current, a faction demanding democratization of the ruling party. When their efforts were rebuffed and they were expelled from the PRI, they entered the 1988 presidential election as part of a left-of-center, multiparty coalition, called the National Democratic Front (FDN). The FDN's presidential candidate was Cuauhtémoc Cárdenas, the former PRI governor of Michoacán and son of Mexico's legendary president.

MEXICO MOVES RIGHT (1940–1970)

Cárdenas's progressive social programs turned out to be somewhat aberrant, a leftward policy swing that was greatly slowed or reversed in the succeeding decades. His policies alienated powerful groups inside Mexico and abroad: the Monterrey business community, large landowners, segments of the military, portions of the middle class, and American oil companies, among others. Faced with an impending recession and a large budget deficit at the close of his term, Cárdenas moderated his policies and chose a centrist politician, Manuel Avila Camacho, as his successor.

Both Avila Camacho (1940–46) and President Miguel Alemán (1946–52) stressed economic growth and industrialization, rather than redistribution, as their primary policy objectives (see chapter 6). Indeed, from the 1940s into the 1960s government policy adversely influenced rural living standards by supporting capital transfer from the countryside to the cities. "Though each president [during this period] gave lip service to agrarian reform, the largest part of the federal government's annual expenditures went to promote the development of basic industries."[51] Within the agricultural sector itself, the state largely channeled agricultural credits and technology to large commercial farmers rather than *ejidatarios.*

At times, progressive presidents such as López Mateos (1958–64) and Luis Echeverría (1970–76) revived agrarian reform and increased government assistance to the *ejido* peasantry. But their efforts could not overcome the prevailing pattern of rural poverty.[52] More recently, Carlos Salinas officially brought to an end the agrarian reform program, once a centerpiece of the Revolution, and opened the door for privatization of *ejido* plots.* While it is too early to determine the effects of this change, critics fear it will increase income inequality and rural poverty.

The relationship between organized labor and the state has also been transformed since the 1940s. Whereas Cárdenas had mobilized the working class and supported it during labor-management disputes, Avila Camacho and, especially, Alemán were decidedly pro-business. Though the subject of considerable government criticism under Cárdenas, Monterrey's powerful business leaders were praised by President Avila Camacho as people "who dream and plan for the prosperity and greatness of Mexico."[53] At the same time the outbreak of World War II restrained labor militancy. As part of the war effort, the CTM's member unions agreed to limit wage demands and strike activity as part of a "social truce" between labor, management, and the state. Organized labor abandoned class struggle in favor of "national unity." Symbolizing its more centrist ideology, the CTM changed its marxist rallying cry, "For a Classless Society," to the more nationalistic motto, "For the Emancipation of Mexico."[54]

The radical union leaders who had helped Cárdenas build the labor movement in the previous decade were purged from their positions. Most important, the CTM's founding father, Vicente Lombardo Toledano, was replaced by Fidel Velázquez, a far more conservative union boss who has dominated the labor movement ever since. In response to the CTM's swing rightward, several of the country's largest industrial unions established a rival confederation. These dissidents included the railroad, electric power, petroleum, mining and metalworking, telephone, and textile unions. But Alemán squashed the opposition leadership and restored CTM dominance.[55] As a consequence, the rate of strikes diminished nationally and wage demands were contained in order to encourage greater capital investment.

For the next three decades, heavy state and private sector investment stimulated vigorous economic growth. By the 1970s, Mexico had become one of the Third World's most economically developed nations. But critics of this "economic miracle" note that its benefits were very inequitably distributed, leaving behind millions who remained marginalized and mired in poverty.[56] As the EZLN rebels in Chiapas have noted years later, the country's peasants were most neglected, especially rural Indians. Still, as long as economic growth re-

---

* The Chiapas uprising was partly directed against Salinas's 1992 Agrarian Law. In an effort to restore stability, the government resumed very limited land redistribution, but only in Chiapas.

mained robust, enough benefits trickled down to the bottom levels of society to forestall political unrest.

The post-Cárdenas era also witnessed additional changes in political institutions. In 1946, President Avila Camacho changed the official party's name once again, this time from the PRM to the Institutional Revolutionary Party (PRI). Unlike the previous name change, this one was not accompanied by structural reorganization. But the new name itself had symbolic import. The use of the word *institutional* indicated that the radical Cardenista phase of the Revolution was over and that it was now time to consolidate (or, sometimes, roll back) reform. Henceforth, change would have to come through more gradual, formal channels.

At the same time, successive administrations deepened civilian control over the armed forces, thereby reducing the military's political influence. The tradition of citizen-soldier presidents prevailing since the Revolution came to an end. Like the presidents that preceded him, Manuel Avila Camacho had been an army officer. Unlike them, however, he never was a military leader. Indeed, his detractors derisively called him the "unknown soldier." His relations with the armed forces had been damaged by his suspect electoral victory over Juan Andreu Almazán, a respected general who had gone on leave to enter the race. Andreu Almazán had broad support among his fellow officers, and thirty-four generals had also taken leave to campaign for him. When Andreu Almazán lost the fraud-tainted election, he challenged the results. Conscious of the general's backing in the military, many Mexicans anticipated a coup.

Though the army never attempted a takeover, Avila Camacho had obvious motivation for further limiting the military's political influence after he took office. He soon disbanded the PRM's military sector (created for soldiers and officers of the army and marines), a scant two years after Cárdenas had created it.[57] When Avila Camacho left office in 1946, he chose Miguel Alemán as his successor, the first civilian (other than an interim president) to serve as president since 1920. All chief executives since that time have been civilians. The military's political influence continued to diminish at least into the 1960s. That change was reflected in its shrinking share of the national budget: from 21 percent in 1940 to 10 percent in 1950 and 3 percent in 1980.[58]

That is not to say that the armed forces is currently without political clout. Its influence in the critical area of national security makes it an important political player.[59] Still, when compared with that of the armed forces in other Latin American nations, the Mexican military's political power currently ranks among the lowest. No other country in the region has been free of military rule for so long. Considering Mexico's earlier history, that surely ranks as one of the Revolution's more outstanding accomplishments.

By Latin American or Third World standards, Mexico has been quite stable for nearly seventy years. Yet it has also experienced serious political strains in recent decades. In the late 1950s, for example, the long-quiet labor movement was shaken by a surge of rank-and-file discontent over union corruption and declining living standards. In the most bitter labor conflict, the government used army troops to crush a nationwide railroad strike led by radical insurgents.[60] During the 1960s and 1970s, marxist guerrilla movements were organized in several rural regions, most notably in the state of Guerrero. And in 1968, as the country prepared to host the summer Olympics, student activists in Mexico City mobilized mass protests against the government. The government's massacre of demonstrators at the Plaza de Tlatelolco and the arrest of student leaders severely eroded the regime's legitimacy. As a result, the next two presidents, Luis Echeverría (1970–76) and José López Portillo (1976–82), sought ways to regain the Mexican people's support.*

THE SEARCH FOR RENEWED STABILITY (1970–)

Since the 1968 student upheaval, a series of political and economic crises have further undermined the government's legitimacy. Most recently, the prolonged economic decline of the 1980s has been followed by the EZLN rebellion in Chiapas, the assassination of Luis Donaldo Colosio, and the collapse of the peso. In response, successive administrations have tried to coopt or circumvent the opposition by opening up the electoral system, restructuring Congress, and facilitating more honest electoral counts.

Presidents Echeverría and López Portillo also tried to bolster PRI support by lavishly spending on populist economic programs. But in the aftermath of the 1982 debt crisis and a worldwide trend toward fiscal conservatism the de la Madrid (1982–88) and Salinas (1988–94) administrations sharply reduced state economic intervention. At the same time, Mexico's recent presidents faced considerable pressure to accelerate political reform.

When Luis Echeverría took office, he faced the difficult task of disassociating himself from the Tlatelolco massacre and the previous administration's other repressive policies. After all, as President Gustavo Díaz Ordaz's secretary of government he had overseen many of those very policies.[61] But as president, Echeverría shifted from the right to the reformist wing of the PRI in a feat of considerable political dexterity. Associating himself with the Cardenista tradition, he became one of the country's most progressive postwar presidents.

In part, Echeverría's transformation was intended to regain the support of social groups that had been alienated by his predecessor, particularly disaffected students and intellectuals. The president's shift left was true to the "pendulum" theory of Mexican politics, which holds that presidents frequently take positions that differ ideologically from their predecessor's (though within clearly circumscribed boundaries) in order to appeal to political constituencies that had been estranged by the past administration.[62]

Echeverría put a populist imprint on both his domestic and his foreign policies. At home, he released student leaders, lowered the voting age, in-

---

* The delegitimizing effect of the Tlatelolco massacre at home and its negative impact on Mexico's image abroad in many ways paralleled the effects of China's Tiananmen Square massacre twenty-one years later.

creased opposition party representation in Congress, and augmented the economic role of the state considerably. Abroad, he allied Mexico more closely with the nonaligned bloc and periodically upset Washington over relations with Cuba and Israel.[63]

Many of these policies aimed to secure the support of the university students, intellectuals, and professionals whose skills were badly needed by the government bureaucracy and the PRI. As Peter Smith has noted:

> For decades after the Revolution, intellectuals tended to collaborate with state authorities. . . . Then came 1968. The massacre . . . suddenly disrupted the long-standing agreement between the intellectual and political establishments . . . and essayists began to question the basic legitimacy of [the] regime. . . . The universities became . . . hotbeds of opposition. . . . Echeverría was unable to complete a ceremonial visit to National University and had to flee from angry student crowds.[64]

That initial hostility from professionals and intellectuals was particularly detrimental to Echeverría because his administration was especially dependent on their talents. His was the first Mexican government to be dominated by technocrats (*técnicos*) rather than career politicians (*políticos*), that is, to be led by trained professionals (many with postgraduate degrees) whose expertise had carried them to the top of the bureaucratic ladder.[65] Consequently, the president was anxious to mend fences with his disaffected critics. To a remarkable degree he succeeded. Many former student activists were coopted into the government, while a number of prominent, progressive intellectuals took high-profile administration positions.

But, while Echeverría liberalized the political system in a number of ways, democratization had its limits, constrained by conservative forces within the government and by the president's own authoritarian tendencies. Thus, when university students staged antigovernment demonstrations in 1971, the police allowed, and likely encouraged, right-wing goon squads to attack them. Between thirty and fifty students were killed and many more injured. Despite his professed commitment to political reform, Echeverría concentrated political power more exclusively in his own hands than had previous presidents.[66] He was also intolerant of media criticism directed against him. Thus, after initially promoting greater press freedom, his administration later forced the leftist journal *Por Qué?* out of business and ousted the editorial board of *Excelsior,* Mexico's most highly regarded newspaper at the time.

In the final accounting, Echeverría's administration has been judged a tremendous failure. He accumulated excessive budget deficits and antagonized the business community, leaving behind a legacy of private-sector capital flight, a devalued peso, government corruption, and rumors of an impending military coup. The 1976 presidential election, in which José López Portillo ran virtually unopposed, contributed to public apathy and declining voter turnout.

In order to rekindle public support for the electoral process, López Portillo introduced a far-reaching electoral reform law. The 1977 law was the most ambitious effort yet to create an enlarged, but still controlled, congressional opposition.[67] Opposition parties were allocated one-fourth of the seats in the expanded Chamber of Deputies. In addition, the law made it easier for small political parties to attain legal recognition and gain access to the mass media (chapter 4).

López Portillo's reforms did not significantly democratize Mexico. The PRI still controlled about three-fourths of the Chamber of Deputies and the entire Senate until the cataclysmic election of 1988. Moreover, congressional powers themselves remained quite limited relative to the president's. Still, government recognition of several new leftist parties and the expansion of opposition seats in the Chamber of Deputies added greater texture to the political fabric. Increased opposition party participation also helped to reduce public apathy. The rate of voter turnout in the 1982 presidential race was the highest in thirty-six years.[68]

Presidents Miguel de la Madrid (1982–88), Carlos Salinas (1988–94), and Ernesto Zedillo (1994–) have further liberalized Mexican politics but to date have failed to complete a full transition to democracy. While the political system has become more open and less repressive, elections are still not evenly contested. The number of seats allocated to opposition parties in both houses of Congress has increased, and for the first time the government has recognized opposition party victories for the Senate and for governor. Finally, recent electoral reforms permitted perhaps the most honest vote count since the Revolution in the 1994 presidential election. But fraud continues to poison the state and local electoral systems. And the PRI still enters national campaigns with such enormous resource advantages that even with an honest count, elections cannot yet be called truly fair.

In response to popular discontent in the late 1960s and early 1970s, the Echeverría administration had also tried to redress some of the socioeconomic inequities that had unleashed student, worker, and peasant unrest. The president saw an enlarged state sector as the vehicle for social reform. Seeking to create new jobs and increase public resources, his administration greatly increased the number of state-owned enterprises.[69] It also augmented spending on roads, schools, clinics, and agricultural production. While Echeverría's populist projects yielded some positive results, including more equitable income distribution, his administration's excessive deficit spending and external borrowing, coupled with a falloff in private-sector investment, precipitated a recession at the close of his term.

Not surprisingly, José López Portillo began his presidency more cautiously, moving to the political center as he tried to mend fences with powerful business groups that Echeverría had alienated. But following the government's discovery of enormous petroleum reserves, the president threw caution to the wind and adopted an expansionist economic policy that outstripped his predecessor's. Because of the country's vast new petroleum riches and the expectation of future increases in oil prices, Mexico gained access to enormous foreign credit. Borrowing heavily from abroad, the government undertook overly ambitious programs designed to accommodate a broad array of interest groups from big business to the rural poor. When Luis Echeverría took office in 1970, the public sector's external debt was $4.2 billion. By the time that López Portillo stepped down in 1982, that debt had risen to $85 billion, the second largest in the developing world.[70]

When petroleum prices subsequently fell far below expectations, the result was inevitable. In 1982, the Mexican government announced that it could no longer meet its foreign debt obligations, setting off a decade-long economic crisis throughout Latin America. Further foreign credit was curtailed, painful economic austerity programs were introduced, inflation soared, purchasing power declined, and unemployment rose to the worst levels since the Great Depression. To address the nation's large trade and budgetary deficits, Presidents Miguel de la Madrid and Carlos Salinas reversed decades of economic nationalism and state economic intervention. Abandoning the country's import-substitution, industrialization model, they promoted industrial exports and opened the country to foreign imports and investment (chapter 6). Mexico belatedly joined the General Agreement on Tariffs and Trade (GATT) and later championed the North American Free Trade Agreement (NAFTA) linking Mexico's economy to that of the United States. At the same time, de la Madrid and Salinas scaled back the state's economic role substantially and privatized major portions of the public sector.

The debt crisis of the 1980s and the government stabilization and adjustment programs enacted to remedy it have cut deeply into Mexican living standards. In addition, the deteriorating economy and the reduced size of the state sector have decreased public support for the political establishment by curtailing its ability to fund programs and dispense patronage.* Ironically, other positive, long-term social developments inadvertently have also diminished support for the government and the PRI. As Mexico's population has become more educated and more politically informed over the years, the public has become more intolerant of the corruption and fraud that pervades their country's political system. Carlos Salinas's suspect victory in the 1988 presidential election deepened the regime's legitimacy crisis.

Ernesto Zedillo is committed to continuing the neoliberal reforms of his predecessors. Indeed, as a member of Salinas's cabinet he helped craft that market-oriented economic course. But the fall of the peso and the sharp drop in living standards during his first year in office have cut short Mexico's economic recovery and exposed its excessive dependence on foreign capital. Zedillo has tried to regain public support by more vigorously pursuing political reform than previous presidents have and by reducing presidential domination. Unfortunately, his more conciliatory style has been perceived (to some extent, correctly) as a sign of weakness.

---

* An important exception to this trend was President Salinas's National Solidarity Program (PRONASOL) begun in the late 1980s. This sizable public works and social development program became a major source of support for Salinas's administration and the PRI (chapter 6).

CONCLUSIONS

In 1992–93 Mexico witnessed a bitter debate over government efforts to rewrite the nation's elementary school history texts. The intensity of that controversy, noted Jorge Castañeda, reflected the tremendous importance of historical symbols in the culture. "Mexican history," he observed, "appears to be one long continuum, with great and long constants and underlying continuities."[71] In trying to change the perspective of Mexican textbooks on the war with the United States, the Porfirian dictatorship, and the Tlatelolco massacre, the administration hoped to make the nation's official history congruent with the government's current neoliberal economic policies and the country's closer ties to the United States. But Mexican nationalists (including much of the intellectual establishment) considered the proposed changes unacceptable.

Because the pull of history is so strong and because symbols such as the Revolution and the struggle against foreign domination remain so powerful, major political and economic change must be legitimized by the past. Whereas historical legacies in the nineteenth century—conservative Catholicism, anticlerical liberalism, ethnic heterogeneity—tended to divide the country, the twentieth-century symbols of the Revolution and Cardenismo have been forces for unity. Small wonder that the ruling party continues to call itself the party of the Revolution (in spite of its current free-market orientation) or that the Chiapas rebels named themselves after Zapata, Mexico's most revered revolutionary hero. As it enters the twenty-first century, Mexico will need to alter its authoritarian and inegalitarian historical traditions without letting those important transformations once again divide the nation.

Notes

1. Robert Ryal Miller, *Mexico: A History* (Norman: University of Oklahoma Press, 1985), 3–65; Robert Wauchope, *The Indian Background of Latin American History: The Maya, Aztec, Inca and Their Predecessors* (New York: Alfred A. Knopf, 1970).

2. Sherburne F. Cooke and Woodrow Borah, *The Indian Population of Central Mexico: 1531–1610* (Berkeley: University of California Press, 1960).

3. Charles Cumberland, *Mexico: The Struggle for Modernity* (New York: Oxford University Press, 1968), 50.

4. Michael C. Meyer and William L. Sherman, *The Course of Mexican History*, 2d ed. (New York: Oxford University Press, 1983), 211 and 208.

5. Population data are based on Agustín Cué Cánovas, *Historia social y económica de México (1521–1824)* (México, 1972), 134, as cited in Meyer and Sherman, *Course of Mexican History*, 218.

6. Robert E. Quirk, *Mexico* (Englewood Cliffs, N.J.: Prentice Hall, 1971), 29–33.

7. Cumberland, *Mexico: The Struggle for Modernity*, 41.

8. Meyer and Sherman, *Course of Mexican History*, 218; Cumberland, *Mexico: The Struggle for Modernity*, 56, presents quite different data indicating that the Indian and Mestizo populations were nearly equal by 1800. To some extent such statistics are "guesstimates."

9. Alan Riding, *Distant Neighbors: A Portrait of the Mexicans*, 2d ed. (New York: Vintage, 1984), 3.

10. Ibid., 292. The 1990 census indicated that Indians constitute 8.5 percent of the population. This, however, is an undercount since it excludes children under the age of five. Some experts believe that the true percentage is about 15 percent. See Wayne A. Cornelius and Ann L. Craig, "Politics in Mexico," in *Comparative Politics Today*, ed. Gabriel A. Almond and G. Bingham Powell, 5th ed. (New York: Harper Collins, 1992), 465 and 513 n. 3.

11. *New York Times*, 15 June 1994.

12. Meyer and Sherman, *Course of Mexican History*, 292.

13. Jan Bazant, "The Aftermath of Independence," in *Mexico since Independence*, ed. Leslie Bethell (New York: Cambridge University Press, 1991), 3.

14. Agustín Cué Cánovas, *Historia social y económica de México: La Revolución de Independencia y México independiente hasta 1854* (México: Editorial América, 1947), 60.

15. Frank Tannenbaum, *Peace by Revolution*, 2d ed. (New York: Columbia University Press, 1966), 85.

16. On early Mexican liberalism, see Charles A. Hale, *Mexican Liberalism in the Age of Mora, 1821–1853* (New Haven: Yale University Press, 1968).

17. Friedrich Katz, "The Liberal Republic and the Porfiriato," in *Mexico since Independence*, 82.

18. Luis González y González et al., *La república restorada: la vida social*, vol. 3 of *Historia moderna de México*, ed. Daniel Cosio Villegas (México: Edición Era, 1957), 643, 692–94.

19. Miller, *Mexico: A History*, 250–51.

20. Eric R. Wolf, *Peasant Wars of the Twentieth Century* (New York: Harper and Row, 1968), 13; Friedrich Katz, "The Liberal Republic and the Porfiriato," in *Mexico since Independence*, 51.

21. Katz, "Liberal Republic and the Porfiriato," 59–60.

22. Quirk, *Mexico* 77.

23. Frank R. Brandenburg, "Causes of the Revolution," in *Revolution in Mexico*, ed. James W. Wilkie and Albert L. Michaels (New York: Alfred A. Knopf, 1969), 22.

24. Judith Adler Hellman, *Mexico in Crisis* (New York: Holmes and Meier, 1978), 2.

25. Wolf, *Peasant Wars*, 20.

26. Katz, "Liberal Republic and the Porfiriato," 49–124.

27. Ibid., 15.

28. Kenneth F. Johnson, *Mexican Democracy: A Critical View*, rev. ed. (New York: Praeger, 1978), 29.

29. Meyer and Sherman, *Course of Mexican History*, 458.

30. John Womack, Jr., *Zapata and the Mexican Revolution* (New York: Vintage, 1968), 42–43.

31. Quirk, *Mexico*, 78.

32. Meyer and Sherman, *Course of Mexican History*, 459.

33. Crane Brinton, *The Anatomy of Revolution* (New York: Vintage, 1957).

34. Robert E. Quirk, *The Mexican Revolution, 1914–1915: The Convention of Aguascalientes* (Bloomington: Indiana University Press, 1960), 82.

35. Henry Bamford Parkes, *A History of Mexico*, 3d ed. (Boston: Houghton Mifflin Co., 1960), 326.

36. Quirk, *Mexican Revolution*, 135–38.

37. Wolf, *Peasant Wars*, 35.

38. See John Womack, Jr., "The Mexican Revolution, 1910–1920," in *Mexico since Independence*, 125–200.

39. Cumberland, *Mexico: The Struggle for Modernity*, 241 and 245. The 16–17 million figure is a projection of what Mexico's population would have been in 1921 without the war. Cumberland estimates some 2 million deaths, while others have suggested lower figures.

40. Ibid., 233.

41. Ibid., 234.

42. Nora Hamilton, *The Limits of State Autonomy* (Princeton, N.J.: Princeton University Press, 1982), 177–78; Hellman, *Mexico in Crisis*, 68–74.

43. Meyer and Sherman, *Course of Mexican History*, 602.

44. Hellman, *Mexico in Crisis*, 70–71.

45. Barry Carr, "Labor and the Political Left in Mexico," in *Unions, Workers and the State in Mexico*, ed. Kevin J. Middlebrook (La Jolla: University of California–San Diego Center for U.S.-Mexican Studies, 1991), 131.

46. Daniel Levy and Gabriel Székely, *Mexico: Paradoxes of Stability and Change* (Boulder, Colo.: Westview Press, 1983), 59; Alan Knight, "The Rise and Fall of Cardenismo," in *Mexico since Independence*, 272.

47. On labor under Cárdenas, see Joe C. Ashby, *Organized Labor and the Mexican Revolution under Cárdenas* (Chapel Hill: University of North Carolina Press, 1963).

48. Hamilton, *Limits of State Autonomy*, 161.

49. Knight, "Rise and Fall of Cardenismo" 282; Ashby, *Organized Labor*, 237.

50. Hamilton, *Limits of State Autonomy*, 183.

51. Quirk, *Mexico*, 105.

52. Steven E. Sanderson, *The Transformation of Mexican Agriculture* (Princeton: Princeton University Press, 1986); Merilee S. Grindle, *Bureaucrats, Peasants, and Politicians in Mexico: A Case Study of Public Policy* (Berkeley: University of California Press, 1977): Grindle, *Searching for Rural Development: Labor Migration and Employment in Mexico* (Ithaca, N.Y.: Cornell University Press 1988).

53. Knight, "Rise and Fall of Cardenismo," 297.

54. Hellman, *Mexico in Crisis*, 41–42.

55. Kevin J. Middlebrook, "State-Labor Relations in Mexico: The Changing Economic and Political Context," in *Unions, Workers*, 6–7; Victor M. Durand, *Las derrotas obreras, 1946–1952* (México: Universidad Nacional Autónoma de México, 1984).

56. There is an abundant literature on this phenomenon in both Spanish and English. For a very readable, nontechnical summary, see Riding, *Distant Neighbors*, especially chaps. 7, 11, and 14. While the book is now about a decade old, conditions for the poor are, if anything, worse as a result of the country's steep economic decline in the 1980s.

57. Dale Story, *The Mexican Ruling Party* (New York: Praeger, 1986), 25–26; Edwin Lieuwen, "Depoliticization of the Mexican Revolutionary Army: 1915–1940)," in *The Modern Mexican Military: A Reassessment*, ed. David Ronfeldt (La Jolla: University of California–San Diego Center for U.S.-Mexican Studies, 1984), 59–61; Edwin Lieuwen, *Mexican Militarism: The Rise and Fall of the Revolutionary Army* (Albuquerque: University of New Mexico Press, 1968).

58. Edwin Lieuwen, "Depoliticization of the Mexican Revolutionary Army," 61; see also James W. Wilkie, *The Mexican Revolution: Federal Expenditures and Social Change since 1910* (Berkeley: University of California Press, 1967), 102–3.

59. David Ronfeldt, "The Mexican Army and Political Order," in *Modern Mexican Military*, 63–86.

60. Howard Handelman, "The Politics of Labor Protest in Mexico: Two Case Studies," *Journal of Inter-American Studies and World Affairs* (August 1976); Evelyn P. Stevens, *Protest and Response in Mexico* (Cambridge, Mass.: MIT Press, 1974).

61. While there is debate among scholars as to the degree of Echeverría's personal responsibility for the massacre, students and other dissidents generally blamed him for it. See Miguel Angel Centeno, *Democracy within Reason: Technocratic Revolution in Mexico* (University Park: Pennsylvania State University Press, 1994), 78 n. 10.

62. Levy and Székely, *Mexico: Paradoxes of Stability*, 111.

63. Samuel Schmidt, *The Deterioration of the Mexican Presidency: The Years of Luis Echeverría* (Tucson: University of Arizona Press, 1991), 121–35.

64. Peter H. Smith, "Leadership and Change: Intellectuals and Technocrats in Mexico," in *Mexico's Political Stability: The Next Five Years*, ed. Roderic A. Camp (Boulder, Colo.: Westview Press, 1986), 104–5.

65. Roderic A. Camp, "The Political Technocrat in Mexico and the Survival of the Political

System," *Latin American Research Review* 20, no. 1 (1985): 97–117; Peter Smith, *The Labyrinths of Power: Political Recruitment in Twentieth Century Mexico* (Princeton: Princeton University Press, 1979).

66. Manuel Villa Aguilera, *La institución presidencial* (México: UNAM, 1987).

67. Kevin J. Middlebrook, "Political Liberalization in an Authoritarian Regime: The Case of Mexico," in *Transitions from Authoritarian Rule: Latin America,* ed. Guillermo O'Donnell, Philippe C. Schmitter, and Laurence Whitehead (Baltimore, Md.: Johns Hopkins University Press, 1986), 123–47.

68. Ibid., 141.

69. Levy and Székely, *Mexico: Paradoxes of Stability,* 148; Riding, *Distant Neighbors,* 206.

70. Morgan Guarantee Trust, "Mexico: Progress and Prospects," *World Financial Markets,* May 1984, 2; Levy and Székely, *Mexico: Paradoxes of Stability,* 149.

71. Jorge G. Casteñeda, "Ferocious Differences," *Atlantic Monthly,* July 1995, 75.

3

The Structure of Government

At first glance the structure of Mexican government appears quite similar to that of the United States government. It is a federal system, encompassing thirty-one states and the Federal District (Mexico City), with each state having an elected governor and legislature. As in the United States, the executive branch is headed by a popularly elected president and his cabinet. Congress consists of two houses, the Senate and the more powerful Chamber of Deputies. Mexico also has a judicial branch including federal and state systems headed by the Supreme Court.

But in this case appearances are deceptive, and the many similarities to the American political system are more superficial than real. In fact, Mexico has a very centralized government in which the states depend on the national government for funding and remain subservient to Mexico City. Until the late 1980s, state governors (all of whom were then from the PRI) were effectively chosen and tightly controlled by the chief executive. Presidents may still replace governors who have not performed satisfactorily or whose election has been challenged. In recent years the chief executive has used that power occasionally to remove elected or sitting governors who have embarrassed the administration. These have included unpopular or corrupt incumbent governors as well as winning PRI candidates who were not permitted to take office because their victories were suspect.

Presidential supremacy also characterizes the executive's relations with the other branches of the national government. Indeed, so great is the executive's authority that the Mexican political system is sometimes described as a presidential dictatorship with six-year term limits. Because the PRI perennially controls Congress and because its delegation has slavishly followed presidential directives, at least until now, the legislature has been a rather weak body (though it has shown modest signs of independence under Zedillo).

The judiciary also does not offer a counterweight to the executive branch. To be sure, the Supreme Court has asserted some independence at times, but it always has been careful not to challenge the president's priorities. Moreover, the constitution permits only limited judicial review in which the courts may overturn executive orders or congressional legislation.

This chapter describes the structure and behavior of Mexico's government and examines the informal procedures governing recruitment of the political elite.

THE PRESIDENCY

Presidential Authority.   "Within the Mexican system, the chief executive is accorded a wide range of rights, prerogatives, and functions that together enable him to play the determining role in plotting the nation's course."[1] Through much of the country's history, strongman rule alternated with political disorder and instability. In the last decades of the nineteenth century, Porfirio Díaz closed an era of political instability by concentrating power in his own hands. Years later, fighting for the principle of "effective suffrage, no reelection," the Mexican revolutionary leadership toppled Díaz and established a single-term limit on elected office. At the same time, however, the new order continued to concentrate overwhelming power in the president's hands. Indeed, the enormous chaos and destruction brought on by the insurrection and the ongoing conflict that followed it convinced the revolutionary elite that political stability required an all-powerful presidency.

Some Mexican presidents have been stronger than others (the current chief executive, Ernesto Zedillo, seems particularly weak), but the political system concentrates power in all of them. For example, all important legislation originates in the executive branch. During the first half of his term, Carlos Salinas's administration proposed approximately 90 percent of *all* bills passed by Congress.[2] Because the PRI has enjoyed a congressional majority for decades and because the party exercises tight discipline over its legislators, it has been a foregone conclusion that presidential proposals will be adopted. By capturing nearly half of the Chamber of Deputy's seats in the 1988 election, opposition parties temporarily reduced presidential dominance. As a result of the PRI's strong comeback in the 1991 and 1994 congressional elections, however, the executive branch regained much of its previous power.

Presidentialism (presidential political supremacy) fulfills several important functions. Symbolically, the head of state is the bearer of the revolutionary tradition and a source of unity for a geographically and socioeconomically diverse nation.[3] To solidify that position and legitimize the electoral process, all PRI presidential candidates campaign intensely, even when the election's outcome is a foregone conclusion.*

> To supporters of the *status quo*, ["presidentialism"] signifies arrangements appropriate to Mexico's reality: a strong, centralizing institution, personified in a figure who can preserve order amid conflict and underdevelopment while advancing the Revolutionary projects. . . . Critics on both the right and the left, [however], view presidentialism as the core institutional flaw of a system that permits no checks on the personal power of the incumbent.[4]

Until recently, the president's importance as a national symbol inhibited

---

* As we have seen, PRI presidential candidates routinely won at least two-thirds of the vote until 1988. In the last two presidential elections, however, the official party candidates have faced far more serious opposition. But while elections have become more competitive, it is still unclear whether the ruling elite is ready to allow an opposition party candidate to win the presidency.

criticism of him in public discourse, including the press. Thus, while it was acceptable for journalists to find fault with administration policies, personal criticism of the president was out of bounds, at least for the mainstream press. Only since the 1980s has that begun to change.

In his study of the Mexican presidency, Jorge Carpizo notes the broad scope of executive power.[5] The president dominates the PRI and uses its ties to labor unions, peasant organizations, and professional groups to advance his own agenda. Within government, neither Congress nor the Supreme Court has yet seriously challenged presidential power. The professionalized military, unlike its counterparts in much of Latin America, accepts civilian, presidential control. Finally, until now Mexico's presidents have selected their own successor, though Zedillo has promised to end that practice.

As each president approaches the close of his term, he begins to evaluate various *precandidatos* (precandidates) as the potential PRI presidential nominee. For many years political custom has dictated that precandidates must be individuals with cabinet-level positions in the incumbent administration who are considered presidential material.[6] As candidate selection time approaches, media pundits and the public speculate intensely about the president's final choice, while the decision-making process remains shrouded in secrecy. Not until 1988 did the incumbent even reveal the identity of precandidates on his short list. In the lead-up to the past two elections, however, they have been named, and they have even "campaigned" among PRI leaders and influential interest groups. To date, however, the final choice has remained exclusively the president's. After consulting behind the scenes with leaders of major party factions and powerful interest groups, he has revealed his selection. At that point PRI leaders have dutifully rallied behind the anointed successor and nominated him as their candidate, though in recent years some of those unhappy with the final choice (most notably union leaders) have, for the first time, publicly signaled their displeasure.

Despite his enormous powers, however, the chief executive is not an entirely free agent able to pursue whatever policy he pleases. The stability of the political system requires him to consult on major issues with his cabinet, presidential staff, and influential interest groups. Labor bosses, most notably the longtime leader of the Confederation of Mexican Workers (CTM), Fidel Velázquez, have been particularly influential, though less so in recent years. The popular wing of the PRI articulates to the president the policy preferences of influential white-collar unions and professional groups.

Big business, though outside the PRI's formal structure, also limits the chief executive's options. Most presidents are conscious of the private sector's economic strength and consult regularly with major business groups, especially the powerful conglomerates based in Monterrey (chapter 5). Presidents Echeverría (1970–76) and López Portillo (1976–1982) demonstrated the dangers of going it alone. Echeverría's impulsive style alienated private-sector leaders who already disliked his populist policies. Consequently, business disinvestment and capital flight set off a serious financial crisis at the close of his term. Although Echeverría's successor, José López Portillo, initially tried to mend fences with the private sector, his nationalization of the country's banking system at the close of his term without having consulted those most deeply affected by that action had catastrophic consequences. Both the Echeverría and López Portillo administrations ended disastrously, in part because they had made critical economic policy decisions without adequate input from the business community.

Finally, presidents have had to work closely with the U.S. government and international financial community, particularly since the start of Mexico's economic crises. That too has limited the president's economic policy options. For example, when the Bush and Clinton administrations each helped Mexico renegotiate its foreign debt and engineer international loan packages, they insisted that the Salinas and Zedillo governments impose fiscal restraints at home.

The current economic crisis has also weakened President Zedillo domestically. His administration's poor handling of the peso devaluation has emboldened some PRI deputies to question government policy.

Presidential Recruitment.   Because of executive branch dominance and the concentration of power in the presidency, it is important to understand how Mexico's most influential political leaders are recruited through a process quite distinct from that of established democracies. Movement up the political hierarchy takes place through a complex web of patron-client relations. Aspiring politicians and technocrats wishing to be successful must first attach themselves to an influential patron who can protect and advance them.[7] The higher an aspirant hopes to rise, the more powerful his or her patron needs to be. In return for that patronage, clients owe their mentors loyalty and support.[8] Ambitious politicians and bureaucrats often have more than one patron and may switch mentors as their careers advance. Similarly, patrons have many clients. In short, Mexico's power structure consists of "interlocking chains of patron-client relationships," called *camarillas,* linking virtually all actors to patrons above them and clients below them.[9]

Politicians and technocrats frequently establish initial contacts with their patron during their university days, frequently being taken under the wing of a politically well-connected professor. Virtually all of Mexico's most important leaders first secured a very powerful mentor at the start of their career, and frequently they follow him up the political ladder. As Roderic Camp has noted, "every major national figure is the 'political child,' 'grandchild,' or 'great grandchild' of an earlier, nationally known figure."[10] Of course, since each powerful patron has many clients, only the most talented and ambitious make it to the top. Moreover, as they advance, successful politicians and technocrats usually join several *camarillas,* often belonging to more than one at the same time. The tops of important *camarillas* reach to the president's cabinet, and it is from the cabinet (dominated by the incumbent's clients) that the next president is chosen.

The careers of recent PRI presidential candidates illustrate the importance of clientelism and powerful political patrons. Thus, the young Luis Echeverría acquired an influential mentor when he married the daughter of a former state governor. The following year he was appointed personal secretary to General Rodolfo Sánchez Taboada, who soon became president of the PRI and later served as secretary of the navy. With Sánchez Taboada's support, Echeverría climbed the bureaucratic hierarchy to the national cabinet and was then elected president, without having previously run for any public office.[11] As political power has shifted from career politicians to the *técnicos,* most recent presidents have made their careers in the government bureaucracy, without the benefit of having previously held elected office.

Echeverría's successor, José López Portillo, was born into a politically well-connected family including a grandfather who had been a governor and the secretary of foreign relations. Another of his early political mentors was Emilio Martínez Manatou, who later served as secretary of the presidency. The young López Portillo was also Luis Echeverría's law school classmate at the UNAM (Mexico's massive National Autonomous University, located in the capital) and maintained a lifetime friendship with him. When Echeverría became president he appointed him to the cabinet and subsequently selected him as his successor.[12]

Miguel de la Madrid's family had been politically influential in the state of Colima for over two hundred years. Like most of the nation's political elite, however, he was raised in Mexico City. His first political patron was his uncle, Ernesto Fernández Hurtado, who later headed the Bank of Mexico under Echeverría.[13] At the same time, de la Madrid was also López Portillo's student at the UNAM law school. Years later, López Portillo appointed him to the cabinet and then tapped him for the presidency.

Carlos Salinas also was born into a politically influential family, and his father had served in President Adolfo López Mateos's cabinet. As Salinas's career progressed, he secured family, school, and professional ties linking him to nearly every cabinet member responsible for economic planning since the 1940s.[14] Consequently, his rapid ascent to the top of the Finance Ministry and Treasury was propelled not only by his impressive talent and intellect (manifested by his Harvard Ph.D.), but also by his *camarilla* ties to Miguel de la Madrid and others. Beginning as de la Madrid's student at the UNAM, Salinas later served under him at the Finance Ministry. He also worked for López Portillo, then Echeverría's Treasury secretary. Appointed to de la Madrid's cabinet at the age of thirty-four, six years later Salinas became the youngest Mexican president in modern times.

After returning from university studies in the United States and Europe, twenty-nine-year-old Luis Donaldo Colosio attached himself to Carlos Salinas (then a rising young star in the technocracy). When Salinas became Miguel de la Madrid's secretary of budget and planning, Colosio served under him. Colosio was next elected to the Chamber of Deputies, making him one of the country's few elite *técnicos* who also held an elected office. In 1988, newly elected President Salinas chose Colosio to head the PRI, then appointed him to his cabinet. Finally, five years later he designated him as the PRI's presidential candidate, a candidacy cut short by Colosio's assassination.

Mexico's current president, Ernesto Zedillo, also was a Salinas protegé. Like the two presidents who preceded him, Zedillo had a career that took him through several powerful government bureaucracies involved with economic planning (as well as a brief and rather disastrous stint as minister of education). With a Yale doctorate in economics, he was representative of Mexico's highly educated governing elite. But precisely because he was a technocrat with no prior electoral experience, his selection as the PRI nominee was poorly received by the party's *políticos* and labor leaders.

As these cases illustrate, Mexico's political elite tend to share a number of social characteristics. Overwhelmingly, they come from urban, middle-class, politically connected families. Ernesto Zedillo is a clear exception in this respect, a man of lower-class background who sold newspapers on the street as a boy to help support his family. A large and growing number of the nation's governing elite have been raised in Mexico City or have been educated there if they were born elsewhere. Typically they receive their first degree from the UNAM, with an increasing number of them earning postgraduate degrees in the United States. Between 1970 and 1994, more than one-third of the country's cabinet members came from the nation's capital, but under Presidents de la Madrid and Salinas that proportion rose to over 50 percent.[15] About half the people serving at all levels in the Salinas administration were born in the Federal District, and an even larger portion had graduated from the UNAM.[16]

As we have noted, in recent decades political power has shifted from politicians (*políticos*) who rose through the ranks as elected officials and party activists, to the hands of trained *técnicos* who have climbed the bureaucratic hierarchy, with little or no electoral experience. In fact recent presidents have rarely served previously in *any* elected capacity. Instead, they have typically developed careers and built *camarilla* contacts in economic planning ministries and other government agencies as springboards for success. Thus each of the last four presidents had headed an economic-policy-making ministry in the preceding administration. Not surprisingly, career politicians resent the *técnicos*' rapid ascent (Salinas and Zedillo, for example, shot to the top far more quickly than any *político* could have) and accuse them of being out of touch with the grass roots.[17]

As Mexico has modernized, its presidents, cabinet members, and others in the technocratic elite have become increasingly well educated. Since the early 1980s all PRI presidential candidates and many other precandidates have held postgraduate degrees in the social sciences from prestigious American universities, often from Ivy League schools. One expert has observed that Salinas's first cabinet was the most well-educated group of its kind anywhere in the world.[18] More recently, all of the precandidates in the 1994 presidential election had earned masters degrees or doctorates from elite universities such as Yale, Columbia, the University of Pennsylvania, and Stanford. Presidents Zedillo and Salinas hold Ph.D.'s from Yale and Harvard, respectively, while de la Madrid also received a postgraduate degree from Harvard.

THE CONGRESS

The Mexican Congress consists of two houses: the more powerful Chamber of Deputies (currently containing 500 seats) and the Senate (now 128 seats). Deputies serve three-year terms and are all elected concurrently. As a result of the 1993 electoral reform, the Senate now includes four senators from each of the country's thirty-one states and the Federal District, each serving a six-year term.* Since the early 1990s, senatorial elections have been staggered, with one-half of the chamber standing for election every three years. By the end of the decade, however, the entire Senate is scheduled once again to be elected concurrently with the president. Like all Mexican elected officials, neither deputies nor senators may be reelected, but congressmen who complete a term in one chamber are allowed to seek election to the other.

Unlike Latin American nations such as Brazil, Ecuador, and Peru, Mexico has never experienced sharp conflicts between the executive and legislative branches. If anything, relations have been plagued with excessive harmony. The PRI's continuous control of Congress has permitted presidential dominance. Thus, during the 1950s President Adolfo Ruiz Cortínez noted that "the chambers [of Congress] and the governors' offices belong to the president."[19] In Congress little has changed since that time. PRI congressional candidates have needed the president's prior approval. Once they are in office, they remain bound to the chief executive because he controls their chances of continuing their political careers after their term in office is over. The president's legislative proposals are virtually never defeated and, until recently, rarely have been seriously challenged.

As public pressure for democracy has increased in recent years, Mexico's political elite has responded periodically by enlarging the Chamber of Deputies in order to permit greater opposition party representation. Currently 300 deputies are elected from "uninominal" seats (i.e., electoral districts with a single deputy). As table 3-1 indicates, an overwhelming proportion of those seats are still won by PRI candidates. Only in 1988, when opposition parties captured a total of sixty-eight districts (23 percent of the uninominal total), has the opposition won more than 10 percent of them.

At the same time, however, the Chamber of Deputies currently also has 200 "plurinominal" seats that are elected through proportional representation (PR) from five large electoral regions. Under PR, each political party receives a portion of the plurinominal seats that is roughly proportional to the percentage of the popular vote that they have won in the region. Nevertheless, electoral regulations have stipulated that opposition parties receive all or, since the 1980s, almost all of these seats. Since the 1960s a series of electoral reform laws has enlarged the number of party or plurinominal seats in the Chamber.

---

* A new electoral reform law was announced in early 1996 as this book goes to press. It will alter the size and composition of both houses of Congress. Its final passage, however, has been delayed by PAN and PRI accusations against the government of voter fraud.

Table 3-1. Composition of the Chamber of Deputies: Selected Years, 1961–1994

Year	Deputies	PRI	Opposition Parties
1961		172	6
1964	uninominal	175	3
	party	—	32
1976	uninominal	195	2
	party	—	41
1979	uninominal	296	4
	plurinominal	—	100
1988	uninominal	232	68
	plurinominal	28	172
1991	uninominal	290	10
	plurinominal	30	170
1994	uninominal	277	23
	plurinominal	23	177

Sources: Roderic Camp, "Mexico's Legislature: Missing the Democratic Lockstep?" in *Legislatures and the New Democracies in Latin America*, ed. David Close (Boulder, Colo: Lynne Rienner Publishers, 1995), 29; Arturo Alvarado, "Los comicios y la información general," in *Las elecciones de Salinas*, ed. Arturo Sánchez Gutiérrez (México: Plaza y Valdes, 1992), 162; María Amparo Casar, *The 1994 Mexican Presidential Elections* (London: Institute of Latin American Studies, 1995), 15.

At the same time, various legal regulations allocated all or most of those seats to opposition parties (i.e., not the PRI). Thus during the three most recent elections, over 85 percent of the plurinominal deputies have been from the opposition (table 3-1). With the expansion of those seats and the modest growth of uninominal districts won by the opposition, PRI dominance of the Chamber of Deputies has decreased. While some 96 percent of all deputies belonged to the official party in 1961, that figure fell to 52 percent by 1988 (rebounding to 62 percent in 1991). Under the 1993 electoral law the majority party can win no more than 315 seats under any circumstance and no more than 300 if it receives less that 60 percent of the national vote.

Prior to the 1994 election, the various reforms broadening opposition party congressional representation had all affected only the Chamber of Deputies. In contrast, the Senate, composed of two senators from each of Mexico's thirty-one states and the Federal District, remained an exclusively PRI preserve until 1988. Despite growing electoral support for the PAN and the PRD since that time, as recently as the 1991–94 session the PRI retained 61 of the 64 seats. However, the 1993 electoral reform extensively restructured the Senate, doubling its size. Barring further reform, each state and the Federal District are to elect four senators. More important, voters cast their ballots for a political party slate, rather than an individual candidate. In each state the party gaining the most votes is awarded 3 seats, while the runner-up wins the remaining seat.[20] That formula guarantees opposition parties a combined total of at least 32 seats (25 percent of the body). Following the 1994 national election, the PRI held 95 Senate seats, the PAN 25, and the PRD 8.[21]

Electoral reforms mandating greater opposition party representation have strengthened the legislative branch marginally by modestly increasing its independence from the executive. As the number of PAN, PRD, and minor-party legislators has grown, there has been somewhat closer congressional scrutiny of administration policy and more serious debate. While outnumbered by PRI congressman, an opposition deputy or senator can expose flaws in government policy or proposed legislation. For example, Carlos Salinas was allegedly so troubled by Senate criticisms of his policies that he complained to the PRI's sixty-person delegation that a single PRD Senate leader, Porfirio Muñoz Ledo (head of the four-person opposition bloc at the time), was making all of them look bad.

Until the Zedillo administration, however, congressional reform has scarcely altered the underlying balance of power between the branches of government. The PRI has almost always maintained an overwhelming majority in both houses. Only during the Chamber of Deputies' 1988–91 session has the opposition bloc come close to a majority (table 3-1). As long as that continues, and as long as the PRI delegation loyally supports the president, Congress will remain weak relative to the executive branch.

In one important area the executive's control has been reduced. Until recently, Mexican presidents advanced their agendas by introducing substantial numbers of constitutional amendments, which Congress dutifully passed. But as a result of opposition party gains since 1988 the PRI has lacked the two-thirds majority in the Chamber of Deputies needed to pass constitutional amendments (table 3-1). More important, since the latest electoral law stipulates that no party may win more than 315 (of 500) seats in the Chamber of Deputies, it is no longer possible for any party to pass an amendment on its own. Thus Salinas and Zedillo have been forced to negotiate with PAN or other opposition deputies when they wished to alter the constitution.

Other than that, Congress remains a weak institution that offers opposition parties only a very circumscribed role. Not surprisingly, the legislature's limited influence and prestige make it an unattractive career path for talented political leaders. Moreover, once in office it is difficult for congressmen to develop leadership skills or build a power base because of the ban on reelection. Not surprisingly, few of Mexico's recent national leaders have ever served in the national Congress. Gustavo Díaz Ordaz (1964–70) was the last president to have served previously in Congress, and the PRI's slain 1994 nominee, Luis Donaldo Colosio, was one of the few national leaders in recent years with congressional experience.[22] The PRI often rewards aging politicians and union leaders at the twilight of their careers by nominating them for the Senate. But Congress is not considered a launching pad for younger politicians heading to the top.

If Congress is to be strengthened in the future, two important changes are required: First, local party organizations or primary voters, and not the president, need to select PRI candidates. Second, opposition party strength must increase to the point where Congress becomes more than a rubber stamp for presidential initiatives.

In accordance with current PRI policy, Ernesto Zedillo has given local and state party organization greater latitude to nominate candidates. Consequently recent gubernatorial candidates were selected at state conventions rather than by the president. If similar procedures are extended to the nomination of PRI congressional candidates, the legislature may eventually achieve greater independence from the president. So far, though, however desirable in theory, in practice decentralization of candidate selection has generally transferred the decision to state and local party bosses who are far less receptive than the president is to meaningful democratic reform.

More than any president in recent times, Ernesto Zedillo has begun to share some power with the legislative branch. He has met regularly with congressional leaders, had contacts with leaders of the major opposition parties, and tolerated a higher degree of congressional independence. Thus, for example, when his administration presented legislation in 1995 to reform the social security system, it accepted some sixty congressional amendments.

THE JUDICIAL BRANCH

As in the United States, the Mexican judiciary has local, state, and federal components. Levels of professionalism are frequently low in local and state courts, and many are riddled with corruption. Unfortunately, the problem has worsened in recent years with the growing influence of narcotics dealers on the political system. At the same time, the executive branch occasionally pressures, manipulates, and intimidates judges into rendering the decisions it wants. In 1995, for example, the government wished to prosecute several union leaders but was stymied when Superior Court Judge Abraham Polo ruled that there was insufficient evidence to issue an arrest warrant against the men. Subsequently, the judge publicly charged that he had been pressured to change his decision by the chief justice of his own court. Polo, a longtime PRI activist, refused to back down. Several months later he was gunned down by an unknown assailant.[23]

Not all of the judiciary has been compromised. For example, the country's Supreme Court is generally respected for its professionalism. But it has limited independence and rarely challenges the president's wishes. Some experts, such as Martin Needler, have argued that "the judiciary . . . does have a limited measure of independence from the executive, and has rendered decisions against it." But even Needler concedes that "the judiciary normally limits itself to a nonpolitical role and has not mounted frontal challenges to Mexican presidents, as the U.S. Supreme Court has sometimes done . . . to presidents of the United States."[24]

Mexico's most important form of judicial review is the *amparo* suit. Established in 1857 through Article 102 of the constitution, the suit may be brought by plaintiffs who believe that the government has violated their rights. The courts are then empowered to issue a writ of *amparo* restraining the government. Occasionally they have used that power to protect individuals against unconstitutional government behavior.[25] So, at least in theory, "the constitutional jurisdiction potentially available to the Mexican Supreme Court is similar in scope to that exercised by the Supreme Court of the United States."[26]

In reality, however, the Supreme Court avoids ruling against important administration policies or forging new constitutional rights. For example, it has never applied *amparo* writs when the government has been charged with violating the plaintiff's *political* rights. Nor has it challenged presidential actions that affect the economy (such as the nationalization of the banking system in 1982). Most important, because individual Supreme Court decisions apply only to the *specific* case under review, judicial rulings do not establish legally binding precedent. For that to happen, the Court must issue the same *amparo* ruling for five consecutive, essentially identical, cases.[27]

Even were the judicial branch to assert its independence, until recently it has been in no position to challenge the executive. Prior to 1988, if the Supreme Court had ruled against the government on an important case, the president had the option of using the PRI's huge congressional majority to amend the constitution (as we have noted, the Mexican constitution is amended quite frequently). That amendment could overturn the Supreme Court's ruling or might even further limit the Court's power of review. Since 1988, however, as we have noted, the PRI no longer has the two-thirds majority in the lower house necessary for amending the constitution, thereby limiting the president somewhat.

Ernesto Zedillo took office strongly committed to political reform. With the economy in tatters and the political scene awash with assassination conspiracy rumors, political liberalization appeared to offer the most promising vehicle for restoring government legitimacy. The administration's first initiatives in this areas were constitutional reforms designed to increase the independence and integrity of the judicial system. The proposals attracted considerable support across the political spectrum. Consequently they passed the Senate by a vote of 108 to 0 (the PRD and some PAN senators abstained) and then sailed easily through the Chamber of Deputies.

Perhaps the most important new reform empowered the Supreme Court to declare laws unconstitutional under specially stipulated circumstances. The Court may now invalidate a law or regulation in cases of conflict between different levels of government (a state challenge to a federal law, for example). It may also rule on the constitutionality of any federal law when there is a legal challenge supported by 33 percent of either congressional chamber (similarly, it can rule on state laws that are challenged by 33 percent of that state's legislature). That means that should the opposition parties in the Chamber of

Deputies join forces, as the PAN and PRD already have on occasion, they are in a position to challenge a law's constitutionality.

The 1994 reforms also affected the selection and tenure of justices. The size of the Supreme Court was reduced from a rather unwieldy twenty-six to just eleven. In order to reduce the common practice of using judicial appointments as a political reward, it is stipulated that individuals who have just stepped down from elected office can no longer be appointed to the bench. The law also now requires judicial nominees to have ten years of prior legal experience so as to raise professional standards.

Other changes altered the procedure for Supreme Court appointments, intended to reduce presidential dominance. Previously justices were nominated by the president and then submitted for Senate approval. Because the PRI held almost all Senate seats until 1994, making approval essentially automatic, the president really controlled the Court's composition. Under the new procedure the president submits a list of candidates to the Senate, which must then approve them with a two-thirds majority. So, with the recent Senate restructuring guaranteeing opposition parties at least 25 percent of the seats, those parties are within striking distance of the 34 percent needed to block a presidential nominee. For now, however, the PRI still has more than the necessary two-thirds majority.

Yet another reform changed the tenure of Supreme Court members. Previously appointed for life, justices now serve staggered fifteen-year terms. In theory this should allow for a periodic infusion of new blood into the Court. At the same time, however, the abolition of lifetime tenure could reduce judicial independence. In fact, while the judicial reform package has some positive aspects, it is far from clear that it will establish an independent judiciary. For example, the restructuring and downsizing of the Supreme Court required all justices to resign while President Zedillo nominated a new slate. As the Senate readily approved all of them, it appears that, for now at least, presidential dominance persists.

THE MILITARY

Although the military is not a branch of government, it deserves attention in this chapter because it occupies a special place in Latin American politics. As recently as the early 1980s, most of the countries in the region were governed by military regimes.[28] Furthermore, even when the armed forces does not control the government, it often exerts considerable influence over policies relating to defense, internal security, and foreign affairs. In some countries such as El Salvador and Guatemala, the military has kept civilian governments on a short leash.

But modern Mexico has been an exception to this pattern. Of course the army had dominated national politics prior to the Revolution and remained influential into the 1930s. But there has not been a successful military coup since 1920, the longest period of sustained civilian rule anywhere in Latin America.* There were, of course, several attempted military uprisings in the 1920s and 1930s, but none of them succeeded, and no others have been attempted since 1938. Today, many scholars view the relationship between the government and the armed forces as "a model of civil-military tranquility."[29] Furthermore, Mexico's per capita military expenditure is among the lowest in the hemisphere.[30]

Several factors help explain the Mexican armed forces' acceptance of civilian (i.e., presidential) supremacy and the absence of coups. For one thing, major political actors have implicitly agreed to restrict their activities to the civilian arena. By contrast, disgruntled opposition parties and interest groups (most notably business groups) elsewhere in Latin America frequently encourage the military command to oust governments that these groups oppose. But in Mexico, even when recent economic crises and political scandals unleashed broad public discontent, the country's political culture has precluded military intervention as an acceptable solution.

Thus, despite the worst economic decline in many decades, public opinion polls in the late 1980s indicated that over 60 percent of the population opposed *any* military involvement in politics at all (much less a coup). Elsewhere in Latin America, economic elites have often been the leading promoters of military takeovers. But in Mexico opinion surveys reveal that the wealthy are among those most strongly opposed to armed forces political intervention.[31] Norms of civilian political supremacy have permeated the military as well, with officers "show[ing] no signs of coveting . . . political leadership."[32]

But the most significant deterrent to military intervention has been the strength of Mexico's political institutions.[33] In other developing countries, the army is most likely to intercede in politics during periods of instability, particularly when disorder threatens the military's hierarchical structure.[34] During the 1960s and 1970s, for example, the growth of marxist political parties, militant labor unions, radical peasant organizations, or revolutionary guerrilla groups triggered coups in Argentina, Brazil, Chile, and Uruguay. In contrast, despite extended economic decline, the EZLN uprising in Chiapas, a string of high-profile assassinations, and revelations of corruption in high places, Mexico's political system has so far maintained sufficient stability to deny the military a reason for intervention. The rate of labor unrest is quite low, the Zapatista insurgency has been contained, the leftist electoral opposition is, if anything, weakening, and there have been no significant civil disturbances.

To be sure, at times military commanders have been concerned about political instability and quite unhappy over the government's management of internal unrest. Following the Tlatelolco massacre in 1968, for example, the generals were infuriated with President Díaz Ordaz and Secretary of Government

---

* As we have noted (chapter 2), from 1917 through 1946 all Mexican presidents first launched their careers in the army. But they were citizen-soldiers who subsequently left the armed forces when they started their political careers. Most important, they subsequently reached the presidency by political rather than military means, that is, through elections, however noncompetitive, not through coups.

Luis Echeverría for mishandling the student demonstrations and making the armed forces the object of public indignation. In the mid-1970s, as President Echeverría's relations with the private sector deteriorated and the economy floundered, there were frequent rumors of impending coups. Most recently, military commanders were reportedly incensed at Carlos Salinas's failure to heed their warnings of incipient guerrilla activity in Chiapas and his subsequent fumbling response to the Zapatista uprising. Yet throughout the economic collapse of the 1980s, the Chiapas upheaval, and the current financial crisis, the armed forces has not attempted a coup.

But although civilian supremacy has been maintained, the political and economic difficulties that have gripped the country since the 1960s have increased the military's political influence.[35] From the student unrest of the 1960s to the war on drugs to the Zapatista uprising, perceived security threats have drawn the armed forces more deeply into the political system.

As the army has become more involved in "civic action programs" promoting rural development, in antiinsurgency campaigns, and in the war on drugs, it has become more preoccupied with Mexico's political and socioeconomic problems. Military schools such as the Escuela Superior de Guerra (Superior War School) and Colegio de Defensa Nacional (National Defense College) train elite officers to deal with these politically sensitive issues. Experience elsewhere in Latin America indicates that advanced officer training on such political, social, and economic issues usually increases "the potential for the military's greater knowledge of, interest in, and inclination for politics."[36] In Brazil and Peru, for example, politically related courses at the advanced war colleges increased military preoccupation with internal security matters and opened the door to political intervention.[37]

Following the Zapatista rebellion, several army officers publicly criticized the Salinas administration's handling of the revolt and complained privately about being shut out of decision making. Mexican newspapers reported that army intelligence spied on the peace negotiations between government negotiator Manuel Camacho and the EZLN.[38] Such unprecedented insubordination indicated how far Chiapas had raised military doubts about the president's ability to maintain public order. Those concerns were heightened further by a wave of kidnappings of wealthy businessmen, a series of high-profile assassinations, and the political intrigue that marked the closing years of Salinas's term.[39]

CONCLUSIONS

The recent debate on democratization in Mexico has focused primarily on the importance of a competitive party system along with honest and transparent elections (chapter 4). But Mexican authoritarianism is also manifested by overly centralized political institutions. Full democracy will require a better balance of power between the branches of government so that the Congress and judiciary can impose reasonable checks on the president and reduce his dominance. Such reform would not only establish greater protection against presidential excesses, but also ultimately contribute to more honest presidential elections. Should the PRI become confident that yielding the presidency to the opposition will not lead to the official party's ruin, and should it be possible to exercise some power through the Congress and state government, the political elite might become more receptive to fair presidential elections.

Notes

1. Luis Javier Garrido, "The Crisis of *Presidencialismo*," in *Mexico's Alternative Political Futures*, ed. Wayne A. Cornelius, Judith Gentleman, and Peter H. Smith (La Jolla: University of California–San Diego Center for U.S.-Mexican Studies, 1989), 421.

2. Roderic A. Camp, "Mexico's Legislature: Missing the Democratic Lockstep?" in *Legislatures and the New Democracies in Latin America*, ed. David Close (Boulder, Colo.: Lynne Rienner Publishers, 1995), 25.

3. For the manifestations of presidentialism in the past three decades, see Carlos Monsiváis, "'En virtud de las facultades que me han sido otorgadas. . .' Notas sobre el presidencialismo a partir de 1968," in *La transición interrumpida: México 1968–1988* (México: Nueva Imagen, 1993), 113–25.

4. John J. Bailey, *Governing Mexico: The Statecraft of Crisis Management* (New York: St. Martin's Press, 1988), 29.

5. Jorge Carpizo, *El presidencialismo mexicano*, 3d ed. (México: Siglo XXI, 1983), 25–26.

6. Peter H. Smith, "The 1988 Presidential Succession," in *Mexico's Alternative Political Futures*, 391–415. Smith notes that technically the term *precandidato* refers only to the candidate selected by the president but not yet nominated by the party. In practice, however, Mexicans use the term for all viable presidential contenders.

7. Roderic A. Camp, "Camarillas in Mexican Politics: The Case of the Salinas Cabinet," *Mexican Studies* 6, no. 1 (Winter 1990): 85–107.

8. On patron-client relationships more generally, see Luis Roniger, *Hierarchy and Trust in Modern Mexico and Brazil* (New York: Praeger, 1990).

9. Wayne A. Cornelius and Ann L. Craig, *The Mexican Political System in Transition* (La Jolla: University of California–San Diego Center for U.S.-Mexican Studies, 1991), 39.

10. Camp, "Camarillas in Mexican Politics," 106.

11. Samuel Schmidt, *The Deterioration of the Mexican Presidency: The Years of Luis Echeverría* (Tucson: University of Arizona Press, 1991), 5.

12. Bailey, *Governing Mexico*, 39–40.

13. Ibid., 57.

14. Miguel Angel Centeno and Jeffrey Wilson, "A Small Circle of Friends," paper presented at the International Congress of the Latin American Studies Association, Washington, D.C., April 1991.

15. Cornelius and Craig, *Mexican Political System in Transition*, 30.

16. Camp, "Mexico's Legislature," 22, based on data drawn from *Diccionario biográfico del gobierno Mexicano* (México: Presidencia de la República, 1989); Roderic A. Camp, *Politics in Mexico* (New York: Oxford University Press, 1993), 99, data drawn from Camp, *Mexican Bibliographical Project*, 1991.

17. On the rise of the new technocratic elite, see Miguel Angel Centeno, *Democracy within Reason* (University Park: Pennsylvania State University Press, 1994).

18. George Philip, *The Presidency in Mexican Politics* (London: Macmillan, 1992), 241.

19. Jorge Alcocer V., "Recent Electoral Reforms in Mexico: Prospects for Real Multiparty

Democracy," in *The Challenge of Institutional Reform in Mexico,* ed. Riordan Roett (Boulder, Colo.: Lynne Rienner Publishers, 1995), 70.

20. One of the most recent analyses of Mexico's ongoing electoral reforms is ibid., 57–75; also, Silvia Gómez Tagle, "Electoral Reform and the Party System, 1977–1990," in *Mexico: Dilemmas of Transition,* ed. Neil Harvey (London: Institute of Latin American Studies, 1993), 64–90; Camp, "Mexico's Legislature."

21. *LAWR,* 15 September 1994, 420.

22. Camp, "Mexico's Legislature," 21. This section draws heavily on Camp's work.

23. *New York Times,* 7 June 1995, 7.

24. Martin C. Needler, *Mexican Politics: The Containment of Conflict* (New York: Praeger, 1990), 90.

25. Joel Verner, "The Independence of Supreme Courts in Latin America: A Review of the Literature," *Journal of Latin American Studies* 16 (1984): 463–506.

26. Richard D. Baker, *Judicial Review in Mexico: A Study of the Amparo Suit* (Austin: University of Texas Press, 1971), 268.

27. Carl Schwartz, "Jueces en la penumbra: la independencia del poder judicial en los Estados Unidos y en México," *Anuario Jurídico* (México: UNAM, 1977), 144–45; Camp, *Politics in Mexico,* 141.

28. On the military in Latin American politics, see Karen L. Remmer, *Military Rule in Latin America* (Boulder, Colo.: Westview Press, 1989); Abraham F. Lowenthal and Samuel J. Fitch, eds., *Armies and Politics in Latin America,* 2d ed. (New York: Holmes and Meier, 1986).

29. William S. Ackroyd, "Military Professionalism, Education and Political Behavior in Mexico," *Armed Forces and Society* 18, no. 1 (Fall 1991): 81.

30. Arturo Sánchez Gutiérrez, "El estado y los militares en los años ochenta," in *El nuevo estado Mexicano: estado y política,* ed. Jorge Alonso et al. (México: Nueva Imagen, 1992), 22; Needler, *Mexican Politics,* 80.

31. Data from Miguel Basáñez, *El pulso de los sexenios: 20 años de crisis en México* (México: Siglo XXI, 1990), 238–40.

32. Edward J. Williams, "The Evolution of the Mexican Military and Its Implications for Civil-Military Relations," in *Mexico's Political Stability: The Next Five Years,* ed. Roderic A. Camp (Boulder, Colo.: Westview Press, 1986), 155.

33. Because of its highly closed nature, little has been written on the Mexican armed forces, and our knowledge of them remains somewhat limited. The best recent English-language study is Roderic A. Camp, *Generals in the Palacio: The Military in Modern Mexico* (New York: Oxford University Press, 1992), esp. 212–30.

34. See Howard Handelman, *The Challenge of Third World Development* (Englewood Cliffs, N.J.: Prentice Hall, 1996), chap. 8 ("Soldiers and Politics"); Eric Nordlinger, *Soldiers in Politics* (Englewood Cliffs, N.J.: Prentice Hall, 1977).

35. See, for example, Martin Edwin Andersen, "Civil-Military Relations and Internal Security in Mexico: The Undone Reform," in *Challenge of Institutional Reform in Mexico,* 155–80; for an earlier discussion of the effects of modernization on the military's political influence, see David Ronfeldt, ed., *The Modern Mexican Military: A Reassessment* (La Jolla: University of California–San Diego Center for U.S.-Mexican Studies, 1984); Williams, "Evolution of the Mexican Military and Its Implications."

36. Camp, *Generals in the Palacio,* 169.

37. Alfred Stepan, "The New Professionalism of Internal Warfare and Military Role Expansion" in *Armies and Politics in Latin America,* 134–50.

38. Andersen, "Civil-Military Relations," 170.

39. Ibid., 170–71.

4

Elections and the Party System

Like so much of Mexico's politics, neither its elections nor its party system is what it appears to be at first glance. To the casual observer, the country seems to have a competitive, multiparty electoral system. Anyone visiting during its last national election might encounter mass rallies by the PRI, the PRD, the PAN, and several lesser competitors. Opposition party campaign literature and posters, though sparser than the PRI's, are freely available. Thus, unlike most authoritarian regimes, Mexico has elections that are usually vigorously contested.

But of course electoral contestation only goes so far. The PRI and its predecessors have won every presidential race since the formation of an official party in 1929, and prior to 1988 had won virtually every election of any import. Indeed, only in the past two elections has the PRI presidential candidate even faced serious opposition.* Thus, until recently national elections served a far different function than they do in pluralist democracies. Their purpose was not to determine the winners, normally a foregone conclusion, but rather to offer the public a sense of participation in the political process and thereby to legitimize PRI control. Indeed, for many years the government's primary electoral concern had been to insure sufficient electoral opposition to maintain the facade of truly contested elections. As Alan Riding observed: "Without formal opposition, elections would be meaningless. And without elections the system would lose its mask of democratic legitimacy."[1]

The 1988 election, in which both Carlos Salinas and the PRI congressional slate officially received only half the vote, raised the possibility that the party's monopoly on power might be coming to an end. To be sure, the PRI's strong victories in the 1991 and 1994 elections indicated that the country still lacks a fully competitive party system. But the PAN's strong performance in the 1995 state and local elections showed renewed signs of party competitiveness.

This chapter will first examine the origins of the Mexican political party system. It will then analyze the structure and goals of the PRI, in order better to appreciate how single-party dominance has reinforced political stability

---

* To be sure, many observers felt that General Juan Andreu Almazán, the 1940 candidate of the Revolutionary Party of National Unity, was denied victory through fraud. Whatever the truth of those charges, however, his official total barely exceeded 6 percent of the vote.

while simultaneously corrupting the political system. Subsequently, we will consider changes in the nation's social structure and in electoral procedures since the 1960s that have strengthened opposition parties. Finally, we will discuss the recent emergence of stronger political challenges from parties on the right and left, and then consider the continuing obstacles to truly competitive elections.

THE ORIGINS OF SINGLE-PARTY DOMINANCE

The creation of Mexico's official party, first called the National Revolutionary Party (PNR), can be best understood in the context of the intensive conflict that preceded it. As we have seen, throughout the nineteenth century national politics had oscillated between disorder and dictatorship. In the early years of the twentieth century, the Porfirian dictatorship gave way to revolution, civil war, military revolts, and religiously based uprisings. Even after the warfare came to an end, selective political violence continued through the next decade. Finally, the assassination of President-Elect Alvaro Obregón in 1928 convinced President Plutarco Elías Calles and the revolutionary elite that an official party was needed that could bring together regional political bosses and their contending organizations. Only then could there be political stability and a more orderly means of selecting national leaders.

As Pablo González Casanova has noted, the initial purpose of the government party was "the control of *caudillos* and *caciques* [regional and local strongmen]" and a rationalization of the party system. At the time that the PNR was founded, the country had fifty-one registered parties and ten others that fielded candidates in the 1929 election. Within four years, that number was reduced to four, as politicians and their organizations climbed aboard the official party machine.[2] While the revolutionary elite allowed and even encouraged opposition parties, it did not seriously consider alternating control of government through truly competitive elections.[3] Indeed, there was little precedent for that. The election of 1911, won by Francisco Madero, was the freest the country had ever enjoyed, but at the end Madero faced no opposition when his opponent, General Bernardo Reyes, dropped out of the race. Venustiano Carranza (1917) and Alvaro Obregón (1920 and 1928) had similarly one-sided contests, winning over 95 percent of the vote.

In subsequent years, the government party changed its name, its organizational structure, and its purpose. Under the leadership of Lázaro Cárdenas (1934–40), it evolved from a conglomeration of political elites and regional machines to a mass-based party with a corporatist structure. Rather than enhancing worker and peasant political input, however, the party became a vehicle for elite control. Because labor unions and peasant federations were so tightly linked to the ruling party, they were stripped of their capacity for independent political action.

The military, long a mainstay of national politics, was also initially represented in the PNR. But after Calles and Cárdenas had reduced the military's political power, President Manuel Avila Camacho terminated the party's military sector in 1940.[4] While some former officers continued to hold important party posts until the early 1960s, the military itself has lacked the same independent political influence that its counterparts have exercised in most of Latin America.[5]

Shortly after the military was removed from the official party, a new branch was added. Called the "popular" sector, it has represented unionized white-collar workers (especially government employees), professionals, small businessmen, and a broad array of other groups whose underlying bond is their middle-class status. In 1946, the official party (by then called the PRM) changed its name once again, this time to the PRI (Institutional Revolutionary Party). As we have noted, the current name reveals the conflict between the regime's desire to institutionalize stability and its continued identification with the ideal of revolutionary change. For more than half a century, stability has taken precedence.

THE PRI: A CATCHALL PARTY

In many single-party systems, the governing party defines the dominant political ideology and makes most important policy decisions that the government then carries out. That model currently prevails in Cuba and China, as it did formerly in the Soviet Union and Eastern Europe. In Mexico, however, the ruling party was created by the government elites and has always served their needs. It has lacked a clearly defined ideology, and its primary purpose is not to make policy but to garner votes for establishment candidates and to back the president's political objectives. Seeking support from all social classes and casting its net across the ideological spectrum from left to right, the PRI is a "catchall" party.* Its greatest support, however, has traditionally come from the rural population and from government employees.

In return for their support, the party provides its constituents with a range of services and channels many of their demands to government bodies. In short, the party integrates peasants, farmers, blue-collar workers, white-collar employees, professionals, and small businessmen into the political system while establishing significant government control over their political activity.

The Structure of the PRI.   At the top of the PRI's organizational pyramid stands the party's National Executive Council (CEN) and its president. While some party presidents have shown flashes of independence, they and the CEN more generally are at the service of the country's president. The CEN controls the party's National Assembly, National Council, and nominating convention.[6] At all levels of the party, from the CEN to the local branches, power and

---

* Catchall parties differ from parties of the left or right (socialists, conservatives, etc.) that draw their primary support from particular social classes or other sectors of the population.

authority flow from the top down through a web of patron-client relations, as they do in almost all of Mexico's political structures.

The PRI is also divided into three functional branches: the labor, agrarian, and popular sectors. Theoretically, they provide the lower and middle classes access to the political system.

The agrarian sector is built around the National Peasant Confederation (CNC), an organization representing beneficiaries of the agrarian reform. Created by President Cárdenas to promote rural change while also deradicalizing the peasantry, the sector has lost considerable political influence since the 1940s and no longer protects peasant interests effectively.[7] Though it allegedly represents nearly four million peasants (an inflated number), the sector suffers from the isolation of its members and their lack of political experience. It is surely the weakest of the PRI's three branches.[8]

Almost half the labor sector's roughly six million members belong to the Confederation of Mexican Workers (CTM), an umbrella group that includes thirty-six national unions. Representing many of the nation's blue-collar workers, the labor sector is perhaps the most well organized, well disciplined, and effective of the PRI's three wings. But it has used its power cautiously in its dealings with the national government. Because the state has substantial power over labor-management relations, including the determination of whether a strike is legal, unions have felt obliged to moderate their demands and have hesitated to carry out work stoppages. Thus, during the economic crisis of the 1980s, even though Mexican workers suffered some of the sharpest declines in real earnings anywhere in Latin America, they went on strike at a lower rate than their counterparts in countries such as Argentina, Brazil, and Peru.[9]

Labor's political clout has benefited its rank and file and its leaders in a number of ways. Government subsidies on food, housing, utilities, and other consumer items were particularly beneficial for many members of the working class. During Mexico's postwar economic expansion, powerful unions such as the petroleum workers and the electric power workers secured comparatively generous wages and benefits for their members. Union bosses, most notably CTM chief Fidel Velázquez, until recently have been closely connected to the president and have helped shape government economic policy. And trade union leaders still constitute a sizable portion of the PRI's congressional delegation.

On the whole, however, most labor unions have not represented their members as effectively as they could because they are notoriously boss-dominated and corrupt. Within the PRI the labor sector has been among the fiercest opponents of democratic reform as union chiefs struggle to protect their own fiefdoms. Since the early 1980s, organized labor's political influence has declined considerably as it has been marginalized by neoliberal economic reforms. A number of independent, reformist unions have emerged but so far have had limited success (chapters 5 and 6).

Finally, it should be noted that since less than 25 percent of Mexico's urban labor force is unionized, organized labor can hardly claim to speak for the entire working class.[10] As in many countries, unions have had the most success organizing in larger industries, particularly those in the more modern sectors of the economy. These include petroleum, steel, telecommunications, electric power, and automobiles. But most of the industrial workforce is employed in smaller firms such as machine shops, bakeries, and garment shops. Rarely unionized, these workers gain little from the CTM or the PRI labor sector.

The third branch of the PRI, called the CNOP or "popular sector," represents major segments of the Mexican middle class. The most important actors in the CNOP are unions representing public-sector employees, most notably schoolteachers and white-collar workers in the state bureaucracy. In addition, there are associations representing professionals, owners of small businesses, commercial farmers, and disparate occupations such as taxi drivers, street vendors, and mariachi musicians. While the CNOP primarily represents the middle class, it also includes lower-income groups such as urban slum dwellers and shoe-shine men.

With less than four million members, the popular sector is considerably smaller than the labor wing. In addition, because of its very heterogeneous composition, many analysts feel that it is less politically effective than the labor sector. On the other hand, the CNOP's members have higher education levels and greater political skills than the other PRI sectors. Thus Judith Adler Hellman has argued that "to the extent that crucial policy decisions are fought out within the party, the popular sector clearly has the upper hand in terms of financial, educational, technical and personal resources."[11] In recent years the allocation of PRI seats in the Chamber of Deputies has reflected the CNOP's influence. In the seven national elections held between 1967 and 1988, nearly half the PRI deputies were popular-sector members, while the labor and agrarian sectors each held about one-fourth of the seats.[12] Since the Salinas administration, however, the role of the CNOP has been reduced substantially. In 1990, the president announced plans for eventually phasing out the popular sector.[13]

The PRI's Ideological Wings.   In addition to its organizational divisions, the PRI is split informally along ideological lines. In the past, the party's progressive wing has been more nationalistic, more favorable to state economic intervention, and more committed to internal party democracy. During the mid-1960s, PRI president Carlos Madrazo tried to establish greater grassroots control over the candidate selection process. Ultimately, his efforts were defeated by PRI conservatives, and he was marginalized from power. When he was killed in a commercial plane crash in 1969, many Mexicans suspected foul play. Nearly two decades later, the reformist Democratic Current launched a broader struggle for party democracy. But they and their titular leader, Cuauhtémoc Cárdenas, were expelled from the PRI. Subsequently another PRI reform movement, the Corriente Crítica, succeeded the Democratic Current, but it too left the party.

For decades Mexican presidents rejected the progressive wing's reformist agenda, clinging steadfastly to the ideological center. From that position they could attack the PAN, the major conservative opposition party, as being beholden to big business, insensitive to the people's needs, and insufficiently nationalistic. At the same time, they could dismiss the left opposition as being too radical.

But while staking out the political center, individual presidents over the years have swung modestly to the right or the left of their predecessors as circumstances and the need to win back disaffected constituencies dictated. Perhaps the most dramatic example was Luis Echeverría. Having taken office as the former point man of a right-wing, law-and-order president, he shifted to the left to win support from disaffected students and intellectuals.

At times presidential shifts have resulted in a strange mix of policies and ideologies. For example, even though the PRI has been affiliated with the international organization of democratic socialist parties, President Salinas pursued free market policies that were more akin to British Prime Minister Margaret Thatcher's brand of conservative capitalism. Presidents López Portillo and de la Madrid implemented conservative economic programs at home while maintaining close ties with marxist regimes in Cuba and Nicaragua.

Ultimately, a key element of the PRI's "ideology" has been pragmatism, a determination to do whatever is necessary to win elections and maintain political stability. Since the early 1980s, the party's progressive wing has weakened considerably. Market-oriented reforms have sharply diminished the state's economic role, while NAFTA and other trade openings have undermined economic nationalism. Many PRI progressives were expelled from the party or left it to join the Cardenistas. This does not mean that the progressives have been without influence. In recent years, many of the old Cardenista demands for honest national elections have been adopted, and under Zedillo there have been some initial signs of democratization within the PRI itself (and evidence of PRI resistance to change as well). As the corporatist sectors of the party have weakened in recent years and as the ability of sectoral leaders to deliver their members' votes has diminished, PRI/government leaders have begun to transform the party. One important change has been creating territorially based (state and local) structures that make it easier to join the party for individuals and groups who are not affiliated with the three party sectors.[14] Thus, the party's corporate structure will likely be phased out.

THE EVOLVING ELECTORAL SYSTEM

As we have noted, prior to 1988, Mexico's governing party had never lost a gubernatorial race, lost only one campaign for the Senate, and won virtually all Chamber of Deputies seats chosen in single-member districts.* Electoral dominance was achieved in a number of ways. Initially PRI manipulation of

---

* Single-member (or uninominal) districts, like those in the U.S. House of Representatives and the British House of Commons, are each represented in the legislature by a single person. In addition, however, a portion of the Mexican Chamber of Deputies (currently 40 percent) is elected through proportional representation in multimember districts (see chapter 3).

nationalistic and revolutionary symbols made it seem near treasonous to support the opposition. During one congressional election in the 1970s, for example, this author recalls seeing political wall posters all over Mexico City and
Guadalajara warning that a PRI defeat would mean "foreign domination,
hunger and disorder." PRI resources far outstrip the opposition's, and until recently the party drew liberally on government funds. Until now the party has
ignored legal limits on private contributions and attracted large donations
from businessmen who have extensive dealings with the state. In addition,
Mexican media coverage, particularly television, is strongly slanted in favor of
the official party. It remains to be seen whether a new reform law scheduled for
early 1996 will better equalize campaign spending and media access among
the political parties. Finally, like any powerful machine, the PRI makes liberal
use of government patronage. It not only dispenses government jobs, but controls the licenses for taxi drivers, shoe-shine men, newspaper vendors, and
many others who dutifully work for the PRI every election.

Government resources are also used as a carrot to lure votes at the community level. Peasant villages and urban slum neighborhoods understand that
their prospects for securing new schools, irrigation or potable water systems,
paved streets, and other needed projects hinge on delivering a strong PRI vote.
In 1995, the Civic Alliance, a widely based citizens' watchdog group, observed
Mexico's state elections and found that in 60 percent of the polling places that
it was monitoring, government officials had threatened to reduce state aid to
the district if the PRI did not win there.[15] The government/PRI has particular
leverage in rural communities where peasants not only depend on the state for
schools, roads, and irrigation systems, but have also been subject to state controls on the marketing of farm products.[16]

Until recently, low-income, urban neighborhoods typically had no contacts with any party organization other than the PRI's. Susan Eckstein's study
of the urban poor notes the PRI's ability to deliver social services. It was "the
only party with a grass-roots organization and local social service agencies [in
the poor neighborhoods that she studied]. District PRI offices offer[ed] classes
in sewing, cooking, hairdressing, and typing, and medical and barber services. . . . Furthermore, it [was] the only party which regularly solicit[ed] the
government for social and urban facilities on behalf of residents."[17]

After his narrow victory in the 1988 presidential election, Carlos Salinas
introduced a massive public works and welfare program, called the National
Solidarity Program (PRONASOL). While of definite value to the poor, Solidarity's purpose was also to build support for his administration in urban
slums and rural villages. As we will see (chapter 6), PRONASOL in fact succeeded in building Salinas's popularity and strengthening the PRI's vote in the
1991 and 1994 national elections.

When necessary, authorities have also used force and intimidation to further the PRI/government agenda. To be sure, Mexico has never experienced
the blatant political repression that Argentina, Brazil, Chile, El Salvador, and
Uruguay have suffered from in the recent past or that Guatemala still endures.

On occasion, however, the authorities do intimidate opposition figures, particularly those in leftist parties (chapter 5). For example, from 1988 to 1994 dozens, if not hundreds, of activists in Cuauhtémoc Cárdenas's National Democratic Front (FDN) and its successor, the PRD, were murdered. In 1994, a truck mysteriously crashed into a car carrying the PRD's gubernatorial candidate in Chiapas, at the very spot where a PRD worker had been hit not long before.

If all else has failed, the PRI has resorted to fraud. Of course, political machines throughout the world engage in fraud, but until now it has been a particularly fundamental strand in the Mexican political fabric. Electoral manipulation has included exclusion of opposition party supporters from the voter rolls, voter intimidation, ballot-box stuffing, and voting multiple times by PRI enthusiasts. Vote counts often have been falsified, particularly in rural areas where opposition parties often lack the manpower to monitor the process. While all political parties are legally entitled to provide observers at the country's voting stations (currently numbering about ninety-six thousand), only the PRI has had enough activists to provide observers in all locations. In the 1988 presidential election, many rural districts in the states of Chiapas, Nuevo León, Guerrero, Oaxaca, Veracruz, Sinaloa, Puebla, and Yucatán allegedly cast *all* of their votes for the PRI (sometimes casting more votes than the number of registered voters).[18]

While state and local elections have become increasingly competitive of late, until recently the PRI could win most elections without resorting to fraudulent vote counts. Hence, in most cases the purpose of electoral manipulation was not so much to win as to pad the PRI's margin of victory. As one Mexican analyst has noted:

> The PRI commits fraud, not only to reverse unfavorable results, but when they [really] *win* as well. Why? To be able to show absolute dominance, and also to continue the internal competition within the PRI hierarchy. . . . Winning a larger share of the vote than one's rival [in the PRI] determines the pecking order.[19]

Over the years, however, a number of factors have eroded the PRI's electoral dominance. Mexico's modernization since the 1940s—rapid industrial growth, rural-to-urban migration, increased education, and greater media penetration—has significantly altered its demographic map. In 1950, nearly 60 percent of the population lived in rural communities. By 1980 that proportion had fallen to only 34 percent.[20] From 1940 to 1992 the nation's literacy rate grew from 52 percent to 96 percent. The number of students attending secondary school and university also grew rapidly. Social and economic modernization, in turn, swelled the ranks of the middle class.

Over time, such changes inevitably had important political implications. For one thing, the official party has traditionally drawn its strongest support from rural voters. Because peasants depend heavily on the state for agricultural credits, irrigation, technical aid, and marketing their produce, they are more easily manipulated by rural political bosses. Thus urbanization favors opposition parties as it produces more independent voters. Similarly, the growing

Table 4-1. Presidential Election Results: 1929–1994

Year	PRI	PAN	FDN or PRD	Other
1929	93.55	—	—	6.45
1934	98.19	—	—	1.81
1940	93.89	—	—	6.11
1946	77.90	—	—	22.10
1952	74.31	7.82	—	17.87
1958	90.43	9.42	—	0.15
1964	88.82	11.05	—	1.03*
1970	84.13	13.85	—	2.03*
1976	92.27	—	—	7.63*
1982	71.00	15.68	—	15.89*
1988	50.74	16.80	32.50	—
1994	53.40	28.60	18.00	—

* Total includes anywhere from 1.1% (1964) to 6.7% (1976) cast for "loyal left" parties that supported the PRI candidate.
Sources: Pablo González Casanova, El estado y los partidos políticos en México, 3d ed. (México: Ediciones Era, 1986), 132–34; Dale Story, The Mexican Ruling Party (New York: Praeger, 1986), 52; María Amparo Casar, The 1994 Mexican Presidential Elections (London: Institute of Latin American Studies, 1995), 14 and 18; CFE and IFE; Ann Craig and Wayne Cornelius, "House Divided: Parties and Political Reform in Mexico," in Building Democratic Institutions: Party Systems in Latin America, ed. Scott Mainwaring and Timothy Scully (Stanford, Calif.: Stanford University Press, 1995), 258.

middle class, being less dependent on government patronage, is more free than the urban poor to support opposition candidates. At the same time, the spread of literacy and broadcast media has raised public political awareness and increased indignation over government corruption and electoral fraud.

Tables 4-1 and 4-2 reveal that there has been a gradual erosion of PRI dominance since the 1970s leading up to the Cardenista electoral upheaval in 1988 and the PAN upsurge in 1995.

Table 4-1 shows the erosion of support for PRI presidential candidates since the early 1980s. While the ruling-party candidate once routinely received over 80 percent of the vote, he received only slightly over 50 percent in the past two elections. Two factors reduced the PRI's congressional strength: declining voter support and electoral reform. From 1964 to 1994, the party's share of the congressional vote declined from 86.3 to 50.3 percent (table 4-2). At the same time, a series of electoral reforms first facilitated the registration of opposition parties and later guaranteed them a larger number of seats in the Chamber of Deputies (table 4-3) and more recently in the Senate as well. These changes were a response to public discontent and the regime's weakening legitimacy.

As far back as 1964, the government set aside a relatively small number of "party seats" in the Chamber of Deputies for opposition parties (chapter 3). The pressure for democratic reform intensified in the late 1960s and early 1970s, following the Tlatelolco massacre and an economic downturn.[21] A steady decline in voter turnout indicated the electorate's discontent. Although

Table 4-2. Elections for the Chamber of Deputies: 1976–1994 (Percentage of the Valid Vote)

Year	PRI	Independent Left	Loyal Left	PAN
1964	86.3	—	2.1	11.5
1967	83.8	—	3.6	12.5
1970	83.6	—	2.2	14.2
1973	77.4	—	5.8	16.5
1976	85.2	—	5.6	8.9
1979	74.2	5.0	5.0	11.4
1982	69.3	5.6	5.0	17.5
1985	68.2	4.5	6.1	16.3
1988	50.4	29.6	—	18.0
1991	61.4	8.9	8.3	17.7
1994	50.3	16.7	2.7	26.8

The 1994 totals, unlike the others, includes annulled votes. The party totals, therefore, add up to only 96.5% and are not comparable to those of other years.

Sources: Federal Electoral Commission and Federal Electoral Institute (1976–91); Federal Election Institute (1994); 1964–88 data aggregated in Kathleen Maria Bruhn, "Taking on Goliath: The Emergence of a New Cardenista Party and the Struggle for Democracy in Mexico," Ph.D. diss., Stanford University, 1993, 3.; Joseph L. Klesner, "Realignment or Dealignment," in *The Politics of Economic Restructuring,* ed. Maria Lorena Cook, Kevin J. Middlebrook, and Juan Molinar Horcasitas (La Jolla: Center for U.S.-Mexican Studies, University of California–San Diego, 1994), 162; Germán Pérez Fernández del Castillo et al., *La voz de los votos: Un análisis crítico de las elecciones de 1994* (México; FLACSO, 1995), 259.

President Echeverría introduced modest political reforms in the early 1970s and reduced government repression of leftist political groups (the "democratic opening"), he failed to alter an electoral system that still offered opposition parties few opportunities.[22]

Responding to the public's growing political alienation, in 1977 the López Portillo administration passed the Federal Law on Political Organizations and Electoral Processes. Its purpose, said Minister of Government Jesús Reyes Heroles, was to open

> political representation in such a way that [elected bodies] would include the complex, national ideological mosaic, made up of the majority faction [the PRI] and the lesser factions [opposition parties] that diverge from the majority, but also form part of the nation.[23]

Requirements were eased for the registration of political parties so that smaller ones could get onto the ballot. In addition, opposition parties were given modest financial support from the Federal Electoral Commission and increased (though still limited) access to radio and television. Most important, to compensate for the PRI's overwhelming lead in uninominal districts, the Chamber of Deputies was enlarged to four hundred seats. Three hundred of those would be elected in uninominal districts (i.e., districts with a single deputy). The PRI

Table 4-3. Party Representation in the Chamber of Deputies: 1976–1994
(Percentage of Seats)

Year	PRI	PAN	FDN/PRD	Other
1976	82.0	8.5	—	9.5
1979	74.0	10.8	—	7.8
1982	74.8	12.5	—	12.7
1985	72.7	10.3	—	17.0
1988	52.0	20.2	27.6*	—
1991	63.9	17.8	8.2	10.2
1994	60.0	23.8	14.2	2.0

* Total for all parties supporting Cárdenas in 1988.
Sources: Juan Molinar Horcasitas, El tiempo de la legitimidad (México: Cal y Arena, 1991),
152; Alberto Aziz Nassif and Jacqueline Peschard, Las elecciones federales de 1991 (Méx-
ico: CIIH, 1992), 230; María Amparo Casar, The 1994 Mexican Presidential Elections
(London: Institute of Latin American Studies, 1995), 15; Daniel C. Levy and Kathleen
Bruhn, "Mexico: Sustained Civilian Rule without Democracy," in Politics in Developing
Countries, ed. Larry Diamond, Juan J. Linz, and Seymour Martin Lipset (Boulder, Colo.:
Lynne Rienner Publishers, 1995), 188.

has continued to win almost all of those seats, except for the 1988 election. But
the remaining one hundred seats would be divided among the opposition parties in order to allow them greater representation. Based on the principle of
proportional representation (PR) each party would receive a share of the plurinominal seats proportional to their percentage of the vote in large, multimember electoral regions. In 1986, the number of deputies elected through PR was
increased to two hundred, while at the same time the allocation formula was
altered so as to allow the PRI to win some of those (see table 3-1).

In the 1961 congressional election, the PRI won an overwhelming 90.2
percent of the vote.[24] But two years later one of Mexico's first electoral reform
laws was passed. Since that time the PRI has received a declining share of the
vote in eight of the last ten legislative elections, all but 1976 and 1991 (table
4-2). The 1977 electoral reform permitted the registration of additional political parties and stimulated an increase in opposition party votes. In 1988,
spearheaded by Cuauhtémoc Cárdenas's candidacy, opposition parties won
sixty-eight single-member districts, some ten times their normal performance.
With only a thin majority in the Chamber of Deputies (52 percent of the seats),
the PRI faced its most formidable congressional opposition ever, coming from
both the left and the right of the political spectrum (table 4-3).

Let us now examine the PRI's most important conservative and leftist opposition in recent years.

THE CHALLENGE FROM THE RIGHT

For more than forty years the National Action Party (PAN) was the PRI's
only significant opponent (see tables 4-1 and 4-2).[25] The party was established
in 1939 by businessmen, professionals, and Catholic intellectuals who op-

posed Lázaro Cárdenas's reforms and much of the revolutionary agenda.[26] Initially the PAN embraced Catholic conservatism. While it has maintained its religious underpinnings, over the years it has entertained a range of political ideologies, shifting its orientation periodically. In addition to proclerical and probusiness conservatives, its ranks have included progressive Christian Democrats and other democratic reformers.[27] But a common thread that has bound these different factions together is their conviction that the Mexican state has accumulated too much power. In recent years the party has become a leading champion of honest elections and clean government. Under that banner, it has attracted considerable support, especially within the Mexican middle class. The vote for the party's presidential candidates has grown steadily from under 8 percent in 1952 to 28.6 percent in 1994.*

During the 1960s, the PAN was influenced by Christian Democratic reformers who wished to temper the free enterprise system with greater social justice and economic equity. Following the economic crises of the mid–1970s and 1980s, however, the party moved sharply to the right. Shaken by President Luis Echeverría's economic populism and President López Portillo's nationalization of the banking system, many wealthy businessmen took a more active role in politics, particularly through the PAN.[28] The country's most powerful and most conservative entrepreneurs, centered in the city of Monterrey, were particularly important.

By the early 1980s, the PAN's most avid supporters of free market policies, known as the "neopanistas," took control from the party's centrist wing. Often educated in the United States, these conservative leaders were energized by the Reagan administration's attacks on big government and its unbridled commitment to free enterprise. Troubled by their party's shift to the right, a number of moderate PAN leaders resigned.[29] In time, Carlos Salinas's market-oriented reforms had stolen the neopanistas' thunder by implementing much of their economic program. Consequently, during the 1994 presidential race Diego Fernández's campaign stressed political reform and democratization rather than conservative economics. In fact, in a throwback to the PAN's more progressive days, Fernández argued that the effects of market reforms on the nation's poor needed to be cushioned, a position surprisingly similar to the left's.

By convincing many voters that he, rather than Cuauhtémoc Cárdenas, was the leading voice for democracy, Fernández unexpectedly returned the PAN to its longtime second-place standing. With 28.6 percent of the presidential vote, its best showing ever, the party accelerated its steady growth over the past half century (table 4-1).

The PAN's electoral strength is greatest in the north (a region especially influenced by American values), the western state of Jalisco (a bastion of conservative Catholicism), and the southern state of Yucatán (historically dis-

---

* The PAN boycotted the 1976 presidential election.

trustful of the central government). Its support is most pronounced among younger, more urban, more highly educated, and more affluent voters. While the PRI receives its strongest backing from government employees and (decreasingly) peasants, the PAN's support is highest among students and white-collar workers in the private sector.[30] By 1995, it controlled four statehouses (including Jalisco's, Mexico's second most populous state) and some 150 municipal governments.[31] Thus, nearly one out of five Mexicans currently resides in a state with a PAN governor.

THE CHALLENGE FROM THE LEFT

Although Mexico's leftist parties share many of the PAN's political objectives—democratization and reduced corruption—they differ with it sharply on economic policy and the role of the state. Prior to de la Madrid's and Salinas's market-oriented reforms, the PAN used to assail PRI governments for promoting an overly interventionist state. By contrast, the left has always endorsed greater state economic intervention and faulted the government for failing to achieve a more egalitarian and just society.

In view of Mexico's inequitable income distribution and extensive poverty, leftist parties might be expected to garner considerable support from workers, peasants, and the urban poor. Prior to 1988, however, they seemed to convince few voters that they were the true bearer of the nation's revolutionary values. Instead, building on revolutionary mythology and Lázaro Cárdenas's far-reaching reforms, the ruling party has used progressive rhetoric, often unmatched by government behavior, to steal the left's thunder. At the same time, starting with Presidents Obregón, Calles, and Cárdenas, the party effectively organized workers and peasants, thereby coopting the left's natural constituencies.

The Mexican government has long been more antagonistic toward the left than toward the PAN and, consequently, has placed more obstacles in its path. In fact, the regime benefits from having a critic on the right since its attacks make state policies appear to be progressive. On the other hand, the left's rhetoric could potentially remind voters of the government's failure to fulfill its revolutionary promises.

Prior to the 1977 electoral reforms, government regulations made it difficult for leftist parties to register legally. As Wayne Cornelius has noted, until then the government refused to recognize "the existence of a legitimate political opposition to the left of the PRI."[32] While parties on the left can now register and compete more easily, electoral authorities still deny them some of their electoral victories. As far back as 1975, the Popular Socialist Party candidate is believed to have won the governor's race in the state of Nayarit, but government authorities altered the count.

More recently, PRD candidates have won a number of municipal state legislative, and Senate elections. To date, however, the PRD has failed to win a single gubernatorial election including a few races in which it may have been denied victory through fraud. During the Salinas administration, several allegedly fraudulent PRI gubernatorial victories prompted considerable public protest. In response, the president removed a few PRI victors and replaced them with interim governors, twice appointing a governor from the PAN. Never, however, did Salinas rectify or overturn a suspect PRD defeat. Thus it remains to be seen when the government will allow a PRD victory at the state level.

Frequently the left has compounded the problems it faces from government fraud and harassment, through internal ideological divisions and factional fighting.[33] Unable to agree on a common program, for years a handful of small leftist parties competed amongst themselves for a small percentage of the vote. Though brought together by Cuauhtémoc Cárdenas in 1988, they have been torn by discord once again.

THE LEFT BEFORE THE CARDENISTA CHALLENGE

Analyzing the Mexican left shortly before the 1988 presidential election, Barry Carr divided it into three groups:[34]

1. The "Loyal" or "Satellite" Left. Despite their professed radical ideologies, some leftist parties loyally supported PRI presidential candidates and endorsed government policy for years in return for political and financial favors. These "satellite" parties often justified their behavior by insisting that Mexico did not yet have the proper socioeconomic conditions for a marxist transition. Parties of the loyal left included the Popular Socialist Party (PPS) and the Socialist Workers Party (PST). In 1987, a major faction of the PST broke away to form the Party of the Cardenista Front for National Reconstruction (PFCRN), which supported Cuauhtémoc Cárdenas's presidential candidacy. Other formerly (but no longer) loyal left parties also supported Cárdenas.

2. The Independent Left. Independent leftists have tried more vigorously than has the satellite left to mobilize the poor and the working class. At the same time they have resisted the potential benefits that they could have gained from cooperating with the government. Instead, they have accused the PRI of subverting the ideals of the Revolution and have been especially critical of the government's current neoliberal economic policies. The most important independent leftist parties have included the Labor Party (PT), the Revolutionary Workers Party (PRT), and the Mexican Socialist Party (PMS). Like the loyal left, these parties were divided by the Cardenista phenomenon. The PMS supported Cárdenas's candidacy in 1988 and gave its party registration to his newly formed Party of the Democratic Revolution (PRD) the following year, thereby permitting the PRD to gain a place on the ballot. A portion of the PRT also broke away from that party in order to join the Cardenistas.

3. The Cardenista Left. During the late 1980s, the so-called neocardenist

movement became the dominant force on the Mexican left and the most potent challenger that the PRI has ever faced at the ballot box. Built around the candidacy of Cuauhtémoc Cárdenas, the movement first emerged from the PRI's progressive wing that his father had once led. In 1985, Cárdenas along with Porfirio Muñoz Ledo and other PRI dissidents had formed the reform movement Democratic Current.[35] But their demand for democratic selection of the PRI's presidential candidate was rejected, and they were subsequently ousted from the party. Consequently the Cardenistas joined with four other political parties and entered that alliance, the National Democratic Front (FDN), into the 1988 presidential campaign.[36]

THE RISE OF CARDENISMO

Unlike other leftist leaders who are very much the outsiders, Cárdenas (a former PRI governor of Michoacán and former senator) and Muñoz Ledo (previously the president of the PRI and Mexico's ambassador to the United Nations) come from the peak of the country's political establishment. Moreover, they were never marxists, though many PRD activists were. Instead, Muñoz Ledo defined the Cardenistas as a "populist-nationalist" movement.[37] Although its solutions to Mexico's political and economic problems are sometimes vague, the movement skillfully articulates the widespread belief that the Revolution's egalitarian goals must be rekindled.

In his 1988 and 1994 campaigns, Cárdenas's electoral platform was certainly more statist than the PRI's or the PAN's, but it was not socialist. He accepted some of the government's market-oriented economic reforms, but rejected others as too harsh. While acknowledging the value or inevitability of a free trade agreement with the United States (though he has since backed away from that stance), Cárdenas charged the government with inadequately protecting Mexican interests in the NAFTA negotiations and with failing to construct a safety net for Mexican workers displaced by free trade. Like his conservative PAN opponents, Cárdenas criticized government corruption and authoritarianism, but he appeared more intransigent than they in protesting electoral fraud. Following the 1994 election, for example, he initially seemed to encourage his followers to take part in nonviolent resistance.

The FDN coalition brought together for the first time several populist and leftist political parties and factions that had been notoriously divided in the past.* Drawing on popular discontent over the country's prolonged economic decline and its falling living standards, the FDN not only exceeded the PAN's vote but raised an unprecedented challenge to PRI dominance. Officially, Cárdenas received 32 percent of the vote, the largest proportion ever won by an opposition candidate since the official party was created in 1929. In fact, his

---

* The FDN included the Democratic Current, three leftist parties (the PFCRN, the PMS, and the PPS), one center party (the PARM, formerly a PRI satellite), and MAS, a splinter of the Trotskyist PRT.

real total was probably higher. FDN leaders insisted that Cárdenas had actually defeated Carlos Salinas by a margin of 42 to 37 percent and had been robbed of his victory. Many Mexicans agree. While the true count will never be known, one extensive postelection poll suggested that had there been an honest tally Salinas would have still won, but only by a margin of 3 or 4 percent rather than the official gap of 18 percent.[38]

One year after the 1988 election, the newly created Party of the Democratic Revolution (PRD) absorbed much of the FDN coalition. In subsequent local elections the PRD won control of eighty-nine municipal governments, nearly three times as many as the PAN governed (though most of the PRD victories were concentrated in Cárdenas's home state of Michoacán).[39] Thus, it appeared that the Cardenista movement was poised to mount a serious challenge to PRI dominance.

THE DECLINE OF CARDENISMO

Yet despite its early success, the PRD has faded badly in the 1990s. Several factors have contributed to its difficulties. The party has occasionally been the victim of government harassment and repression, particularly at the grass roots. According to nonpartisan human rights groups, there were up to a hundred politically motivated murders during the Salinas administration, most of them committed against PRD activists. The government also has used nonviolent "dirty tricks" to discredit municipal governments controlled by the PRD. "In [the city of] Morelia, for example, the PRI-affiliated garbage workers union struck shortly after the PRD took over. As the garbage piled up, ... [progovernment] newspapers proclaimed Morelia a dirty city and called the PRD incompetent."[40]

Equally important, the Cardenistas have suffered from the PRI's ability to rejuvenate itself and from the PRD's own organizational weaknesses and internal divisions. During his presidency, Carlos Salinas was remarkably adept at outflanking the left and coopting its potential support. His Solidarity Program (PRONASOL) provided clean drinking water, sewage systems, sports facilities, health clinics, and other public works to many poor neighborhoods and villages throughout the nation (chapter 6). The program invited grassroots organizations, including those formed by the left, to participate in the implementation of those projects. By transferring substantial government resources to poor communities, by incorporating neighborhood organizations into the decision-making process, and through his campaign of highly publicized visits to Solidarity projects, Salinas developed a strong following among the nation's poor.

PRONASOL's large budget was particularly targeted toward areas where it could give the PRI optimal political payoff. For example, seeking to head off a potential PRD victory in Michoacán's 1992 gubernatorial election, the Salinas administration devoted a huge proportion of Solidarity's budget to that single state. Later it channeled substantial development funds into Chiapas following the Zapatista uprising.

The Cardenistas also have been weakened by lackluster performances by many of the local governments that they control and by political infighting within the PRD. The FDN's strong showing in the 1988 national election and in the succeeding municipal elections depended heavily on Cuauhtémoc Cárdenas's personal appeal. Other important FDN and PRD leaders such as Porfirio Muñoz Ledo offered the party considerable political talent and know-how. But below its upper echelons, the PRD organization and local officials lack political experience and have frequently appeared disorganized and inept.

Finally many party activists, who range from former members of the PRI's progressive wing to ex-activists in various marxist parties, have little in common with each other beyond their opposition to the regime and their support for Cárdenas. Even the founding fathers of the FDN and PRD have had serious differences. During the 1994 campaign, for example, Cárdenas and PRD president Muñoz Ledo clashed over the party's position toward the electoral reform law. Following his disastrous performance in Mexico's first presidential campaign debate, Cárdenas's voter support plunged and he eventually finished a disappointing third in the 1994 election. Since that time the PRD has been split between Cárdenas's more confrontational faction that tends to oppose the administration at every turn, and Muñoz Ledo's moderate faction that favors dialogue with Zedillo. As Cárdenas has moved further to the left, he seems to be losing touch with Mexico's mainstream. By the mid-1990s the PRD was in some disarray and had dropped well behind the PAN in public support.

ELECTORAL REFORM, BUT STILL NO LEVEL PLAYING FIELD

The 1993 electoral reform law made considerable progress toward creating a more honest process. It reconstituted the Federal Electoral Institute (IFE) so that it could independently oversee the voting process as well as the vote count. Unlike its predecessors, the IFE has been largely freed of outside political influence and is respected for its independence and integrity. Indeed the 1996 reform law is expected to further its independence. Sophisticated voter identification cards and other new safeguards have been introduced to prevent illegal voting and ballot-box stuffing. In the past, the political parties themselves supplied the poll watchers at the thousands of voting stations throughout the country. With huge numbers of party activists available for that task, the PRI had been able to cover many voting stations that opposition parties could not.[41] Under the new procedures, poll watchers are chosen by lottery from a list of the citizens in the district.

In addition, in recent elections thousands of additional (unofficial) observers from Civic Alliance have blanketed the nation's polling stations. In 1994 they were joined by several hundred foreign observers whom the government had reluctantly accepted as the result of considerable international pressure. All of these reforms produced the most honest ballot count in Mexican history (though still with certain irregularities). For the most part, the 1995 state election counts also seem to have been relatively clean. That does not mean, however, that elections are now fully fair. To the contrary, the PRI retains so many advantages in the campaign itself that there is still little semblance of a level playing field.

One of the PRI's greatest advantages is its favored treatment in media coverage.[42] Because only about 10 percent of the population read newspapers, television is the major source of news for as many as 75 percent of all Mexicans.[43] And to an extraordinary degree television broadcasting is dominated by the networks of the Televisa conglomerate. Owned by multibillionaire Emilio Azcarraga, Televisa accounts for 85 percent of the nation's television audience and carries 90 percent of all advertising.[44] Its nightly news program *24 horas* (24 hours) is such a pervasive source of news that its anchor, Jacobo Zabuldovsky, has often been called Mexico's best-known personality after the president.

Televisa enjoys a symbiotic relationship with the government, presenting slavishly supportive news coverage in return for favors such as new licenses for local stations (sixty-two of them in 1993 alone). At an infamous 1993 dinner with some of the country's richest men, President Salinas reportedly solicited $25 million from each participant for the PRI electoral campaign. As a sign of his commitment to the ruling party, Azcarraga allegedly pledged three times that amount (though all of the commitments were rescinded after news of the dinner leaked to the press).[45]

Televisa's news programs during the presidential campaign frequently began with an interview of the PRI candidate or an extended clip from a speech that he had made that day. That lead might be followed by brief shots of the PAN or PRD candidate, typically with an announcer's voice-over. A study of 1994 campaign coverage on *24 horas* and *Hechos* (the major news show of the far smaller competing network, Televisión Azteca) revealed the extent of television news bias.[46] Over a four-month period, the two PRI presidential candidates, Colosio then Zedillo, received 43 percent of the air time devoted to the presidential race, Fernández (PAN) had 12 percent, and Cárdenas (PRD) 11 percent. In the three months preceding his assassination, Luis Donaldo Colosio appeared as the lead story in the nightly news twenty-three times. Ernesto Zedillo was the lead twenty-three times in only the first month of his campaign. Conversely, during those same four months, the Cárdenas and Fernández campaigns each were given the lead on the nightly news only once.

Although Mexican newspapers and news magazines have modest audiences when compared with television, the most respected ones have considerable influence because they are read by the country's professionals and intellectual elite. Moreover, publications such as *Proceso, La Jornada, El Financiero,* and *Uno Más Uno* offer more independent political analysis than television does, frequently criticizing the government. Yet a study of election

Table 4-4. Newspaper Coverage in the 1988 Campaign

Newspaper	PRI	PAN	FDN
El Universal	46.4%	12.5%	11.4%
Excelsior	52.0	5.5	14.0
La Jornada	40.9	19.8	14.0

Source: Kathleen Maria Bruhn, "Taking on Goliath: The Emergence of a New Cardenista Party and the Struggle for Democracy in Mexico," Ph.D. diss., Stanford University, 1993, 158.

coverage in three of the country's most prestigious daily newspapers during a single week of the 1988 campaign revealed that even they gave disproportionate space to the PRI (table 4-4). A more extensive examination of both the Mexico City and provincial press during six months of the campaign indicated a similar pattern, with the PRI getting two and one-half times as much coverage as the PRD and three times as much as the PAN.[47]

In the recent past Mexico has seen its share of government intimidation of the press, and muckraking journalists are occasionally still killed under highly suspicious circumstances. But the imbalance in news coverage demonstrated in table 4-4 has less to do with government pressures than with its ability to manufacture news. Because government officials are overwhelmingly from the official party, there are endless opportunities for events (ribbon cuttings at new public works projects or the like) that showcase the PRI incumbent and benefit the party's candidate for succession. In addition, with far more financial resources than its opponents, the PRI can more readily stage newsworthy stories. All of these factors explain why even a moderately leftist paper like La Jornada, which favored the PRD, still gives the PRI far greater coverage (table 4-4).

To be sure, press objectivity has improved over the years. Influential publications such as Proceso, La Jornada, and El Financiero can now criticize the government fairly freely, and there has even been modest improvement on television. For example, during the 1994 campaign independent monitoring groups credited the press as well as Televisa's smaller competitor, Televisión Azteca, with becoming more objective. NBC's recent acquisition of minority ownership in Azteca may further promote that network's professionalism. Still, Televisa so thoroughly dominates news coverage and remains so blatantly biased that even if opposition parties received balanced coverage in the rest of the media, which they don't, they would still be at a great disadvantage.

In the long run the future of Mexico's party system will depend, not only on clean election counts, but also on the government's willingness to allow fairly contested elections at all levels. Both the PRI and the government itself are divided between factions wishing to permit a more open political system and those adamantly trying to preserve the old order (the "dinosaurs"). Ironically, members of the reformist faction are often government technocrats and administrators who have reached the top by climbing the rungs of the government bureaucracy rather than by running for elected office. Many, like the past three presidents, have studied abroad, hold advanced degrees in the social sciences, and have been convinced of the need to modernize the political system. On the other hand, the group adamantly defending the status quo includes many career politicians whose advancement depends not only on winning their own elections but on having other members of their political clique win handsomely as well.

Presidents de la Madrid and Salinas, themselves technocrats, supported political liberalization, but set limits on how far they were willing to go. For example, while the Salinas administration was the first to allow opposition party candidates to win gubernatorial races, it restricted that opening to the PAN and was considerably less receptive to the PRD.

Ernesto Zedillo is seemingly committed to extending democratization, most notably by separating the government from the official party and giving the party greater independence from the president. As we have seen, he has allowed PRI state organizations to select their gubernatorial candidates rather than having the president dictate the choice. Zedillo has also indicated that he will let the party organization choose the next PRI presidential candidate in the year 2000, rather than unveiling the candidate himself.

But transferring power to the party organization is not necessarily a progressive change. Candidate selection will generally reside in the hands of party *caciques,* and conservative dinosaurs will continue to exert considerable power in the PRI and in the labor movement. In fact, during economic crises such as the one Zedillo inherited the president is particularly dependent on those bosses to get out the vote and dampen discontent. Finally, while the 1993–94 electoral reforms have achieved honest electoral counts at the national level, they apply to state elections only if the state legislature votes to accept them. While some states, notably those with strong PAN representation, have accepted reform, others have refused. Thus, while considerable progress has been made toward democratization much remains to be done. The major political parties continue to discuss further reform.

CONCLUSIONS

Predicting Mexican political trends is not as easy as it used to be. The party system, once so simple and stable, has become more complex. In one highly respected volume on Mexican politics published in 1987, not one of the contributing experts correctly anticipated the following year's surge of voter opposition to the PRI.[48] With Cuauhtémoc Cárdenas's strong showing in the 1988 presidential race the country finally appeared to be moving toward a competitive electoral system. Then the PRD's decline and the PRI's resurgence in the 1991 congressional elections suggested that while the PRI was no longer as dominant as it had been, it would likely continue to govern for the foreseeable future. But most recently, the PAN's 1995 victories in three gubernatorial elections and its strong showing in local elections indicate that a powerful conservative opposition party is emerging for the first time since the Revolution.

Some recent electoral trends have been contradictory. While national elections have become more honest, in some parts of the country fraud in local election has worsened. Pressured by public opinion, civic groups, and the opposition parties, Presidents de la Madrid, Salinas, and especially Zedillo have tried to modernize the electoral system and eliminate blatant fraud. But as the electoral system has become more competitive, reactionary PRI machines at the local and state level have intensified their efforts to manipulate the vote in order to protect their own interests.

Shortly before the 1994 presidential election a national survey indicated that most Mexicans expected the elections to be cleaner than in the past.[49] And while there were some foul-ups and some public discontent on election day, most Mexicans seemed to view the results as legitimate. So too did a contingent of distinguished foreign observers, who concluded, after monitoring the vote on election day, that the process was essentially clean.[50] Civic Alliance was more critical (alleging widespread electoral violations), but still saw no pattern of fraud sufficient to have affected the outcome. The PAN also accepted the essential integrity of the election. Only Cuauhtémoc Cárdenas, who claimed that once again he had been the victim of massive fraud, refused to accept the results.

While vote counts have become increasingly honest, the PRI's continued electoral strength in the 1990s reflects the party's continuing campaign advantages. We have already noted the tremendous pro-PRI bias in the mass media, particularly on television. The party's financial resources also dwarf those of its opponents. While it no longer uses government resources to the extent that it used to, it is still able to extract vast sums from the private sector. Until now it has continued to ignore legal limits on campaign contributions in many campaigns. Thus in Tabasco's 1994 gubernatorial race, the PRI spent $70 million to court a mere five hundred thousand voters, outspending the opposition by a margin of sixty to one and shattering legal spending limits. In the 1994 national elections the PRI spent more than three times as much as all of its opponents combined.

In 1996 the government is expected to announce yet another electoral reform law, this one emerging from months of secret negotiations between the PRI, PAN, and PRD. The law would further remove the IFE from government control by taking it out of the Ministry of Government's jurisdiction. More significantly, it is expected to establish more balanced electoral competition by strictly limiting campaign spending and awarding candidates equal access to radio and television time. If these rumored provisions are actually implemented and enforced, they would introduce a sea change in Mexican electoral competition. Unfortunately, PRD and PAN charges of PRI electoral fraud are delaying a reform accord.

Even so, the major opposition parties still have their own internal problems that leave them at a disadvantage. The left suffers from two major weaknesses. First, many voters who supported it in 1988 and 1994 did so out of a personal allegiance to Cárdenas and what his name represents. Consequently, the PRD or its successor party on the left will not necessarily inherit that support when he leaves the political stage. Equally important, Cárdenas's initial popularity tended to cover up the ideological divisions that have long plagued the left. As his star has begun to fade, the PRD and other left political parties have once again found it difficult to formulate a unified agenda.

Leftist support in the 1988 and 1989 elections also was closely linked to the country's severe economic crisis. Survey data reveal that the more optimistic voters were about the economy, the more they were prone to vote for Salinas, while pessimists tended to prefer Cárdenas.[51] Not surprisingly, the economic recovery in the early 1990s restored faith in the system and weakened opposition parties, at least temporarily. It is too early to know exactly how the latest economic crisis will affect public opinion. But as voters once again become disillusioned with the government, the PAN, rather than the disorganized PRD, has been the major beneficiary of their discontent.

On the political right, PAN has begun to develop a national following beyond its electoral base in the north. It has already demonstrated its ability to elect governors in several states. As the country urbanizes further and as the middle class grows, the PAN's support should increase correspondingly. For now, however, the party still faces difficult challenges. Ironically, it has suffered somewhat from the PRI's appropriation of its program. President Salinas's policies of privatizing state enterprise, supporting the private sector, and promoting free trade with the United States and Canada coopted much of the PAN's core economic agenda. As the economic policy differences between the PRI and the PAN narrowed considerably, *panistas* had some difficulty defining what their role should be as an opposition party. While some were ready to work closely with Salinas or Zedillo, several PAN leaders left the party in 1992 charging that it had become insufficiently critical of the PRI and lacked a distinct identity. Diego Fernández's strong showing in the 1994 presidential race indicates that the PAN's future electoral success may depend on its ability to project itself as the party of democratic reform rather than the champion of conservative economics.

Notes

1. Alan Riding, *Distant Neighbors* (New York: Vintage, 1984), 135.

2. There were also several dozen other parties seeking legal status at the time. Pablo González Casanova, *Democracy in Mexico* (New York: Oxford University Press, 1970), 34.

3. Lorenzo Meyer, "La democracia política: esperando a Godot," *Nexos,* no. 100 (April 1986).

4. Edward J. Williams, "The Evolution of the Mexican Military and Its Implications for Civil-Military Relations," in *Mexico's Political Stability: The Next Five Years,* ed. Roderic A. Camp (Boulder, Colo.: Westview, 1986), 144. On civil-military relations, see also David Ronfeldt, ed., *The Modern Mexican Military: A Reassessment* (La Jolla: University of California–San Diego

Center for U.S.-Mexican Studies, 1984); Adolfo Aguilar Zinser, "Civil-Military Relations in Mexico," in *The Military and Democracy*, ed. Louis Goodman et al. (Lexington, Mass.: Lexington Books, 1990).

5. Daniel Levy and Gabriel Székely, *Mexico: Paradoxes of Stability and Change* (Boulder, Colo.: Westview, 1983), 40.

6. John J. Bailey, *Governing Mexico: The Statecraft of Crisis Management* (New York: St. Martin's Press, 1988), 92–97; *PRI: Documentos básicos* (México: Talleres Gráficos de la Nación, 1984), 156–215.

7. Arnaldo Córdova, *La política de masas del cardenismo* (México: Era, 1974); Cynthia Hewitt de Alcántara, *Modernizing Modern Agriculture* (Geneva: UNRISD, 1976).

8. Roger Bartra, "Campesinado y poder político en México," in *Caciquismo y poder político en el México rural*, ed. Roger Bartra et al. (México: Siglo XXI, 1975).

9. Howard Handelman, "The Politics of Economic Austerity in Latin America," in *Latin America and Caribbean Contemporary Record*, vol. 7, ed. James Malloy and Eduardo Gamarra (New York: Holmes and Meier, 1990).

10. Martin Needler, *Mexican Politics* (New York: Praeger, 1990), 64. See also Kevin Middlebrook, ed., *Unions, Workers and the State in Mexico* (La Jolla: University of California–San Diego Center for U.S.-Mexican Studies, 1991); and Alberto Aziz Nassif, *El estado Mexicano y la CTM* (México: La Casa Chata, 1989).

11. Judith Adler Hellman, *Mexico in Crisis* (New York: Holmes and Meier, 1979), 50.

12. Bailey, *Governing Mexico*, 100. Popular sector members held from 40.8 percent to 53 percent of the single-member districts. The agrarian sector received 21.3 percent to 31.7 percent and the labor sector won 14.6 to 25 percent.

13. Viviene Bracher-Márquez, *The Dynamics of Domination* (Pittsburgh: University of Pittsburgh Press, 1994), 163.

14. Ann L. Craig and Wayne A. Cornelius, "Houses Divided: Parties and Political Reform in Mexico," in Scott Mainwaring and Timothy R. Scully, eds., *Building Democratic Institutions: Party Systems in Latin America* (Stanford, Calif.: Stanford University Press, 1995), 282.

15. *Mexico and NAFTA Report* (Latin American Regional Report), 15 June 1995, 4.

16. Samuel Aguilar and Hugo Andrés Araujo, *Estado y campesino en la Laguna: la lucha campesina por la tierra y el excedente* (Saltillo: Universidad Autónoma Agraria Antonio Navarro, 1984).

17. Susan Eckstein, *The Poverty of Revolution* (Princeton, N.J.: Princeton University Press, 1988), 127; see also Eckstein, "The State and the Urban Poor," in *Authoritarianism in Mexico*, ed. José Luis Reyna and Richard Weinert (Philadelphia: ISHI, 1977), 23–47.

18. Alberto Aziz Nassif and Juan Molinar Horcasitas, "Los resultados electorales," in *Segundo informe sobre la democracia: México el 6 de Julio de 1988*, ed. Pablo González Casanova (México: Siglo XXI, 1990), 170.

19. Rolando Cordero as quoted in Wayne Cornelius, "Liberalization in an Authoritarian Regime," in *Mexican Politics in Transition*, ed. Judith Gentleman (Boulder, Colo.: Westview, 1987), 30.

20. Wayne Cornelius and Ann Craig, "Politics in Mexico," in *Comparative Politics Today*, ed. Gabriel Almond and G. Bingham Powell (New York: Harper Collins, 1992), 490.

21. The best discussion of earlier electoral reforms is Kevin J. Middlebrook, "Political Liberalization in an Authoritarian Regime: The Case of Mexico," in *Transitions from Authoritarian Rule*, ed. Guillermo O'Donnell, Philippe Schmitter, and Laurence Whitehead (Baltimore: Johns Hopkins University Press, 1986), 123–47.

22. For a more extensive listing of possible reasons for the electoral reform, see Silvia Gómez Tagle, "Electoral Reform and the Party System, 1977–90," in *Mexico: Dilemmas of Transition*, ed. Neil Harvey (London: Institute of Latin American Studies, University of London, and British Academic Press, 1993), 67.

23. Speech by Jesús Reyes Heroles in *Reforma política: Gaceta informativa de la Comisión Federal Electoral* (México: Talleres Gráficos de la Nación, 1977).

24. Lorenzo Meyer, "México o los límites de la democratizacíon neoliberal," paper delivered

at a seminar of the University of California–San Diego Center for U.S.-Mexican Studies, La Jolla, 1991.

25. Leticia Barraza and Ilán Bizberg, "El Partido Acción Nacional y el régimen político Mexicano," in *El nuevo estado Mexicano: estado y política,* ed. Jorge Alonso et al. (México: Nueva Imagen, 1992), 83–111.

26. Donald Mabry, *Mexico's Acción Nacional: A Catholic Alternative to Revolution* (Syracuse, N.Y.: Syracuse University Press, 1973), 1–32.

27. Annelene B. Sigg, "De la ideología confesional a la ideología nacional: el PAN y sus presidentes, 1962–1982," in *La transición interrumpida: México, 1968–1988* (México: Nueva Imagen, 1993), 143–70.

28. Dale Story, "The PAN, the Private Sector, and the Future of the Mexican Opposition," in *Mexican Politics in Transition,* 261–80.

29. Joseph L. Klesner, "Changing Patterns of Electoral Participation," in *Mexican Politics in Transition,* 102–3.

30. Edgar Butler, James Pick, and Glenda Jones, "An Examination of the Official Results of the 1988 Presidential Election," in *Sucesión Presidencial,* ed. Edgar Butler and Jorge Bustamante (Boulder, Colo.: Westview Press, 1991), 21 and 40; Germán Pérez Fernández del Castillo et al., *La voz de los votos: Un análisis crítico de las elecciones de 1994* (México: FLACSO, 1995), 405.

31. *Mexico and NAFTA Report* (Latin American Regional Report), 30 March 1995, 2.

32. Wayne Cornelius, "Political Liberalization and the 1985 Elections in Mexico," in *Elections and Democratization in Latin America, 1980–85,* ed. Paul Drake and Eduardo Silva (La Jolla: University of California–San Diego Center for Iberian and Latin American Studies, 1986), 121.

33. Ibid., 122–23.

34. Barry Carr, "The Left and Its Potential Role in Political Change," in *Mexico's Alternative Political Futures,* ed. Wayne A. Cornelius, Judith Gentleman, and Peter H. Smith (La Jolla: University of California–San Diego Center for U.S.-Mexican Studies, 1989), 368–69.

35. Andrew Reding, "The Democratic Current: A New Era in Mexican Politics: Interviews by Andrew Reding," *World Policy 5,* no. 2 (1988); Jose Carreño Carlon, "El MAS rebasa por la cuenta de la izquierda y lleva a Cárdenas al vacío," *Punto,* May 1988.

36. Jaime Tamayo, "El neocardenismo y el nuevo Estado," in *El nuevo estado Mexicano: estado y política,* 113–34.

37. Reding, "Democratic Current," 35. See also Carlos Gil, ed., *Hope and Frustration: Interviews with Leaders of Mexico's Political Opposition* (Wilmington, Del.: Scholarly Resources, 1992), 149–211.

38. Wayne A. Cornelius, Judith Gentleman, and Peter H. Smith, "Overview: The Dynamics of Political Change in Mexico," in *Mexico's Alternative Political Futures* (La Jolla: University of California–San Diego, Center for U.S.-Mexican Studies, 1989), 20.

39. Kathleen Bruhn and Keith Yanner, "Governing under the Enemy: The PRD in Michoacán," paper delivered at the Latin American Studies Association Congress, Los Angeles, 1992, 1.

40. Ibid., 16.

41. Arturo Sánchez Gutiérrez, "Los partidos políticos: La competencia de 1991," in *Las elecciones de Salinas,* ed. Arturo Sánchez Gutiérrez (México: Plaza y Valdes, FLACSO, 1992), 123–24.

42. Pablo Arrendondo Ramírez, "El Estado y la communicación," in *El nuevo estado Mexicano: estado y sociedad,* ed. Jorge Alonso et al. (México: Nueva Imagen, 1992), 39–66.

43. These estimates come from Sergio Aguayo, the leader of Civic Alliance.

44. *New York Times,* 6 March 1994.

45. *Toronto Globe and Mail,* 24 January 1994.

46. The research was conducted by the Mexican Academy of Human Rights and Civic Alliance.

47. Cited in the *Christian Science Monitor,* 1 June 1994.

48. Judith Gentleman, ed., *Mexican Politics in Transition.* To be fair, the essays in the vol-

ume were written in 1985–86. Still, they all failed to forecast a major electoral upheaval that would take place only two to three years in the future.

49. *Voz y Voto* (México), 17 July 1994.

50. Wayne Cornelius, "Elections in Mexico," *Los Angeles Times,* 25 August 1994.

51. Keith Yanner, "Democratization in Mexico, 1988–1991: The Surge and Decline of Support for the Neocardenistas," Ph.D. diss., Washington University, 1992.

5

Interest Groups and Popular Protest

Though the Mexican political system is only beginning to shed its authoritarian skin, it has long been responsive to a range of organized interest groups and social movements. To be sure, the state imposes limits on mass mobilization and interest group activity. When peasant organizations, labor unions, or student protestors transcend those limits, they may still provoke government repression. Even powerful business associations may be cautious about challenging government authority. But the rules of the political "game" have always left organized interest groups and even protestors some room for political maneuver.

Since the 1970s, a combination of social modernization, economic crisis, and growing public awareness has widened the political space available to these groups. The government's relatively measured response to the Zapatista uprising—where it has looked for political, rather than military, solutions—illustrates that progress.

In this chapter we will discuss two types of group political participation. The first is by "insider" groups—those with sanctioned and regularized access to the centers of political power. The second is by "outsiders." Lacking official incorporation into the PRI (or unable to use such links effectively) and having no other regularized contacts with the government, these groups must resort to demonstrations, strikes, and other forms of protest. Perhaps the two most important insider groups are organized labor and big business. Unions, of course, have institutional links to the state through the labor sector of the PRI, although dissident unions are ill served by that mechanism. Businesses approach the government through their legally sanctioned associations outside the PRI structure. In addition, powerful corporations and conglomerates negotiate directly with government officials. In recent decades, some sectors of the business community have entered party politics, working through the PAN.

Outsider groups—including dissident labor movements, peasant organizations, and associations of the urban poor—face a far more difficult task in articulating their needs since they have fewer political resources or connections. Consequently, such groups must first demonstrate a sufficient "power capability" to convince authorities that the government should negotiate with them. At the same time, however, they must not appear unduly threatening to the status quo. In recent years, the government has been more willing to negotiate with outsider groups, as demonstrated by its ongoing talks with the Zapatista rebels in Chiapas.

ORGANIZED LABOR

Since the time that it organized "Red Battalions" for the Revolution, organized labor has been an active participant in Mexican national politics. Article 123 of the 1917 constitution gave workers a number of rights that were unusually advanced for that time. They included the right to organize, the right to bargain collectively, and the right to strike. In subsequent decades, Presidents Calles and Cárdenas encouraged the growth of trade unions, while at the same time tying the labor movement to the regime.[1]

That bond was formalized when Lázaro Cárdenas created the labor sector of the official party. Of course, while this link to the state offered organized labor certain advantages, it also limited their options. Labor "was under the tutelage of the benevolent hand of the government. . . . At the same time, the segment of labor . . . [that] supported the government of General Cárdenas . . . achieved a position of influence over national economic policy never before realized."[2] That trade-off still exists. The union movement's close ties to the government benefit labor bosses and a portion of the working class, especially those in the modern sector of the economy. The price, however, has been corruption and state-imposed limitations on labor's behavior.

When the official party's labor sector was first created, Mexico was still in the early stages of industrial development. Consequently the working class was still relatively weak. But as a consequence of rapid economic growth from the 1940s to the 1970s, the country developed a substantial industrial base and a larger, politically influential labor movement. The proportion of the urban workforce that was organized was one of the highest in Latin America.[3] By the 1970s, organized labor encompassed some 15 percent of the total economically active population (EAP) and about 35 percent of the EAP in manufacturing.[4] Those percentages were quite high compared with those of other developing nations. In fact, the proportion of Mexico's total EAP that is currently unionized is similar to that of the United States even though Mexico has a much larger agricultural workforce that is generally unorganized. It appears, however, that the percentage of unionized workers has declined since the 1970s.[5] Thus, labor unions may now represent only about 20 percent of the urban EAP and a substantially lower proportion of the total workforce.[6]

But organized labor's political influence is based less on the absolute number of workers it represents than on its extensive organization in essential sectors of the economy such as petroleum, railroads, steel, electric power, and automobiles. For over half a century, a substantial portion of those industries have been state owned, though privatization since the early 1980s has reduced that proportion. In return for labor's loyal support, the state has offered workers in those strategic industries wages and benefits well above the national norm. For their part, the workers in critical industries such as the railroads and public utilities have effectively given up their right to strike.

Like their counterparts elsewhere in Latin America, Mexican labor has a history of internal divisions that has weakened its effectiveness. Some conflicts are jurisdictional or legal. Others pit more radical unions or rank-and-file movements that favor greater labor autonomy against government-affiliated unions that typically are dominated by entrenched labor bosses.

In 1919, shortly after labor gained the right to organize, President Carranza encouraged the birth of the Regional Confederation of Mexican Workers (the CROM), which became the principal umbrella group for labor until the 1930s. Composed of relatively conservative, progovernment unions, the CROM worked closely with President Alvaro Obregón (1920–24), but subsequently broke with his successor, Plutarco Elías Calles. Deprived of state support and disdained by rival communist, socialist, and Catholic federations, the CROM disappeared from the forefront of the labor movement. It still exists today, but has a following in only a few industries and geographic regions.[7]

After a period of declining political influence (1928–34), organized labor flourished under the tutelage of President Lázaro Cárdenas (1934–40).[8] During his administration the percentage of the workforce that was unionized nearly tripled. In 1936 Cárdenas's ally, Vicente Lombardo Toledano, the era's most powerful labor leader, founded the Confederation of Mexican Workers (CTM). Two years later the president incorporated the CTM into the labor sector of his newly created Party of the Mexican Revolution (PRM).

The CTM has been the country's primary labor organization ever since. It still dominates the PRI's labor sector today and speaks to the government on behalf of the organized working class. Yet the confederation's member units represent only some 40 percent of the country's organized workers (though a larger portion of the blue-collar workforce). Another 25 percent are represented by two rival confederations, the Revolutionary Confederation of Workers and Peasants (CROC) and the much smaller CROM. Government white-collar employees, constituting close to 20 percent of all organized workers, have a special legal jurisdiction and belong to the popular sector of the PRI, rather than the labor wing, through the Confederation of Government Workers Unions at the Service of the State (FSTSE). Finally, a number of powerful industrial unions—representing electrical power workers, railroad workers, and miners/metalworkers—have remained autonomous, unaffiliated with any labor federation, though still a part of the PRI's labor sector.[9] In 1966 labor unions representing close to 90 percent of all unionized workers formed a larger umbrella organization called the Congress of Labor (CT). While purporting to speak for all of labor, the CT actually is dominated by Fidel Velázquez and the CTM, the most conservative segment of the union movement.

Cárdenas's successors, Manuel Avila Camacho and Miguel Alemán, abandoned his prolabor orientation, discouraged working-class militancy, and controlled wages in order to promote capital investment. World War II imposed further limits on the labor movement when the government asked workers to renounce class struggle for the sake of national unity. Chastened by the specter of European fascism, organized labor complied, signing a "workers solidarity pact" that precluded strikes for the war's duration. Despite the CTM's cooperation, the government remained uncomfortable with the confederation's secretary general, Lombardo Toledano, a marxist known earlier for his militancy. Consequently, the Avila Camacho administration helped unseat him, supporting in his place Fidel Velázquez, a more conservative union leader and an autocrat who still leads the confederation today. In that span of more than fifty years, he has been one of the country's most powerful political figures, with ready access to a succession of presidents.

Velázquez's ascendancy represented a major turning point in Mexico's labor history. While the CTM had frequently cooperated with the government under Lombardo Toledano, it remained committed to the ideal of erasing class differences. However, following the victory of Velázquez's faction the confederation's marxist motto, "For a Classless Society," was changed to the nationalist slogan, "For the Emancipation of Mexico."[10] Previously influential marxists, anarcho-syndicalists, and other leftists were purged from positions of power in the labor movement.

While many critics of Mexican labor dismiss Velázquez and his associates as conservative *caciques* who support the government to the detriment of their rank and file, the truth is more complex. Like the Mexican left, the CTM has been a champion of economic nationalism. It has endorsed limits on foreign trade and investment, and supported import-substituting industrialization (see chapter 6). And it has battled for higher wages, greater state consumer subsidies, and government welfare policies designed to benefit the urban working class.

At the same time, however, during the country's postwar industrial takeoff, CTM unions constrained their wage demands in order to facilitate capital investment. For much of that period, blue-collar wages failed to keep up with increases in the cost of living. Not surprisingly, critics have accused the CTM leadership of helping business industrialize the country on the backs of the working class. Labor kingpins have further undermined their own image with their authoritarian tactics (including the repression of rank-and-file dissidents) and their lavish lifestyles.

Just as union leaders generally have been restrained at the collective bargaining table, they have been conservative on political issues. As we have seen, they have staunchly opposed democratization of the political system. Since the expansion of the labor movement in the 1920s, many unions have been dominated by corrupt strongmen known as *charros*.* Francisco Zapata notes the

* A *charro* literally means a cowboy. The term was first used in the late 1940s and 1950s to describe Jesús Díaz de León, the autocratic leader of the railroad workers union (the STRFM). Díaz de León, who flaunted his Acapulco penthouse and other ostentatious signs of wealth, liked to dress up in cowboy outfits when attending horse shows. First applied to him, the term *charro* was later applied generically to union bosses.

questionable procedures often used to elect union leaders. "The decision making process in organizations like the CTM, the CT and the national industrial unions is cloaked in secrecy. While it is not clear how election procedures for the higher posts actually function, reelection is typical."[11]

The "social pact" between the government and organized labor during Mexico's postwar industrialization gave the unions considerable influence in areas such as negotiating state contracts and selecting PRI candidates. But as we have noted, labor leaders in turn agreed to support government development policies even if they affected workers adversely. Labor's political support has been particularly important to the regime when it has been under siege—for example, after the 1968 student massacre and during the recent economic crises.

Over the years, organized labor's close links to government have produced benefits for its rank and file, including state-subsidized food and housing, public health care, and, more recently, limited profit sharing.[12] But it is surely the union bosses who have gained the most from the alliance. When its help has been needed, the state has intervened in union affairs to squash rank-and-file insurgencies and protect corrupt *charros*. That intervention has helped entrenched labor chiefs survive in powerful unions such as those of the petroleum workers, miners and metal workers, and railroad workers.

Another benefit for labor leaders has been a share of political positions at the national, state, and local level. For example, in recent decades about 20 to 25 percent of the PRI candidates for the Chamber of Deputies have been drawn from the party's labor sector. Others are selected from the unions of government employees that belong to the PRI's popular sector.[13] Those congressional seats along with their other positions at lower levels of government have afforded union chieftains considerable political clout, patronage, and financial gain.

In years past, a number of internal reform movements have challenged *charro* leadership. For example, in 1958–59 marxist activists led a grassroots revolt in the railroad workers' union (the STFRM), ousted the longtime leadership, and staged a series of rail strikes. However, their uncompromising positions evoked a harsh government response. The insurgents' leaders were sentenced to lengthy prison terms, and the twenty thousand striking workers were given the alternative of returning to work or being fired.[14]

During the early 1970s, President Luis Echeverría initially encouraged antiestablishment labor movements in the hope of securing additional support for his progressive political agenda. Rafael Galván, a former senator from the PRI's left wing, helped create Democratic Tendency, a major reform movement within the union of electrical power workers. The movement allied with militant factions in the teachers', university employees', textile, telephone, steel, brewery, petroleum, and railroad workers' unions. And, with some encouragement from the Echeverría administration, they formed the Revolutionary Union Movement (MSR) as a progressive alternative to the CTM. But the president's declining political strength later forced him to mend fences with Fidel

Velázquez and other union bosses when he needed their support against his private-sector opponents. Consequently, he quietly abandoned the union democracy movement. Since that time, the government has been generally unsympathetic to labor dissidents.[15]

Though reformist movements continued into the next decade, the level of labor insurgency declined perceptibly after Democratic Tendency collapsed in the late 1970s. In recent years the most militant rank-and-file movements have developed in the schoolteachers' and the nuclear power workers' unions. Important dissident activity has also emerged within unions representing bank employees, university workers, state sector bureaucrats, steelworkers, and automobile workers.[16] For the most part, however, dissident labor activity has fallen sharply since the 1980s. Rather than radicalizing labor, the recent economic crises and diminished job security have made workers reluctant to challenge their union leadership. From the mid-1970s to the late 1980s, the number of strikes designed to promote union democracy decreased by 95 percent.[17] Yet there has been some progress. Today, a number of CTM unions have more leadership turnover and more democracy at the lower ranks than many critics of organized labor have recognized.[18]

Soon after taking office, President Carlos Salinas seemed to signal an end to the cozy relationship that had long existed between the government and corrupt union leaders. The president ordered the arrest of one of the nation's most powerful and notorious labor bosses, Joaquín Hernández Galicia (called "La Quina"), who had headed the STRPRM (the petroleum workers' union) since the early 1960s. Protected in his palatial home by a large team of bodyguards (allegedly armed with two hundred Uzi machine guns and twenty-five thousand rounds of ammunition), La Quina could be apprehended only after the government had marshaled a substantial military contingent. But even though his arrest was supposed to demonstrate Salinas's resolve to combat union corruption, that message was soon undercut when the administration endorsed the union's new leader, another corrupt official but one who was more compliant with the administration's desires.

The recent economic crisis has driven a wedge between the CTM leadership and the state, thereby undermining organized labor's political strength.[19] During the country's postwar industrial boom, union leaders had implicitly acquiesced to a social pact that restrained blue-collar wages in return for economic growth, job creation, and increased political influence for establishment unions. But the current economic decline has made it much more difficult for organized labor to support government economic policies. It was one thing for labor leaders to ask their rank and file to restrain their wage demands during a period of expanded employment and rising family income.* It is quite an-

---

* The real income (purchasing power) of many individual workers declined from the 1940s through the mid-1950s and grew haltingly in subsequent years. However, economic expansion created more families with multiple wage earners and, hence, higher family income. Moreover, for the many new workers who had migrated to the cities, even the "lower" real wages in the postwar era were higher than what they had previously earned in the countryside.

other matter to ask workers to accept greater unemployment and a 40 percent reduction in real incomes.

The government's market-oriented policies have also created tensions with organized labor. For example, privatization has resulted in numerous job layoffs and reduced the unions' economic power. The number of strikes annually, which had fallen sharply from the 1930s to the mid-1970s, rebounded somewhat in the 1980s.[20] Previously compliant unions such as the petroleum workers (the STRPRM) began to publicly criticize government policy. When de la Madrid stripped the STRPRM of some of its economic power (and corresponding opportunities for graft), its leader, La Quina, asked his rank and file to support the Socialist Workers Party (PST) in the following congressional election. Hoping to win back union support, the government increased political patronage to the PRI's labor sector. Thus the number of congressional seats allocated to the unions increased appreciably.[21]

Yet despite declining economic conditions and the unions' discomfort with the new direction in economic policy, labor unrest in Mexico has remained relatively limited when compared with that of other industrialized countries in Latin America.[22] Although the CTM's high command criticizes government austerity measures, it ultimately has accepted them without much of a fight. Beginning in 1987, the unions, the private sector, and the administration signed a series of agreements (initially called "Economic Solidarity Pacts") implementing wage and price restraints, as well as reductions in the fiscal deficit. During the latter part of the Salinas administration, as inflation declined and the economy haltingly recovered, real wages began to rise slowly. Unhappily, that process has been reversed since the end of 1994 by the country's latest financial crisis. Once more, however, the unions have responded passively. The CTM reacted angrily to President Zedillo's economic austerity program, initially refusing to join the revived tripartite pact (currently called the Alliance for Economic Recovery). Still organized labor did not stage protest marches or call a general strike, as their counterparts have elsewhere. Fidel Velázquez even asked Mexican workers to give up one day's wages to contribute to an economic recovery.

What accounts for labor's rather muted response to the economic crises and to the government's neoliberal economic policies? The answer lies, in part, in the enormous power that the Mexican state exerts over union organization and labor relations. Although the constitution theoretically guarantees workers an "inviolable" right to strike, subsequent legislation authorized the government to declare any strike illegal and thereby permit the firm to dismiss any employee who refuses to go back to work. Between 1963 and 1988, authorities approved only 2 percent of all union petitions for strike authorization.[23] The state also effectively determines wage levels for most workers through its negotiations with labor leaders. These affect the wages of more workers than do union wage agreements reached through collective bargaining with employers. Finally, the government can determine the fate of a rank-and-file insurgency movement within a union by refusing it legal recognition or, far more rarely, recognizing it as the workers' legitimate representative.

While the CTM may clash with the government over specific policies, its leaders have no interest in a serious confrontation. Normally they prefer behind-the-scenes negotiation. Many of the most vocal critics of government economic policy are insurgent labor leaders and leftist politicians, the very ones that have challenged Fidel Velázquez and the CTM leadership. Not surprisingly, union chieftains are very reluctant to legitimize these labor dissidents by echoing their criticisms of the government. Thus, whatever the CTM's displeasure in recent years over wage policies, the GATT trade agreement, NAFTA, and the privatization of state enterprises, it has ultimately acquiesced in those policies after negotiating whatever concessions it could get.

Labor leaders also have been dismayed by recent political reforms, including the advent of greater electoral competition. Even a modest loss of congressional seats or municipal governments to opposition parties reduces the number of political posts and attendant patronage available to the CTM. Because the unions have been so closely associated with the "dinosaur" wing of the PRI, its candidates have suffered the greatest losses in recent congressional elections. For example, the CTM was particularly humiliated when its leader in Mexico City finished third as the PRI candidate in the capital's 1988 Senate race.

For the most part, labor's political influence has declined in recent years. The growth of the commercial and service sectors of the economy and the movement of industrial jobs to the northern (less unionized) region of the country have reduced the proportion of Mexico's urban workforce that is organized. Within the unions themselves, as workers have become better educated and better informed, they are less easily controlled by traditional labor bosses. Neoliberal economic reforms have also reduced the unions' long-standing influence over hiring and promotion, thereby reducing their control over the rank and file.

As the union leadership's influence over their members has decreased and worker discontent over declining living standards has mounted, organized labor has been more hard-pressed to deliver votes to the PRI. While 75 to 80 percent of all union members supported the official party in the 1982 national elections, that figure has declined to around 50 percent today.[24] Consequently, recent PRI presidential candidates have relied more heavily on the mass media and modern electoral techniques to appeal directly to working-class voters. Labor dinosaurs and other members of the PRI old guard have been fighting a holding action against the technocratic modernizers who have surrounded de la Madrid, Salinas, and Zedillo. Unions also have had decreasing influence in the selection of the PRI's presidential candidate. In 1988, the union hierarchy was visibly angered by President de la Madrid's choice of Carlos Salinas as his successor because Salinas had helped craft the administration's painful austerity policies. Six years later labor had little say in the selection of either Colosio or Zedillo.

Because of Fidel Velázquez's advanced age (he was born in 1900) and his more than fifty years at the helm of the CTM, Mexicans have been speculating for years about the future of the labor movement after he dies (or, as a common joke has it, "*if* he dies"). Hoping to continue his influence after his death, he has placed a younger generation of professionally trained loyalists in top CTM posts. But, as Kevin Middlebrook has observed, Velázquez's machine is based on personal loyalties that will probably not survive him. Moreover, "these younger leaders are unlikely to figure prominently in the transition process because their support base is in the CTM national bureaucracy rather than in major unions with significant mass memberships."[25]

Velázquez's impending death, then, may allow more independent union leaders to emerge who might loosen the ties that have bound labor to the state. At the same time, a growing number of modern Mexican firms and unions wish to negotiate labor contracts through collective bargaining rather than through the Labor Ministry. If this trend continues, the state's control over labor, an important component of the corporatist system, will be further weakened.

BIG BUSINESS

Big businesses's links to government, unlike labor's, lie outside the PRI structure. Consequently, its political activities and positions are more varied and complex. Mexico was one of the earliest Latin American nations to industrialize.[26] Much of its late-nineteenth-century growth was centered in the northern city of Monterrey. Ever since, that city's business conglomerates ("Groups") have been a powerful force in the economy.[27] The country's most significant industrial expansion, however, began in the 1940s. These newer industries were more dependent on the state for subsidies and for trade protection to shield them against foreign competition. Not surprisingly, they have been more receptive to the principle of state economic intervention and more cooperative with the government than the Monterrey barons have been.

In Latin American countries such as Colombia and El Salvador, political and economic elites are closely linked by family, school, and country-club ties. This is less true of Mexico, where the two elites tend to come from different backgrounds. A number of years ago, Peter Smith found that Mexico's political leaders generally come from middle-class, rather than elite, backgrounds.[28] More recently Roderic Camp has found little evidence of a unified "power elite." Business leaders originate disproportionately in the north—particularly from the state of Nuevo León and its principal city, Monterrey—and were typically educated at private schools. On the other hand, the most important political leaders come largely from Mexico City and generally attended public schools.[29]

Partly because of these social differences, until recently relations between the state and the private sector have sometimes been less harmonious than in other Latin American countries. However, these relations have varied considerably from one presidential administration to another and from one business sector to another, depending on how dependent that sector has been on state support.

Presidents Avila Camacho and Alemán established a close working relationship with the private sector that endured until the early 1970s. But President Echeverría's populist rhetoric and reform policies provoked enormous business hostility. As a result substantial capital flight abroad undermined the economy. Echeverría's successor, José López Portillo, was undoubtedly impressed by big business's show of muscle and entered office determined to regain private-sector confidence. But with the discovery of vast state-owned petroleum deposits, the economy became far less dependent on private investment, and López Portillo was free to pursue populist policies. His administration borrowed abroad excessively, and when the economy began to unravel in the early 1980s, he alienated the business community by nationalizing the nation's banking system in an effort to control foreign exchange. Because the bank nationalization was carried out without the normal consultations with the financial sector, it infuriated business leaders. Feeling betrayed, they became far more hostile to the state.[30]

The de la Madrid administration (1982–88) improved relations with big business somewhat and began privatization of the state economic sector. But his administration's painful economic austerity policies left many businessmen unhappy. It was Carlos Salinas who finally restored amicable relations with the private sector. Business appreciated the predictability of his policies, the decline in inflation, and the modest economic upturn. Salinas's neoliberal policies reduced state economic intervention, and his privatization program enabled many well-connected businessmen to make millions by buying state industries at favorable prices. Relations between the state and private sectors were more harmonious than they had been in decades.

Ernesto Zedillo was initially received favorably by business leaders. He was, after all, Salinas's former budget director and seemed likely to continue economic policies that they supported. Soon after taking office, however, the new administration clumsily handled a major devaluation of the peso. Having just assured investors that the government would not devaluate, it allowed the peso to fall sharply against the dollar. That misstep, coupled with the uncertainties caused by the government's ongoing standoff with the Zapatista rebels, precipitated capital flight and a steep decline in the Mexican stock market. It remains to be seen what the long-term effects of the president's early difficulties will be, but Zedillo is certain to continue Salinas's probusiness policies.

Unlike labor, which is represented at least nominally by a single umbrella organization (the Congress of Labor), the business community is organized into a number of specialized associations. The most powerful industrial organization is the National Confederation of Chambers of Industry (CONCAMIN). The National Chamber of Manufacturers (CANACINTRA) is an influential industrial organization as well. The commercial sector is primarily represented by the Confederation of National Chambers of Commerce (CONCANACO). Other influential business organizations include the Mexican

Council of Businessmen (CMHN), the Mexican Association of Insurance Institutions (AMIS), the Entrepreneurial Coordinating Council (CCE), and the
Mexican Employers' Confederation (COPARMEX). Smaller firms are represented by the National Confederation of Small Property Owners (CNPP) and
the National Confederation of Chambers of Small Commerce (CNPC). Mexico's corporatist political system requires all business above a designated size
to join the Chambers of Industry (CONCAMIN) or Chambers of Commerce
(CONCANACO), the private sector's official representatives.

While the country's most powerful business firms must belong to these organizations, they typically are not highly active and do not regard them as the
best channel for communicating with important government officials.[31] Much
of Mexico's private industry and commerce is controlled by holding companies
known as "Groups." Typically they are dominated by a small number of linked
families that control much of the capital and hold key managerial positions.[32]
Some of the most powerful of these conglomerates, based in the country's economic capital, belong informally to the umbrella "Monterrey Group." Although that Group broke up into several smaller Groups in the early 1970s, its
name remains synonymous with Mexican big business, and it continues to be
a very powerful force in the nation's economic and political system. Consisting
of approximately two hundred families, the Monterrey economic elite produces about 25 percent of Mexico's industrial output.[33] At the start of the
1980s, the umbrella Group's six component conglomerates had assets exceed-
ing $13 billion (dollars) and employed over 156,000 workers.[34] Since then,
their holdings have grown through merger and acquisitions, including the purchase of privatized state firms.

Because Monterrey is located closer to the U.S. border than to Mexico
City, its businessmen have traditionally identified with American capitalism
and have distrusted Mexico's powerful state sector. Having founded their firms
prior to the country's postwar industrial boom, they were less dependent than
were later industrialists on state support and tariff protection. Consequently,
they have been more committed to free market policies and more antagonistic
toward big government. That has not prevented them from seeking state support when they have needed it, however. For example, when the Alpha Group
was going bankrupt 1981, it turned to the state for badly needed loans.

Though it has been influential in some business associations such as CO-
PARMEX (a voluntary group) and CONCANACO, the Monterrey Group
usually conveys its position to government through direct contacts with high-
ranking administration officials. Government leaders, for their part, take such
exchanges very seriously.

Unlike most of the private sector, which traditionally either supported the
PRI for pragmatic reasons or stayed clear of party politics, members of the
Monterrey group have frequently supported the PAN. Following President
López Portillo's nationalization of the banks in 1976, business support for the
PAN intensified.[35] The Monterrey Group especially was inspired by the anti-
government rhetoric and policies of the Reagan administration in the United

States and Britain's Prime Minister Margaret Thatcher. During the 1980s, business leaders were active in developing the *neopanistas*, the PAN's most antistatist, neoliberal wing.

But not all business associations share the Monterrey Group's antipathy toward state economic intervention. Rather, their attitudes are colored by the degree to which their sector relies on state support or did in the past. A recent study of Mexico's business associations divided them into five categories ranging from "unconditional [government] supporters" to "strong critics."[36] The confederations representing small property owners and small commerce, the CNPP and CNPC, have enjoyed the closest relationship with the government. Their members are particularly dependent on the state for credit and favorable regulations. On the other end of the spectrum, the associations most hostile to government include COPARMEX (the employers' confederation) and CON-CANACO (the Confederation of National Chambers of Commerce), both of which follow the lead of the Monterrey Group.

Among the organizations representing larger businesses, CANACINTRA (the National Chamber of Manufacturers) is the most receptive to government economic intervention. Primarily speaking for the automotive, chemical, food, and metallurgical industries, the chamber is a part of CONCAMIN (the larger group of industrialists) but tends to operate independently. From its inception in 1941, it has represented industries that are dependent on state support. Indeed, CANACINTRA works so closely with the government that some analysts have labeled it a "captive" of the state. Moreover, several chamber leaders have subsequently assumed important government posts. For example, Jesús Reyes Heroles, an early spokesperson, later headed the PRI during the Echeverría administration and then served in both the López Portillo and de la Madrid cabinets. Because of their more centrist politics, CANACINTRA members also tend to be more conciliatory in their dealings with organized labor.

That does not mean, however, that the chamber has slavishly supported the government. Like the rest of the private sector, it was hostile toward Echeverría and embittered by López Portillo's bank nationalization. More recently, as its members have viewed increased foreign trade as either an opportunity or a threat, they have divided over issues such as Mexican entry into the GATT (chapter 6).[37] Many CANACINTRA firms feel threatened by the government's free trade policies since the early 1980s.[38]

On the other hand, two other voices of big business, CONCANACO and COPARMEX have been great champions of free trade and vehement opponents of state economic intervention. Until recently they have also favored confrontational tactics in opposing government policy. Following President López Portillo's nationalization of the banks, for example, CONCANACO called a business strike to express private-sector indignation. However, when CANACINTRA and other industrial associations on favorable terms with the government refused to join the strike, it floundered.

During the 1980s, very conservative businessmen toyed with the idea of creating a new opposition party representing business interests.[39] When that project failed, many of them became more active in the *neopanistas*, the PAN's right-wing faction. As a result of their efforts, the party nominated a particularly confrontational presidential candidate in the 1988 campaign. As we have noted, the Mexican economic elite had previously avoided party politics, preferring to work behind the scenes. Thus, by becoming actively involved in the PAN and pushing it to the right, conservative businessmen, particularly those from Monterrey, were entering unchartered waters.[40] Through much of the 1980s, they broadened the divide between the PRI and the private sector.[41]

But during the Salinas administration (1988–94), relations between business and the government improved considerably. Salinas reduced government economic intervention, privatized most state enterprises, and reduced trade protectionism. All of those policies conformed to the private sector's neoliberal agenda. Business confidence was also bolstered by lower taxes, lower interest rates, modest economic growth, and a falling inflation rate. As domestic and foreign capital poured in, the Mexican stock market soared.

Wealthy businessmen with close connections to the Salinas administration often had the inside track for purchasing privatized industries. Many were sold at bargain prices, netting the purchasers instant fortunes. In fact, the Salinas era was an excellent time for the very rich. One year before he took office, Mexico had only a single billionaire. By the close of his term, there were twenty-four Mexican billionaires in *Forbes* magazine's annual list of the world's richest men. Heading the Mexican contingent was Carlos Slim Helu, whose estimated worth of $6.6 billion was higher than the combined Rockefeller family fortune and three times Ross Perot's. Slim, the son of a Lebanese immigrant, was closely linked to Salinas and was the major beneficiary of the privatization of Mexico's telecommunications industry (Teléfonos de México). He also was able to purchase state banking and mining firms at highly favorable prices.

The two dozen Mexican billionaires on *Forbes's* list constituted the fourth highest number for any country in the world (behind the United States, Germany, and Japan), an astonishing figure for a developing nation. In fact, Mexico now seems to have more billionaires than Britain and France combined. Between them those twenty-four men control an enormous portion of Mexico's private sector. Their combined worth, $44 billion, equaled 12 percent of the country's gross domestic product in 1993. Slim's firms alone make up nearly 20 percent of the stock value of the entire Mexican stock market.[42]

The symbiotic relationship between government and this new class of superrich was demonstrated by the notorious private dinner at which Carlos Salinas met with a small group of powerful businessmen not long before the 1994 presidential campaign. Among the guests were Carlos Slim Helu, Emilio Azcarraga (owner of the television giant, Televisa), Adrián Sada (a member of a powerful Monterrey family), and Carlos Hernández (the purchaser of Banamex, the country's largest privatized bank). Many of them had benefited enormously from Salinas's privatization program, from the creation of

NAFTA, and from other administration policies favorable to business. Not surprisingly many were receptive when Salinas asked each of them to contribute $25 million to the PRI's upcoming campaign.[43]

Ultimately, big business desires a number of things from the government: consultation with the private sector on matters that affect it; less state regulation; pragmatic economic policies and rhetoric; predictable and stable long-term government policies; a smaller state sector; reduced government spending; low tax rates; low inflation; secure property rights; realistic foreign exchange rates; and friendly relations with the United States.[44] After several administrations that failed to meet many of those expectations, Carlos Salinas finally gave the private sector what it wanted. To a considerable extent, Ernesto Zedillo seems intent on doing the same.

POLITICAL OUTSIDERS

Most Mexicans, particularly peasants and the urban poor, are far less able to influence state policy than the preceding groups. They lack organized labor's political connections or the business elite's economic leverage. To be sure, a large segment of the peasantry—those whose families once received land through the agrarian reform—are represented in the PRI by the National Peasant Confederation (the CNC), and some of the urban poor are organized into the party's popular sector. But the quality of that representation is generally low. Consequently, the poor often must resort to less orthodox methods such as protest marches and sit-ins in order to be heard. The regime generally tries to coopt protestors and tolerates their activities as long as they do not transcend strict limits on their scope and nature. However, should a group exceed those limits or should the authorities perceive their activities as threatening to political stability, the government will likely repress them, often quite brutally.

Peasant Mobilization.   From the colonial period through the 1920s, Mexico's peasantry were among the most rebellious in Latin America, periodically participating in local and regional uprisings.[45] Rural unrest during the nineteenth century was generally precipitated by state policies depriving the peasants of their land. Led by leaders such as Emiliano Zapata and Pancho Villa, the peasants were a major force in the Mexican Revolution. But during the following decade many of the rural poor turned against the revolutionary government in the enormous, conservative Catholic uprising know as the *Cristero* movement.

In time, Lázaro Cárdenas's agrarian reform and the creation of the official party's peasant sector demobilized the peasantry and turned them into a reliable source of government support. Since then the CNC has uncritically supported government agricultural policy, even when it has affected its members adversely. For example, when government favoritism toward agribusiness forced many peasants to abandon their land in the 1940s and 1950s, the CNC stood by. Today, confederation officials are often notoriously corrupt and rather indifferent to their constituents' needs.[46] Furthermore, within the *ejidos* and other rural communities, village strongmen (*caciques*) often exploit their fellow peasants and use the political and legal systems to their own advantage.

But while the CNC is a weak political voice, it is still an indispensable intermediary between villagers and the rural institutions that provide them with basic services.[47] Peasants, who depend on the state for credit, irrigation, fertilizers, seeds, and other fundamental agricultural inputs, understand that delivering a strong PRI electoral majority in their village may determine how good their access will be to government assistance. Not surprisingly, the rural population has generally been the most dependable source of support for the PRI election machine.[48]

In recent elections, however, the official party's control over the countryside has weakened somewhat. For example, PRI candidates chosen from the ranks of the CNC have run rather poorly of late.[49] In 1988, Cuauhtémoc Cárdenas received a significant portion of the peasant vote in his home state of Michoacán, though that support declined in the most recent presidential election. In Chiapas, the PRI's rural machine rolled up some 90 percent of the vote (with the likely help of fraud) until recently. But in the 1994 election, both Cárdenas and the PRD's gubernatorial candidate received considerable peasant support, a sign of growing rural disenchantment with the government. Many of the state's peasants also have demonstrated their sympathies for the Zapatista movement.

If they are to succeed, peasant protesters must maintain a very delicate political balance. Like any outsider group, they must first demonstrate a sufficient "power capability" to prompt the authorities to consider their demands seriously. Yet, at the same time, they must not pose a threat to political stability. In her discussion of rural Mexico, Judith Hellman describes "the politics of tamales," that very balance between independent peasant mobilization and the knowledge of how and when to work within the system.[50] She focuses on the communist-led Central Union of peasants in the cotton-growing Laguna region. In 1936 the union organized a major strike that eventually convinced President Cárdenas to introduce sweeping agrarian reform to the area. In the succeeding decades, the movement survived periodic repression from less sympathetic administrations. By the 1960s, having demonstrated its strength and ability to survive, the Central Union moderated its demands and its tactics, eventually reaching a beneficial accommodation with the regime. "The Central Union," notes Hellman, "seemed to be more 'successful' in its dealings with each new regime, *opposing the government less, but winning more* in the way of economic benefits for its constituency."[51] Similarly, widespread, but controlled, peasant land invasions in the 1970s convinced the Echeverría administration to redistribute valuable farmland to the peasantry in the state of Sonora.[52]

Since that time, however, the government has first scaled back and then abandoned its constitutional commitment to land redistribution. Instead, it has introduced a number of alternative rural programs over the years designed to raise peasant productivity, improve rural health and education, and raise peasant living standards. The slow death of land reform has contributed to rural unrest in several regions, most notably the Zapatista uprising. But more frequently peasants have responded to the problem by migrating to urban centers rather than by organizing politically. With roughly half the farmland in the country redistributed in earlier years, land reform seems to have reached its limits. Critics call the government's alternative development programs inadequate and point out that in many rural areas poverty and landlessness have been rising.[53] Because the CNC rarely questions government policy, peasants favoring other alternatives must organize independently. The history of autonomous peasant organization during the past two decades demonstrates both the possibilities and the limitations of independent mobilization.

In 1979, eleven state and national peasant organizations, unhappy with the phasing out of land reform, formed the CNPA. More militant than most peasant groups, the organization often staged high-profile demonstrations such as marches on Mexico City. Often it worked closely with sympathetic labor groups such as the national teachers' union.

But the CNPA's "capacity for mobilization [was] far greater than its capacity for negotiation" with the state.[54] Eventually it split into two warring factions: a radical wing that used confrontational tactics to press the government for land redistribution; and a pragmatic group favoring negotiation with the authorities and greater involvement in government rural development programs. Conflict between the two sides became quite violent, and several dozen members of the radical faction were murdered.

The CNPA ultimately failed because it focused its efforts excessively on land reform to the exclusion of other issues. It failed to respond adequately to emerging peasant concerns that grew out of the 1980s economic crisis. Aside from Chiapas and a few other radicalized areas, peasant concerns today focus less on land reform than on "agricultural prices, access to markets, wage rates, the delivery of basic services, and . . . inflation."[55] In addition, the CNPA failed to take advantage of the more competitive electoral system that has emerged since the late 1980s, because its leaders dismissed elections as "a bourgeois game."[56] Forced for the first time to compete with the Cardenistas and even the PAN for the rural vote, the PRI is now compelled to negotiate more seriously with independent peasant groups. Because the CNPA and other radical groups failed to take advantage of this new opportunity, they have been eclipsed by more politically astute peasant organizations such as the UNORCA (the National Union of Autonomous Regional Peasant Organizations).

Although UNORCA is led by marxists, it has been more pragmatic and compromising than the CNPA in its dealings with government authorities. Union leaders have viewed the severe economic recession as reason for pragmatism and retrenchment because in any confrontation with the government peasants would now have fewer resources to fall back on. Furthermore, they realize that there is scant prospect for significant agrarian reform and therefore little sense in making it a prime union objective. Instead, UNORCA has concentrated on other issues: more favorable credit terms, higher agricultural prices, and greater peasant control over agricultural marketing, the very goals too often ignored by the CNPA.

The union also has been adept at forging alliances with influential actors within the political system. For example, it enlisted the support of the Mexican ecology movement by arguing that increased government aid to villagers in Chiapas would raise peasant productivity and thereby reduce their need to clear land in the dwindling Lacandon rain forest. During a dispute with the governor of Chiapas over land rights, UNORCA enlisted the support of the nation's minister of urban development and ecology at the time, Manuel Camacho. Eight years later, President Salinas appointed Camacho as his negotiator with the Zapatista rebels. By that time, Camacho had established a good working relationship with peasant groups in that state.

Occasionally, the union resorts to militant tactics such as blocking roads and occupying government facilities. But such activities are still part of a broader, pragmatic political strategy. The Cardenistas' electoral success at the end of the 1980s forced government officials to deal more seriously with UNORCA and other grassroots peasant groups in the hopes of gaining their support. In response to rural mobilization and the rise of the PRD, the Salinas administration signed a series of "cooperation agreements" (*convenios de concertación*) with sixty-six independent peasant organizations in eighteen states.[57] The purpose was to give them greater input in formulating government agricultural policy. Salinas also created a new umbrella organization called the CAP (Permanent Agrarian Congress), designed to bring Cardenista and marxist peasant groups such as the UNORCA into a closer relationship with CNC and other PRI-affiliated peasant organizations.

As the government has phased out crop subsidies, reduced its role in agricultural credit and marketing, and terminated agrarian reform, the nation's peasants increasingly have been put at the mercy of the free market (chapter 6). Many peasants fear the consequences of these changes and have joined Cardenistas or other leftist groups. Peasant advocates have been particularly disturbed by Salinas's *ejido* reform law that seeks to privatize communal holdings. Though its effects have been limited so far, the law has driven a wedge between progovernment and leftist peasant groups in the CAP.[58] Hoping to maintain rural support, the Salinas administration cushioned the effects of disappearing crop subsidies by providing peasants with fifteen-year fixed subsidies unrelated to production levels. At the same time, it transferred some agricultural marketing activities from the state to independent peasant cooperatives. While these tactics obviously failed in Chiapas, they were fairly successful in maintaining rural peace elsewhere.

The Urban Poor.   Like peasant organizations, groups that mobilize the urban poor must make some basic tactical decisions. They must decide whether to affiliate with the PRI's popular sector or otherwise cooperate with the government, or whether to be more confrontational. Groups that work closely with the regime risk being coopted too easily, letting the government purchase their support at too low a price. But groups that are too strident and militant risk being shut off from needed state resources. In fact, if they appear to pose a threat to political stability, they are likely to face government repression. Like other outsider groups, those representing the urban poor must establish a fine balance between those two options.[59]

Susan Eckstein's study of low-income neighborhoods in Mexico City revealed a wide array of community associations, including labor unions, teachers' unions, church groups, and associations of market vendors.[60] Many of these were affiliated with the PRI. Independent organizations sometimes used more militant tactics, staging rallies in the Zocalo, the city's central square, or camping out near the president's residence. But their ultimate *objectives* were usually fairly pragmatic—neighborhood health clinics, improved bus service, clean drinking water, sewage systems, electricity, paved streets, or an improved local food market.

Once militant neighborhood associations achieve some of their initial demands, the level of grassroots participation tends to decline, and the group's tactics generally become less militant. Frequently, group leaders or the entire group itself is coopted into the PRI. Leaders are tempted by the promise of greater political influence or elected office. Once affiliated with the ruling party, however, they face pressure to demobilize their followers. The price of political access is accepting the rules of the political system. Even idealistic leaders, unwilling to sell out for personal gain, may realize that they must "play the game" if they are to attain substantial benefits for their followers. Cooptation teaches the urban poor to "request," rather than demand, government benefits and services that they are legally entitled to.

Two events have contributed to the growth of independent political activity since the early 1980s. The first has been the extended economic crisis, which has decreased the resources that the state can distribute to low-income neighborhoods, thereby weakening its capacity to coopt. The second was the devastating Mexico City earthquake of 1985. When the government responded to the disaster extremely slowly and ineffectually, many of the city's poor became disillusioned with it and fell back on their own resources. Grassroots groups sprung up all over the city. A politically outspoken former professional wrestler became a local folk hero when he assumed the persona of *super barrio.** Dressed in a mask, tights (revealing a large paunch), and a cape, he became an important spokesperson for low-income families seeking new housing after their homes were destroyed by the earthquake. Inspired by Mexico City, the urban poor elsewhere also created independent, grassroots organizations known as "popular movements."

As far back as the 1970s, young political activists who had emerged from the radical student movement organized Durango's poor into an umbrella neighborhood association called the CDP.[61] In the 1980s, the group organized land invasions for housing space and demonstrated for improved urban so-

---

* The name is a cross between superman and *barrio,* a low-income neighborhood.

cial services. Eventually, the CDP entered electoral politics, initially support-ing Cuauhtémoc Cárdenas and local candidates from the Mexican Socialist Party.

While the PRI remains an important force in Mexico's low-income neigh-borhoods, it has lost the political monopoly it once enjoyed. In cities through-out the country low-income neighborhood associations have responded in varying ways to the emergence of Cardenismo and the PRD: some remain wary of the Cardenistas' long-term prospects and have decided to maintain their ties to the PRI so that they can continue to receive state patronage; others have joined the PRD hoping to see more fundamental social change; and still others have avoided affiliation with any political party.

The Salinas administration responded to the Cardenista phenomenon with a vigorous campaign to coopt urban social movements and regain the support of the urban poor. As in the countryside, the government negotiated a series of "cooperation agreements" with grassroots organizations of all types, from PRI affiliates to the marxist left. All were incorporated into the National Solidarity Program (PRONASOL) (chapter 6).[62] Unlike prior antipoverty pro-grams, Solidarity brought the poor themselves into the organization's decision-making process and opened its doors to radical opposition groups. By bring-ing low-income groups into PRONASOL, rather than the PRI, Salinas created an independent power base for himself while giving grassroots organizations greater political independence than government programs normally have al-lowed. To some extent, local groups have helped shape PRONASOL decisions on neighborhood and village projects. Moreover, activists can negotiate di-rectly with reform-oriented PRONASOL officials, thereby bypassing PRI di-nosaurs.

Solidarity obviously coopted radical groups to some extent by persuading them to work within the political system. But they have not been forced to sac-rifice their independence. In fact, they have been relatively free to oppose gov-ernment policies and even to back opposition parties. Thus, PRONASOL has welcomed into its ranks leftist popular movements that would never join the PRI. By giving the urban poor a partial alternative to the PRI, Carlos Salinas liberalized the political system and loosened the corporatist reins.

Many government critics still insist that PRONASOL was merely a more subtle instrument of cooptation designed to undermine the PRD. Cuauhtémoc Cárdenas urged independent urban movements not to affiliate with Solidarity. Some of the most militant neighborhood associations, such as Mexico City's Asamblea de Barrios, followed his advice. But, many others, including Du-rango's CDP, signed up after concluding that the president's new political ini-tiatives gave them access to government aid without unduly restricting their political independence. Indeed, the CDP remained in PRONASOL even after it had established an opposition party that defeated the PRI in the race for city executive.[63]

THE LIMITS OF INDEPENDENT POLITICAL ACTIVITY

In recent years, the Mexican political system has opened up more space for independent interest group activity and allowed political protesters more latitude. As the public has become more educated and more politically aware, it has put greater pressure on the government to democratize, reduce corruption, and respect civil liberties. For example, media exposure and public outrage helped force President Salinas to abandon the military's initial, heavy-handed tactics in Chiapas and seek an accommodation with the EZLN.

Yet despite these improvements, many peasant and urban militants, PRD activists, and other government critics are still persecuted by government authorities. Government human rights violations are most common at the state and local level. However, prosecutors and police authorities at all levels commit abuses. The growing political influence of drug cartels has further corrupted the law enforcement system. As a result, there have been a number of police attacks against journalists and other independent investigators who have examined the ties between narcotics traffickers and government authorities. Police units trying to apprehend drug lords have sometimes been attacked by other police defending the dealers. Between 1990 and 1992 alone, a total of 270 federal justice department officials and federal judicial police agents were charged with corruption or abuse of power.[64] Unfortunately, corruption has permeated the highest levels of law enforcement, and the number of officials actually charged undoubtedly represents a small percentage of those who are tainted.

To be sure, Mexico's human rights record is not nearly as dismal as that of recent Latin American military dictatorships or of the current civilian governments in Peru and Colombia. But its record is nonetheless flawed. Violations are most common in the countryside, where many peasants, particularly Indians, are evicted from their lands, harassed, or physically attacked. Such violence is particularly widespread in the country's poorest states, including Chiapas, Guerrero, and Oaxaca.[65] A number of political activists who have tried to organize peasants against such abuses have been tortured or killed.

An Amnesty International study of human rights violations in Oaxaca and Chiapas concluded that "a number of peasants . . . have apparently been the victims of deliberate political killings." While Amnesty, a respected human rights watchdog, did not blame the national government for the deaths, it concluded that "local authorities have been involved in murders and . . . criminals regularly act with impunity. . . . Informants say that the killings are the work of assassins hired by landowners and *caciques* who have close ties to the local power elites."[66]

Urban political activists also fall victim to government repression occasionally, though less frequently than in the countryside. For example, several dozen party workers in the PRD and its predecessor the FDN (both urban and rural) were killed during the 1988 and 1991 elections. Fifty-one Mexican journalists were murdered between 1970 and 1988, and many more were attacked or threatened. Very frequently the victims had been investigating politically sensitive topics: election-related fraud or violence; police corruption and mis-conduct; and narcotics trafficking. Human rights monitors have also been ha-rassed or attacked.[67] For example, in 1991 Dr. Víctor Manuel Oropeza, a doc-tor, journalist, and human rights activist in the city of Durango, was stabbed to death, apparently under the direction of the local police. To cover their tracks, the authorities then arrested an alleged suspect who died while in detention as the result of torture. Outraged by the behavior of the police, the Durango Bar Association lodged a protest. Soon afterward their offices were sprayed with bullets.[68]

International exposure of extreme abuses committed by local officials acutely embarrasses the national government, which wishes to project a posi-tive image abroad. The NAFTA debate and the Chiapas uprising have magni-fied foreign scrutiny of Mexico's human rights record, especially in the Amer-ican media. In 1990, not long before meeting with George Bush to launch the NAFTA initiative, President Salinas created a National Commission for Hu-man Rights (the CNDH) to demonstrate his administration's concern in this area. The commission's purpose is to investigate specific human rights viola-tions, propose legislation to improve civil liberties, and educate public officials and the general public. Its member have included a number of respected, inde-pendent jurists and scholars.[69]

International human rights groups such as Amnesty International and Americas Watch as well as the Mexican human rights community have ap-plauded the CNDH's creation and respect its integrity. Its periodic reports fo-cus public attention on specific cases of police torture, penal abuse, and other human rights violations. But the scope of commission activity is rather narrow. It deals with a relatively small number of specific abuses in the judicial process, but its jurisdiction does not cover areas such as systematic attacks against peas-ants or violence carried out by thugs working closely with government officials and police. Nor does the commission probe election-related violence. So, for example, following the murder of three PRD supporters in 1990, the CNDH declared that it had no authority to intervene in election abuses.

President Salinas tried to clean up the notoriously abusive antinarcotics di-vision of the Federal Police and the attorney general's office. But progress was limited, and it remains to be seen whether President Zedillo will be more suc-cessful. Zedillo did take a bold step when he appointed a respected PAN lawyer, Antonio Lozano, as the first opposition party figure ever to hold the politically sensitive post of attorney general. But while the national government has tried to reduce new human rights violations, it has been very hesitant to prosecute past violators, effectively leaving them free to operate with relative legal impunity.

CONCLUSIONS

Since the 1980s, organized labor and the National Peasant Confedera-tion, long the PRI's major pillars of political support, have lost much of their influence. As Mexican society modernizes, new sectors independent of the ruling party will likely gain more political power—most notably, business managers, professionals, and other middle-class groups. Mexico's neoliberal economic reforms, especially privatization and deregulation, are strengthening the hand of the business community and further weakening labor (chapter 6).

These changes may have both positive and detrimental effects on Mexican society. The weakening of corrupt labor unions is reducing rigidities in labor-management relations fostered by the archaic union leadership. For example, some unions are losing their control over the hiring process, a power that gave labor bosses tremendous hold over their rank and file. A critical question is whether independent labor unions will emerge to fill the gap. In the countryside, the deterioration of the CNC and of government controls over the peasant economy also is creating new opportunities for more responsive, independent rural organization. But the rural tradition of *caciquismo* (political bossism) makes independent peasant mobilization more difficult. At the same time, with the traditional urban and rural mass organizations exercising less political influence, the country's already substantial concentrations of wealth and income threaten to worsen.

The increased mobilization of the middle class and the growth of clean-government and human rights groups will hopefully contribute to further democratization. Politically skilled and articulate organizations such as Civil Alliance have already been a force against electoral fraud (chapter 4). Middle-class pressures for democratization will be strengthened if they are complemented by more independent and democratic trade unions.

As the state's economic role has declined and the private sector has become more influential, a segment of the business community has pushed for a more competitive electoral system (throwing their support to the PAN). At the same time, however, powerful economic elites are also likely to resist future efforts to achieve a more equitable distribution of income and may even support nondemocratic practices to maintain the economic status quo, as they have elsewhere in Latin America.

Notes

1. Ruth Berins Collier and David Collier, *Shaping the Political Arena* (Princeton, N.J.: Princeton University Press, 1991), 202–50.

2. Joe C. Ashby, *Organized Labor and the Mexican Revolution under Lázaro Cárdenas* (Chapel Hill: University of North Carolina Press, 1967), 287–88.

3. Joan Davies and Shakuntala de Miranda, "The Working Class in Latin America," in *The Socialist Register,* ed. Ralph Miliband (London: Merlin Press, 1967), 241.

4. Ian Roxborough, *Unions and Politics in Mexico* (Cambridge, England: Cambridge University Press, 1984), 4. It should be understood that estimates of this kind are not very precise and vary considerably from one expert to another.

5. Howard Handelman, "The Politics of Labor Protest in Mexico: Two Case Studies," *Journal of Inter-American Studies and World Affairs* 18 (August 1976): 167–94; Roderic A. Camp, *Politics in Mexico* (New York: Oxford University Press, 1993), 121.

6. Ilán Bizberg, "Modernization and Corporatism in Government-Labor Relations," in *Mexico: Dilemmas of Transition,* ed. Neil Harvey (London: Institute of Latin American Studies, University of London, 1993), 303.

7. For a brief overview of Mexican labor, see Rodney D. Anderson, "Mexico," in *Latin American Labor Organizations,* ed. Gerald Michael Greenfield and Sheldon L. Maram (Westport, Conn.: Greenwood Press, 1987), 549–76; More recent developments are discussed in Kevin J. Middlebrook, ed., *Unions, Workers and the State in Mexico* (La Jolla: University of California–San Diego Center for U.S.-Mexican Studies, 1991).

8. Ashby, *Organized Labor.*

9. Francisco Zapata, "Labor and Politics: The Mexican Paradox," in *Labor Autonomy and the State in Latin America,* ed. Edward C. Epstein (Boston: Unwin Hyman, 1989), 180. For very different percentages, see Víctor Manuel Durand Ponte, "The Confederation of Mexican Workers, the Labor Congress and Mexico's Social Pact," in *Unions, Workers and the State,* 90.

10. Howard Handelman, *Organized Labor in Mexico: Oligarchy and Dissent* (Hanover, N.H.: American Universities Field Staff, 1979), 5; Collier and Collier, *Shaping the Political Arena,* 414–15.

11. Zapata, "Labor and Politics," 178.

12. Peter Ward, *Welfare Politics in Mexico: Papering Over the Cracks* (Winchester, Mass.: Allen and Unwin, 1986). Consumer subsidies for food and other goods grew substantially until 1982, but then fell considerably during the recent economic crisis.

13. John J. Bailey, *Governing Mexico* (New York: St. Martin's Press, 1988), 100.

14. Evelyn Stevens, *Protest and Response in Mexico* (Cambridge, Mass.: MIT Press, 1974), 122–26; Handelman, "Politics of Labor Protest in Mexico."

15. J. Fernando Franco G. S., "Labor Law and the Labor Movement in Mexico," in *Unions, Workers and the State,* 105–19.

16. Enrique de la Garza Toledo, "Independent Trade Unionism in Mexico: Past Developments and Future Prospects," in *Unions, Workers and the State,* 165–80.

17. Ibid., 163.

18. Mark Thompson and Ian Roxborough, "Union Elections and Democracy in Mexico: A Comparative Perspective," *British Journal of Industrial Relations* 20, no. 2 (July 1982): 201–17.

19. Alberto Arroyo, "El Estado Mexicano de los años ochenta y sus trabajadores," in *El nuevo estado Mexicano: estado, actores y movimientos sociales,* ed. Jorge Alonso et al. (México: Nueva Imagen, 1992), 87–123.

20. Zapata, "Labor and Politics," 182–90.

21. Wayne A. Cornelius and Ann L. Craig, *The Mexican Political System in Transition* (La Jolla: University of California–San Diego Center for U.S.-Mexican Studies, 1991), 90.

22. Kevin J. Middlebrook, "State-Labor Relations in Mexico: The Changing Economic and Political Context," in *Unions, Workers and the State,* 10–13; Howard Handelman, "The Politics of Economic Austerity in Latin America," in *Latin America and Caribbean Contemporary Record,* vol. 7, ed. James Malloy and Eduardo Gamarra (New York: Holmes and Meier, 1990).

23. Cornelius and Craig, *Mexican Political System in Transition,* 88.

24. Presentation by Kathleen Bruhn at the International Congress of the Latin American Studies Association (LASA), Washington, D.C., September 1995.

25. Middlebrook, "State-Labor Relations in Mexico," 17.

26. Dale Story, *Industry, the State, and Public Policy* (Austin: University of Texas Press, 1986), 28.

27. Alex M. Saragosa, *The Monterrey Elite and the Mexican State, 1880–1940* (Austin: University of Texas Press, 1988).

28. Peter Smith, *Labyrinths of Power: Political Recruitment in Twentieth-Century Mexico* (Princeton, N.J.: Princeton University Press, 1979), 196–201.

29. Roderic A. Camp, *Entrepreneurs and Politics in Twentieth-Century Mexico* (New York: Oxford University Press, 1989), 54–76.

30. Matilde Luna, Ricardo Tirado, and Francisco Valdéz, "Businessmen and Politics in Mexico, 1982–1986," in *Government and Private Sector in Contemporary Mexico*, ed. Sylvia Maxfield and Ricardo Anzaldúa Montoya (La Jolla: University of California–San Diego Center for U.S.-Mexican Studies, 1987), 18.

31. Camp, *Entrepreneurs and Politics*, 144–46.

32. Nathaniel Leff, "Industrial Organizations and Entrepreneurship in the Developing Countries: The Economic Groups," *Economic Development and Cultural Change* 26 (July 1978): 663.

33. Story, *Industry, the State, and Public Policy*, 91.

34. Maria de los Angeles Pozas, *Industrial Restructuring in Mexico* (La Jolla: University of California–San Diego Center for U.S.-Mexican Studies, 1993), 2.

35. Ricardo Tirado and Matilde Luna, "El estado y los empresarios," in *El nuevo estado Mexicano: estado, actores y movimientos sociales*, 13–31.

36. Luna, Tirada, and Valdéz, "Businessmen and Politics in Mexico," 13–44.

37. Ibid., 24.

38. Story, *Industry, the State, and Public Policy*, 84–88.

39. Luis Felipe Bravo Mena, "COPARMEX and Mexican Politics," in *Government and Private Sector*, 89–103.

40. Roderic A. Camp, "Images of the Mexican Entrepreneur," in *Government and Private Sector*, 139–42.

41. Bailey, *Governing Mexico*, 142–43.

42. *Forbes*, July 1994; *San Antonio Express News*, 6 July 1994.

43. *New York Times*, 10 March 1993. As previously noted (chapter 4), when news of the dinner leaked to the media, it created a major scandal and the donations were returned.

44. Adapted from Bailey, *Governing Mexico*, 140.

45. John Coatsworth, "Patterns of Rural Rebellion in Latin America: Mexico in Comparative Perspective," in *Riot, Rebellion and Revolution: Rural Social Conflict in Mexico*, ed. Friedrich Katz (Princeton, N.J.: Princeton University Press, 1988), 21–62.

46. Merilee S. Grindle, *Bureaucrats, Peasants and Politicians in Mexico: A Case Study of Public Policy* (Berkeley: University of California Press, 1977), 147–63.

47. Merilee S. Grindle, *State and Countryside: Development Policy and Agrarian Politics in Latin America* (Baltimore: Johns Hopkins University Press, 1986).

48. Luisa Paré Ouellet, "El Estado y los campesinos," in *El nuevo estado Mexicano: estado, actores y movimientos* sociales, 125–43.

49. Cornelius and Craig, *Mexican Political System in Transition*, 86.

50. Judith Adler Hellman, *Mexico in Crisis* (New York: Holmes and Meier, 1979), 109–19.

51. Ibid., 116–17; italics added.

52. Graciela Flores Lúa, Luisa Paré, and Sergio Sarmiento, *Las voces del campo: movimiento campesino y política agraria, 1979–84* (México: Siglo XXI, 1988); Steven Sanderson, *Agrarian Populism and the Mexican State: The Struggle for Land in Sonora* (Berkeley: University of California Press, 1981).

53. Merilee S. Grindle, *Searching for Rural Development* (Ithaca, N.Y.: Cornell University Press, 1988).

54. Neil Harvey, "The New Agrarian Movement in Mexico, 1979–1999" (London: Institute of Latin American Studies, 1991), 17; this discussion of peasant mobilization draws heavily from Harvey's article.

55. Merilee Grindle, "Strategies of the Rural Poor," in *Social Responses to Mexico's Economic Crisis of the 1980s*, ed. Mercedes Gozález de la Rocha and Augustín Escobar Latapí (La Jolla: University of California–San Diego Center for U.S.-Mexican Studies, 1991), 147.

56. Harvey, "New Agrarian Movement in Mexico," 20.

57. Ibid., 30.

58. Luis Hernández Navarro, "Cambio y resistencia en el movimiento campesino," *Cuadernos Agrarios* (May-December 1992): 98–132.

59. On the relationship between the state and urban social movements, see Juan Manuel

Ramírez Sáiz, "Entre el corporativismo social y la lógica electoral. El estado y el movimiento urbano popular (MUP)," in *El nuevo estado Mexicano: estado, actores y movimientos sociales,* 171–94.

60. Susan Eckstein, *The Poverty of Revolution,* 2d ed. (Princeton, N.J.: Princeton University Press, 1988).

61. Paul Haber, "Cárdenas, Salinas and the Urban Popular Movement," in *Mexico: Dilemmas of Transition,* 218–45.

62. Wayne Cornelius, Ann Craig, and Jonathan Fox, eds., *Transforming State-Society Relations in Mexico: The National Solidarity Strategy* (La Jolla: University of California–San Diego Center for U.S.-Mexican Studies, 1994).

63. Paul Haber, "Political Change in Durango: The Role of National Solidarity," in *Transforming State-Society Relations in Mexico,* 255–80.

64. U.S. Department of State, *International Narcotics Control Strategy Report 1992: Mexico* (Washington, D.C., 1992), 4.

65. Carole Nagengast, Rudolfo Stavenhagen, and Michael Kearney, *Human Rights and Indigenous Workers* (La Jolla: University of California–San Diego Center for U.S.-Mexican Studies, 1992); Guillermo Bonfil, *México Profundo* (México: Secretaría de Educación Pública, 1988).

66. Nagengast, Stavenhagen, and Kearney, *Human Rights and Indigenous Workers,* 9. The first quote is taken directly from the Amnesty International report, *Mexico—Human Rights in Rural Areas.* The second quote is from Nagengast et al. based on the Amnesty study.

67. Americas Watch, *Unceasing Abuses: Human Rights in Mexico One Year after the Introduction of Reforms* (New York, 1991).

68. *La Jornada* (Mexico City), 20 October 1991.

69. Americas Watch, *Unceasing Abuses.*

6

Mexico's Changing Political Economy

While the beginnings of Mexico's industrial growth date back to the *Porfiriato* (1876–1911), industrialization and economic modernization only started to take off in the late 1930s. During the following decades Mexico was transformed from a predominantly illiterate, rural, agricultural society to a primarily urban, relatively industrialized, largely literate nation. This "economic miracle" was hailed by many social scientists as a model for the Third World.

To be sure, there were serious flaws in the country's development process. The benefits of growth were very inequitably distributed, even by Third World standards. Much of the private sector suffered from low productivity, while the large public sector was rife with inefficiency and corruption. Industrial growth was often linked to large fiscal and trade deficits that subsequently created financial difficulties. Despite such problems, however, growth remained robust through the mid-1970s, when the Echeverría administration's economic mismanagement and its conflicts with the private sector precipitated a severe financial crisis.

By the end of the 1970s, economic growth resumed at a spectacular rate, fueled by the discovery of vast petroleum reserves and extensive foreign borrowing. Yet the petroleum boom proved brief, and by 1982 the country's excessive external indebtedness brought growth to a crashing halt, plunging not only Mexico but all of Latin America into the worst decade of economic decline since the Great Depression.

Presidents Miguel de la Madrid (1982–88) and Carlos Salinas (1988–94) responded by redesigning the nation's economic development model. Their "liberalization" policies substantially reduced the state's economic role and opened up Mexico's formerly protected economy to foreign trade and investment.* By joining the General Agreement on Tariffs and Trade (GATT) and the North American Free Trade Agreement (NAFTA), Mexico embraced free trade

---

* Contrary to what the term suggests to most Americans, economic "liberalization" is used outside of the United States to mean a reduction in the state's economic role and the removal of many regulatory restraints on the private sector. Free-market-oriented reformers such as Mexico's Carlos Salinas and Britain's Margaret Thatcher are called neoliberals.

and tied its economy more closely to the world market, particularly to the United States.

THE NATURE OF MEXICAN STATE CAPITALISM

For many years the state was the engine driving Mexico's rapid economic growth. The country's most influential modern president, Lázaro Cárdenas (1934–40), set the stage. His agrarian reform established rural tranquillity, while the state took control of the agrarian economy, providing peasants with credit, technical assistance, and infrastructure. In subsequent years, however, the very institutions that Cárdenas had created to assist the peasantry were used to control and exploit them.[1]

Cárdenas increased the state's economic power by nationalizing foreign petroleum firms. Petróleos Mexicanos (PEMEX), the government petroleum company that took control of the industry, subsequently became the country's largest corporation.[2] He also took over the railroads and started the nationalization of the country's electric power and telephone industries. In all, Cárdenas helped establish a system of state capitalism in which the private sector owned most of the means of production, while the state controlled much of the economic infrastructure including petroleum production and distribution, electrical power, rail transport, and communications. That control, along with substantial regulatory and fiscal power, gave the national government a central role in Mexico's postwar economic boom.

From the time of the Avila Camacho (1940–46) and Alemán (1946–52) administrations onward, the government actively promoted industrialization and economic development, largely by assisting the private sector. As in other Latin American nations, it promoted import-substituting industrialization (ISI). Designed to make the country more self-sufficient and to correct its international balance-of-payments problems, ISI supported the manufacture of products that had previously been imported from the United States or other economically developed nations. Industrialization was also meant to create employment and raise living standards. In its early stages ISI concentrated on the manufacture of consumer goods such as clothing, footwear, processed foods, and home appliances. Over time, however, the process "deepened," as Mexico began to produce its own capital goods as well (i.e., machinery and other items needed in the manufacture of consumer goods).[3]

The state nurtured industrialization in many ways, subsidizing the private sector by providing rail transport, gasoline, and electric power at prices below their market value. It also provided credit through the state industrial development bank, Nacional Financiera, S.A. (Nafinsa). Indeed, by the late 1940s, Nafinsa was providing nearly 27 percent of the credit available through the country's banking system.[4] It also established firms that the private sector could not or would not develop. Thus, the government invested heavily in sectors of the economy—such as railroads, electric power, petroleum, and steel—

that were vital to national development yet surpassed "either the risk-taking proclivities of the private sector or its capacity to mobilize the capital for the venture."[5] During the 1950s, for example, Nafinsa invested over 50 percent of its budget in infrastructure.[6] Under Presidents Echeverría (1970–76) and López Portillo (1976–82) the government greatly expanded its role in the economy, creating a large number of new parastatals (state-owned enterprises). By the early 1980s state agencies and parastatals employed over one-sixth of the national workforce.[7]

From 1940 through 1952, during Mexico's industrial takeoff, the government's annual share of total economic investment ranged from 37 percent to a peak of 71 percent, averaging about 40 percent.[8] That proportion declined somewhat during the next two decades, but was still about 30 percent.[9] Government tax and credit policy also helped channel private-sector investment into targeted areas of the economy, most notably industry. For example, the 1941 Law of Manufacturing Industries exempted new plants from taxation for a period of five years.[10]

Other government policies also fostered industrial growth. Because incipient Mexican industries were rarely able to compete effectively with imports from industrialized nations, the state protected them from foreign competition, particularly in their infancy. By imposing quotas, licensing requirements, and tariffs, the government limited imports or increased their prices significantly. Without that protection, many Mexican firms (particularly small and midsized companies) could not have survived.

Mexican business also benefited from the state's control over the labor movement. Using the PRI's corporate structure and restrictive labor legislation, over the years the government has restricted strikes and moderated wage demands. In doing so, it has facilitated capital accumulation and increased business investment.[11]

Thus, although the economy remained largely in private hands, the state was a major player in the country's drive for industrialization. The extent of government involvement varied over time. When private-sector investment declined, as it did during the Echeverría administration, the government often stepped in to fill the gap.[12] By 1977, ten of the twenty-five largest enterprises in the country were state owned.[13]

MEXICO'S ECONOMIC MIRACLE AND ITS LIMITS

By most measures, Mexico's postwar record of government-directed economic growth was very impressive. From 1940 to 1970 the gross domestic product (GDP) rose fairly consistently at an annual rate of 6 to 7 percent. Even when population growth is factored in, per capita gains were still about 3.5 percent annually.[14] Moreover, unlike what happened in many other developing economies, rapid growth did not unleash high levels of inflation. During the

Table 6-1. Changing Mexican Socioeconomic Indicators:
1940–1990

	1940	1990
Urban (%)	22	72
In Agriculture (%)	65	24
Literate (%)	52	96
Kilometers of roads	10,000	235,000

Source: Miguel Basáñez, El pulso de los sexenios (México: Siglo
XXI, 1990), 345–59.

1960s, for example, robust annual growth rates of some 7 percent produced inflation of only 3.5 percent.[15]

It was not until the mid-1970s that the economy faltered, largely because of the private sector's loss of confidence in the Echeverría administration. But following the discovery of major petroleum reserves and the massive infusion of foreign credit, economic growth rebounded to even higher levels (8–9 percent) at the close of that decade.

Few Latin American countries have experienced such strong and sustained economic development. Modernization altered Mexico in a number of ways. As the result of extensive rural-to-urban migration, the country changed from a predominantly rural to a largely urban society. By the 1980s, Mexico City was the world's most heavily populated city. Industrialization and urbanization increased the size of the working class and middle class substantially, with each group exercising significant political influence. Mexico's literacy rate rose from 52 percent in 1940 to 96 percent in 1990 (table 6-1). As we have seen (chapter 1), such far-reaching socioeconomic changes have had important political consequences as the public's political awareness grows and new social groups gain influence.

Despite its many accomplishments, however, Mexico's postwar boom was seriously flawed. The benefits of growth were very poorly distributed. And as in the rest of Latin America, the ISI model eventually created economic inefficiencies, balance-of-payments problems, and monetary instability. All of these factors contributed to Mexico's debt crisis in the 1980s.

Furthermore, for the past forty years Mexico's poverty and income inequality have contributed to periodic political unrest, as students, workers, peasants, and the urban poor have protested economic injustices. While these protests have not been sufficient to threaten the political system, they sometimes have been quite destabilizing. The most recent manifestation, of course, is the Zapatista uprising in Chiapas, a thorn in the government's side since the start of 1994.

Prior to the 1980s, Mexico's industrialization model suffered from occasional balance-of-payments difficulties and devaluations of the peso, most notably under President Echeverría. Although the discovery of enormous petroleum deposits during the López Portillo administration masked these

Table 6-2. Distribution of National Income: Selected Nations

| Country | Percentage of total national income earned by | | |
	Poorest 40% of the population	Middle 40% of the population	Richest 20% of the population
Mexico	11.9	32.2	55.9
Brazil	7.0	25.7	67.5
Peru	14.1	34.7	51.4
Morocco	17.1	36.7	46.3
India	21.3	37.5	41.3
Japan	21.9	40.6	37.5

Source: World Bank, *World Development Report 1994* (New York: Oxford University Press, 1994), 220–21.

weaknesses for several years, by 1982 the country confronted its most serious economic crisis in half a century. Mexico's excessive foreign debt plunged it into a deep economic decline and convinced Presidents de la Madrid and Salinas to abandon state-centered ISI in favor of a more outward-looking, market-based development model.

THE PROBLEM OF MALDISTRIBUTION

One of the most severe problems that many Third World nations face is their highly unequal distribution of wealth and income. The upper and middle classes receive a disproportionately large share of the national income, while the poor are left with a correspondingly small portion. Of course, not all developing countries have such skewed income patterns. For example, income distributions in Asian nations such as Bangladesh, India, South Korea, and Taiwan are comparable to those of industrial democracies. A number of Latin America countries, however, including Mexico, Peru, Venezuela, and Brazil, suffer from some of the most extreme income concentration in the world (see table 6-2).[16]

Simon Kuznets has argued that as nations pass through the early stages of modernization and industrialization, and as per capita GDP grows, income inequality tends to worsen. Only when countries develop further and enter the family of higher-income nations do their income distributions become more equitable.[17]

In part, Latin America's severe income inequality (table 6-2) is a legacy of Spanish and Portuguese colonialism, specifically their highly concentrated rural land ownership and their rigid class barriers. During the twentieth century, as countries such as Mexico, Brazil, and Colombia industrialized and entered the group of "middle-income" nations, their income distribution became yet more concentrated as Kuznets's theory would predict.

Consequently, one of reformist president Lázaro Cárdenas's primary objectives was reducing socioeconomic inequality. Agrarian reform was a cornerstone of that effort, eventually redistributing land to nearly half the nation's peasantry. Working through an extensive network of peasant cooperatives (*ejidos*), the Cárdenas administration funneled credit and other aid to the reform beneficiaries to help them compete more effectively with larger, mechanized farmers. At the same time, the state created a potential pressure group for egalitarian government policies by strengthening urban labor unions.

But when the country began its industrialization drive in the 1940s, government policies designed to improve income distribution withered. Indeed, over the next few decades national income became more concentrated (table 6-3). Several factors account for this development. In the countryside, state agricultural policy after Cárdenas favored larger, commercial farmers who the government believed were more productive and, hence, better equipped to produce agricultural surpluses for the domestic and export markets.

> The agricultural sector supported expanding industrialism by providing cheap food for the urban population and by providing the foreign exchange necessary for imported, industrial inputs. Incentives for commercial-export agriculture included massive [state-supported] irrigation projects and green-revolution technology. . . . Meanwhile small and ejidal agriculture was left to stagnate: the proportion of *ejidatarios* [*ejido* members] receiving credit from the government fell from 30 percent in 1936 to 14 percent in 1960.[18]

Landlessness increased, as many peasants were unable to compete with agribusiness and eventually lost their holdings.[19] Although the working class and city poor benefited somewhat from the urban bias of many government economic policies, they were disadvantaged by government restraints on wages, inadequate social services, and capital-intensive industrialization that failed to provide sufficient employment.[20] In time, labor unions were able to secure higher wages for a "working-class elite" of skilled blue-collar workers (petroleum workers, steelworkers, and the like). But most of the working class remained unorganized or poorly represented (chapter 5) and failed to share adequately in the nation's economic growth. By the 1960s, Mexico's income distribution was among the more inequitable in the Third World.

Table 6-3 reveals that the share of national income received by the richest fifth of the population rose from 58.9 percent in 1950 to 64 percent in 1969. At the same time, the portion going to the poorest 50 percent of the population declined from 17.4 percent of national income to 15 percent. In 1958 the poorest 10 percent of the population earned only 2.4 percent of the national income. Yet by 1977 that share had fallen further to 1.1 percent.[21]

This did not mean that the poorest half of the society became absolutely poorer (though the poorest 10 to 20 percent of the population may have). To the contrary, after falling sharply during World War II and the early 1950s, real wages rose steadily during the following two decades. "Trickle down" from a rapidly growing economy raised living standards in a number of ways. Among the major beneficiaries were those who had migrated to the cities from impoverished rural areas and had found factory or other regular employment.[22] As a result of the nation's economic development, the percentage of the population

Table 6-3. Mexican Income Distribution: 1950–1992

	1950	1969	1977	1992
Poorest 50%	17.4%	15.0%	16.7%	18.4%
Middle 30%	23.7	21.0	28.2	27.4
Richest 20%	58.9	64.0	55.1	54.2

Sources: Adapted from Daniel Levy and Gabriel Székely, *Mexico: Paradoxes of Stability and Change* (Boulder, Colo.: Westview Press, 1983), 144; Daniel C. Levy and Kathleen Bruhn, "Mexico: Sustained Civilian Rule without Democracy," in *Politics in Developing Countries: Comparing Experiences with Democracy*, ed. Larry Diamond, Juan J. Linz, and Seymour Martin Lipset (Boulder, Colo.: Lynne Rienner Publishers, 1995), 195.

living in "extreme poverty" declined from about 75 percent in the 1940s to 45 percent three decades later.[23]

Despite such gains, however, the gap between the "haves" and "have-nots" widened, as Mexico's "economic miracle" left substantial portions of the population behind. In 1980, for example, more than three quarters of the population still lived in overcrowded housing.[24] Furthermore, the economic collapse of the 1980s wiped out many of the gains achieved in prior decades. Today, much of the countryside remains mired in poverty, with villagers far less likely than city dwellers to have potable water, sewage systems, electricity, or secondary schools.

THE SEARCH FOR STABILITY AND GREATER EQUITY

By the late 1950s, Mexico's skewed development pattern had begun to generate discontent and occasional political unrest. In parts of the countryside there were outbreaks of peasant land invasions, while militant rank-and-file movements emerged in railroad workers' and teachers' unions. Reacting to these potential threats to stability, the government for the first time in decades began to address the problems of poverty and inequality.[25] For example, in response to rural unrest, President Adolfo López Mateos (1958–64) distributed more farmland to the peasantry than any president had since Lázaro Cárdenas.

But it was not until the 1970s that the government began to fashion a broad welfare package aimed at alleviating poverty.[26] The state provided consumer subsidies for energy and for basic foods such as rice, sugar, and tortillas. CONASUPO (the National Commission of Popular Subsistence), a giant government agency regulating the grain and oilseed markets, provided other subsidized foods.[27] Sometimes the government maintained employment by taking over large private firms that faced bankruptcy.

Luis Echeverría was perhaps the most reform-minded president since Lázaro Cárdenas. He and his successor, José López Portillo, substantially increased government expenditures on social welfare programs. By 1980, rising state consumer subsidies, primarily for basic foods and gasoline, equaled 10 percent of the country's entire GDP.[28] To aid the rural poor, the government offered peasants credit at preferential rates and bought targeted crops at higher prices than their market value. Finally, government policy temporarily halted the long-term trend toward greater income concentration (table 6-3).

ORIGINS OF THE ECONOMIC CRISIS: EXPANDING THE ROLE OF THE STATE

The Echeverría administration increased government expenditures and state economic intervention sharply. The number of state-owned enterprises (parastatals) multiplied as the administration tried to stimulate the economy and expand employment. State economic activity continued to grow rapidly during the López Portillo administration. Between 1970 and 1981 (the end of the economic boom), government expenditure climbed from 20 percent of the GDP to 35 percent.[29] Echeverría believed that

> a country in which the state controlled a larger share of investment, owned more "strategic" sectors (energy, steel, and so on), and regulated more of the price-setting mechanism would be more prosperous, more equitable and less vulnerable to political pressure of the business sector at home and abroad.[30]

Not surprisingly, these policies provoked strong opposition from the business community, particularly the powerful Monterrey Group. The economic elite also opposed Echeverría's nationalistic foreign policy, his restrictions on foreign investment, and his radical political rhetoric. Relations between the government and the private sector sank to a postwar low. As business confidence dwindled, private investment declined and capital flight intensified. Ironically, this only stimulated further state intervention in the economy as it tried to fill the financial gap. Between 1970 and 1975, the state's share of national investment rose from 35.5 percent to 46.2 percent.[31] Still, the government could not compensate for business disinvestment. By the time that Echeverría left office, private-sector capital flight had produced a major financial crisis capped by a 40 percent decline in the value of the peso.

While the government's redistributive and job creation programs in the 1970s and early 1980s addressed an important national need, they required a large jump in government expenditures that was unaccompanied by additional tax revenues to finance them. The Echeverría administration failed to levy new taxes, perhaps fearing the prospect of further capital flight. In any event, the budget deficit soared from an annual average of 2.5 percent of GDP in 1955–72 to a dangerously high level of 8.0 percent of GDP from 1972 to 1976. By 1981, at the end of President López Portillo's term, it had reached 14.1 percent.[32] These enormous deficits were covered by external borrowing, building an ever-mounting foreign debt. Rising fiscal deficits also accelerated inflation, which, in turn, contributed to a growing trade deficit. Anticipating the devaluation of the peso, Mexican investors shifted their funds abroad.

Excessive government spending and borrowing aggravated long-term structural weakness in the economy that had lurked beneath the surface for decades. Like most industrialized nations in Latin America, Mexico had subsidized and protected import-substituting industries for too long. Because protectionism shielded domestic firms from foreign import competition, industrialists had little incentive to invest in more efficient production methods. Worse yet, import-substituting industrialization failed to reduce Mexico's dependence on imports. Instead, expanding domestic industries required increasing amounts of imported raw materials, capital equipment, and technology. The government also overvalued the peso to facilitate importing of consumer goods for the growing middle class. As imports increased, exports failed to grow correspondingly, producing ever-widening balance-of-trade deficits.

Although needed in the early stages of industrialization, protectionism and state subsidies should have been reduced subsequently to force local companies to improve productivity. Had that been done (as it was in East Asia), manufacturers could have competed more effectively in the world market, exporting goods that would pay for imports. Instead, as world trade exploded, Mexico remained relatively inefficient and uncompetitive. The once-impoverished nations of East Asia surged past Mexico and other industrialized nations in Latin America. Thus by 1987, Taiwan, a small nation with a population one-fourth of Mexico's, exported 2.5 times as much, including more than five times as much manufactured goods.[33]

When José López Portillo inherited Echeverría's economic crisis, he tried to remedy his predecessor's mistakes. The new president mended fences with the private sector, consulted with the powerful Monterrey Group, and pledged to control government spending. Not long into his term, however, he threw his initial caution to the wind after PEMEX officials informed him that they had discovered massive offshore petroleum deposits.* Indeed, geological studies indicated that Mexico had discovered one of the world's largest petroleum reserves. Since petroleum experts believed that the price of oil would continue to rise substantially (as it had since 1973), the administration felt that the country had been freed from its previous financial restraints.[34] López Portillo declared that Mexico's major challenge was no longer scarcity, but rather how to deal with its newfound bonanza. The president envisioned a scenario in which his administration could fund new programs for the poor and the middle class while subsidizing the private sector, all without having to resort to tax increases or deficit spending.

Consequently, the government embarked on a spending spree that far outstripped Echeverría's. Consumer subsidies, producer subsidies, and "welfare programs" (for the poor and not very poor alike) were all greatly expanded. For most of López Portillo's term these expenditures stimulated economic

---

* The discoveries actually had been made several years earlier, but were not divulged by PEMEX officials at that time. They were unsure how easily the oil could be extracted and also wanted to maintain the reserves for as long as possible in order to support long-term economic development.

growth and rising living standards. The economy, which had slumped in the mid-1970s, grew at an extraordinary rate of some 8 percent annually in the closing years of the decade. From 1976 to 1981, real income (adjusted for inflation) increased by roughly 25 percent.[35]

Of course, some of the country's oil wealth was wasted through inefficiency, or drained away by corrupt officials. The head of PEMEX, the leader of the powerful petroleum workers' union, and Mexico City's chief of police, among others, amassed millions of dollars in personal fortunes.* Yet amidst the economic surge, these seemed like minor irritants at the time.

While President López Portillo wanted to restimulate the economy as quickly as possible, offshore oil operations take years to set up. Consequently, his administration used its petroleum deposits as collateral for extensive external borrowing. That foreign capital was used to cover Mexico's growing budget and trade deficits. For their part, foreign banks, looking for opportunities to invest their petrodollar surpluses, eagerly lent vast sums to Mexico and other Latin American nations at relatively low (but variable) interest rates. When Luis Echeverría was inaugurated in 1970, the public sector's external debt was under $4 billion. Six years later, when he left office, that debt had mushroomed to $19.6 billion, a 475 percent increase.[36] By the time that López Portillo stepped down it had climbed to $92.4 billion, making Mexico the second largest debtor in the developing world.[37]

After coming to office committed to rectifying Echeverría's economic mistakes, López Portillo instead compounded them greatly. With exaggerated expectations of future petroleum earnings, his administration borrowed and spent recklessly. Because the price of oil had skyrocketed from 1973 (OPEC's first oil shock) through the mid-1970s, industry analysts generally had assumed that prices would continue to rise. Having surged from $3 per barrel in 1973 to over $30, the cost of petroleum seemed destined to top $50 in the 1980s. Had that happened, Mexico's large petroleum holdings would have financed López Portillo's ambitious spending program adequately. Instead, oil prices peaked in 1979 and then declined sharply.

Meanwhile, rising interest rates on the external debt further increased that burden. Like other Latin American nations, Mexico had borrowed at variable interest rates—rates that had been relatively low when it secured the loans in the early and mid-1970s, but climbed at the close of that decade. By 1982, payments on Mexico's external debt accounted for three-fourths of the government's budget deficit and a substantial proportion of its export earnings.[38] In August, no longer able to maintain its payments, Mexico declared a debt payment moratorium. In doing so it shocked the international financial system and caused banks to withhold further loans to all of Latin America, thereby precipitating a decade-long regional economic crisis whose severity exceeded the Great Depression.

As Mexico was gripped by financial panic, López Portillo nationalized the

---

* All three of them were imprisoned by succeeding administrations.

banking system in order to stem the tide of private-sector capital flight. Coming in the last year of his term, the seizure was designed to give the president a place in Mexican history as a heroic economic nationalist. Instead, the unexpected takeover infuriated both the business community and middle-class depositors whose temporarily frozen peso accounts could not be converted to dollars as they were fast depreciating. "The business sector's [already growing] distrust and resentment toward the government had been pushed to the limit."[39] It would take years before the government would begin to win that confidence back and restore the investment that comes with it.

THE LOST DECADE AND ECONOMIC RESTRUCTURING

Restructuring the Economy.   The economic crisis of the 1980s caused Mexico's leaders to reexamine their postwar development model. In contrast to East Asia's export-based manufacturing, Latin American industrialization had been inward-looking, built on import substitution and protectionism. For decades ISI had stimulated economic growth and rising (though inequitably distributed) living standards. But it also had begun to generate massive trade and budget deficits.

Consequently, Mexico's recent administrations have liberalized the economy dramatically, reducing state economic intervention and opening the domestic market to international trade. Economic restructuring began under Miguel de la Madrid and accelerated greatly under Carlos Salinas. Early economic policy making under President Zedillo has been preoccupied with the country's latest financial crisis. Not surprisingly, since he was a leading architect of Salinas's economic policies, Zedillo continues to follow his predecessors' neoliberal path. In any event, Mexico is too far along the path of liberalization to permit a substantial reversal of course.

Shortly before Miguel de la Madrid took office, Mexico signed an accord with the International Monetary Fund (IMF) calling for a reduced budget deficit, diminished state subsidies, and lower real wages in order to lessen inflation. That accord set the tone for subsequent Mexican economic policy. De la Madrid terminated his predecessors' failed experiment in stimulating economic growth through extensive deficit spending and external borrowing. Painful budget cuts slashed consumer subsidies and welfare programs. Meanwhile wage hikes lagged well behind price increases. The payoffs for these painful austerity measures were not apparent under de la Madrid, particularly since he tried to restimulate growth prematurely midway through his term, triggering renewed inflation and a further decline in production. Consequently he left office as Mexico's first postwar president to preside over an overall decline in the country's GDP during his term. At the same time, cumulative inflation from 1982 to 1988 reached 4,600 percent, ten times higher than the rate under President José López Portillo.[40]

But in his last year in office de la Madrid began to turn the corner toward economic recovery by adding a weapon to the government's antiinflationary arsenal. Up to that point his administration had relied, with little apparent effect, on the standard ("orthodox") antiinflationary tools prescribed by the IMF. In December 1987, however, representatives of government, business, and labor agreed to an Economic Solidarity Pact (known to Mexicans simply as "the Pact") binding each party to antiinflationary restraints. For its part, the government committed itself to additional cuts in the fiscal deficit, tightening of the monetary supply, and further trade liberalization. Labor, business, and commercial farmers agreed to wage controls as well as price controls on many consumer goods. The Pact covered a specific time period and was renewed periodically in subsequent years.[41]

The principal "heterodox" (nonorthodox) component of these packages was business and labor's voluntary agreement to wage and price controls. Similar heterodox approaches to confronting inflation have been tried elsewhere in Latin America, generally without long-term success. In Mexico, however, the Pacts were introduced after orthodox measures had already begun to bring the fiscal and trade deficits under control.[42] Soon after Carlos Salinas assumed the presidency, that combination of orthodox and heterodox measures started to reduce the rate of inflation substantially. Equally important, the package stimulated extended economic growth for the first time since the oil boom (though at a much more modest pace). Indeed, the economy grew during each of Salinas's first three years in office (1989–91), the most sustained period of growth since the 1982 crash. During those three years GDP growth ranged from 3.3 to 4.4 percent, levels reached only once in the previous seven years.[43]

At the start of his presidency, Salinas crafted a revised three-party accord entitled the Pact for Stability and Economic Growth (PECE). The revised name signaled that inflation was being brought under control and that the time had come to start stimulating the economy.* Consequently, Salinas restored some of the education, health, and welfare funding that had been slashed under de la Madrid. But he still remained strongly committed to neoliberal policies including deregulation of prices and reduced budget deficits. Most government price controls were lifted by 1990–91. And the budgetary deficit, which had reached 14 percent of GDP in 1982, was transformed into a surplus by 1992.[44]

Stringent monetary policy was accompanied by fundamental structural changes having important long-term impact. After growing enormously under Presidents Echeverría and López Portillo, state intervention in the economy was reduced dramatically. Although de la Madrid initiated these changes, it was Salinas who made structural reforms, such as the privatization of parastatals, the hallmark of his administration. Between 1982 and 1990, the number of state enterprises was reduced from 1,155 to 280.[45] Privatized firms included Teléfonos de México (the telecommunications giant), the country's two leading airlines, copper mines, sugar refineries, steel mills, and food-

---

* The new pact was extended several times and then renamed the Pact for Stability, Competitiveness, and Employment.

processing plants, as well as hundreds of smaller parastatals. From the sale of its ten largest firms alone, the state netted some $3 billion, funds that were used to support social spending and other needed programs.[46] But Mexican public opinion dictated that certain enterprises such as PEMEX (the giant petroleum monopoly), the railroads, and CONASUPO (the government food-distribution agency) remain in government hands.

One of the most fundamental policy changes initiated by de la Madrid and Salinas was dismantling the ISI model of development in favor of export-oriented growth. Two bold government initiatives symbolized the opening of the country's economy to the world: In 1986, after four decades of sitting on the sidelines, Mexico entered GATT, the world's predominant trading group. Seven years later it helped create NAFTA, linking its economy to those of the United States and Canada (chapter 7).

GATT was formed after World War II to reduce tariffs and otherwise facil-itate trade between the world's capitalist nations. Over the years dozens of addi-tional countries enrolled in the GATT as it continued to remove barriers to world trade. For decades, however, Mexico stayed out because of protectionist senti-ment at home (most notably among industrialists and industrial unions) and the logic of its ISI model. Thus, when President de la Madrid finally committed Mex-ico to joining the GATT, his decision provoked considerable domestic opposition because it threatened less efficient companies that had long been protected from import competition. Indeed, opposition from imperiled segments of the private sector had scuttled earlier plans to enter the GATT. The Congress of Labor (CT) also opposed free trade because it threatened jobs in noncompetitive industries and offended labor's nationalist ideology. Only after East Asia's newly industri-alizing countries (NICs) had demonstrated the economic advantages of export-oriented development did Mexico fully embrace the world market.

Stripped of their protectionist trade barriers, Mexican firms have been forced to become more competitive in the international market. Manufactur-ers are now encouraged to produce for export as well as the home market, and many large enterprises have responded vigorously. A surge in manufactured ex-ports temporarily improved Mexico's balance of trade and reduced its depen-dence on petroleum exports. As we will see, however, by the end of Salinas's term the country once again suffered negative trade balances, this time due to mounting imports.

Carlos Salinas proposed the creation of NAFTA in order to integrate the Mexican and U.S. economies more fully and strengthen Mexico's ability to compete in the world market (see chapter 7). Under the agreement, Mexican consumers have gained greater access to imports from the United States and to American retailers such as Wal-Mart.* Similarly, competitive Mexican com-panies now can sell more easily in the North American market. More than any-thing, however, NAFTA reassured Mexican businessmen and foreign investors,

---

* That process was well under way prior to NAFTA, but the agreement guarantees its continua-tion.

burned by past shifts in government economic policy, that the transition to an open economy was irreversible regardless of who might succeed Salinas.

The New *Ejido* Law and the End of Agrarian Reform.   One aspect of President Salinas's neoliberal program, the *ejido* reform law, deserves special attention. As a consequence of Mexico's agrarian reform about half the country's farmland has been distributed since the Revolution to over three million peasant families in cooperatives called *ejidos*.[47] Land in each *ejido* is communally controlled, with the state regulating its tenure and sale. In practice, however, only grazing and forest land (about three-fourths of total *ejido* area) is maintained communally, while agricultural land itself has been divided into family plots that can be passed on from generation to generation.[48] Because the peasantry's struggle for land was so central to the Revolution, maintaining the *ejido* has been considered sacrosanct by its peasant beneficiaries and by all Mexicans who believe in the ideals of the Revolution. To prevent *ejidatarios* (members of the cooperative) from losing their holdings to richer commercial farmers, the law prohibited the sale of community land to outsiders.* Since the Mexican public has judged the agrarian reform to be one of the Revolution's greatest achievements, altering the *ejido* system has been considered as unthinkable in Mexican political discourse as abolishing the Social Security system would be in the United States.

Doubtless the agrarian reform has contributed to rural political stability. Mexican peasants, once among the most rebellious in Latin America, generally have been coopted into the political system. But in many instances *ejidos* are not economically viable. With their small plots of land and limited access to water, villagers are dependent on the state for credit, technical assistance, irrigation, and other agricultural inputs. Consequently, they are at the mercy of government and PRI bureaucrats who are frequently corrupt and arbitrary. In addition, many peasants are exploited by village *caciques,* political bosses from their own ranks, who control access to government agencies.

For the most part, *ejido* farming also is not very productive. Since the early 1940s, villagers have not received sufficient government assistance.** Even when Echeverría and López Portillo increased rural aid, they offered *ejidatarios* few incentives to farm more efficiently. Today, most villagers raise corn for subsistence or for commercial *tortilla* production, with low yields per acre.

The 1980s was a difficult period for Mexican peasants, with a nearly 50 percent decline in crop prices relative to the cost of agricultural inputs.[49] For a few years the effect of that decline was somewhat mitigated by improved export opportunities and unusually good growing weather. But since the late 1980s, decreased government aid and weak crop prices have eroded peasant living standards. Antipoverty programs such as PRONASOL and temporary

---

* In reality that restriction has often been evaded.
** Although the *ejido* plot's small size presents problems, small peasant plots are not inherently unproductive. Many small farms elsewhere in the world have high yields. East Asian peasants, for example, have very high yields on much smaller plots.

government subsidies have helped somewhat, but the long-term prospects for peasant smallholders are not good. Many critics contend that the peasantry's problems could be remedied by giving them greater independence from exploitative government agencies such as BANRURAL (the primary agricultural credit bank) and extending state aid to them more directly. President Salinas's market-oriented advisors, however, did not believe that most *ejidatarios* could ever become competitive and opposed substantial spending to sustain them.

Mexico's entry into NAFTA presents additional problems for many peasants. Since American farmers, on average, produce four times as much corn per acre as Mexicans producers do, the removal of trade protection means that it is generally cheaper to import corn than to grow it. Government neoliberal planners hope that peasants will either switch into the production of higher-value crops that can be exported to the United States (such as tropical fruits and vegetables) or that they will abandon their farms and sell them to more productive farmers.[50]

In 1992, the Mexican Congress amended Article 27 of the Mexican constitution and passed a new *ejido* law. The changes were designed to "permit and even encourage—but not compel—the privatization of previously inalienable community-held *ejido* land."[51] They terminated the government's constitutional obligation to redistribute land to the peasantry, thereby officially ending one of the Revolution's most cherished programs (though, in fact, agrarian reform had been dormant for years). In addition, *ejidatarios* may now rent or sell their plots and may use them as collateral for loans. They may also enter into joint ventures with outside investors (such as packing companies) including foreign firms, which can own up to a 49 percent share of the farm.

Proponents of the *ejido* reform law hope that outside investment and a more open land market will increase production for the domestic and export markets. Opponents of the law fear that it will enable outsiders or richer villagers to buy out poorer *ejidatarios,* thereby contributing to the reconcentration of farmland, greater rural landlessness, and a surge of migration to the cities by displaced farmers. So far, with *ejido* reform still only a few years old, the results have not justified either its supporters' fondest expectations or its critics' worst fears.

To date, few *ejidatarios* have applied for permission to privatize their plots, and fewer still have completed the process. More significantly, *ejido* farms have not attracted great interest from Mexican or foreign investors. Much of the land is too marginal, too depleted, or too removed from good transport to make it commercially viable. Moreover, the privatization of any plot requires the approval of a majority of the *ejido*'s members and must be followed by a detailed land survey. More than two years after the reform law was passed, only about 10 percent of the country's *ejido* plots had even been surveyed. But while the immediate impact of the reform has been limited, the long-term prospect for *ejido* farming is not promising. Partly because so much of their land lacks irrigation and is of poor quality, peasants are rarely able to compete with larger, commercial growers in Mexico or the United States. So when state transitional subsidies are eventually removed, many villagers will be unable to continue farming. Rural economic decline and the privatization of *ejido* plots will likely accelerate rural-to-urban migration. Yet there is little prospect that enough jobs can be created to accommodate these new arrivals.[52]

Restoring Confidence.   Since the early 1980s, another important government objective has been restoring business confidence in the government and the economy. Earlier, President Echeverría's populism and López Portillo's bank nationalization had driven a huge wedge between the private sector and the state. Distrusting their own government and concerned about the declining value of the peso, businessmen had transferred funds into real estate, government securities, and time deposits in the United States. According to a U.S. Treasury Department estimate, between 1975 and 1985 Mexican citizens transferred $55 billion to the United States. Thus, much of Mexico's external debt accrued during that decade merely compensated for capital leaving the country. Indeed, the Morgan Guarantee Trust Company estimated that absent that capital flight, Mexico's external debt would have been only $12 billion at the close of 1985 instead of $97 billion.[53]

In the wake of the debt crisis, the de la Madrid and Salinas administrations both tried to restore the confidence of three crucial constituencies. The first was the Mexican private sector and the middle class. Sustained economic recovery required renewed business investment and the repatriation of capital from abroad. A second targeted group was foreign investors who could provide additional capital and technological skills. All of these groups needed to be convinced that henceforth the government would follow consistent and predictable policies (i.e., that the rules of the game would not constantly switch) and that the peso would stay fairly stable. A final objective was to reassure foreign governments (particularly the United States), international financial institutions (especially the IMF), and foreign private banks regarding Mexico's economic dependability. De la Madrid, Salinas, and, most recently, Ernesto Zedillo enlisted Washington's support to restructure the debt and reassure international financial institutions.

But gaining the trust and support of these groups was not easy. The antigovernment hostility that Echeverría and López Portillo had unleashed within the business community was difficult for President de la Madrid to overcome. By the early 1980s, many business leaders had become active in the PAN. As Wayne Cornelius noted:

> The collaborative state/private sector relationship began to deteriorate in the early 1970s and reached the breaking point with . . . the nationalization of the banks in 1982. De la Madrid . . . made no appreciable progress in repairing the breach, despite the fact that he . . . moved much farther than any of his predecessors in implementing the private sector's own primary agenda—setting market forces free in the Mexican economy.[54]

Moreover, de la Madrid's administration undermined its confidence-building campaign when its own policy errors unleashed a renewed wave of inflation in 1985–86. In addition, Mexico's relations with the United States were strained for much of his term. The Reagan administration was incensed by Mexico's support for the revolutionary Sandinista regime in Nicaragua and its sympathy for the FMLN, El Salvador's marxist guerrillas (chapter 7).

Carlos Salinas, on the other hand, quickly won the confidence of the Mexican private sector and the international financial community. No Mexican president in decades had achieved comparable stature at home and abroad. In part, Salinas merely accelerated the privatization of state enterprises and other free market economic policies introduced by Miguel de la Madrid. But the results were far more positive. Inflation finally was brought under control, and the economy began to undergo sustained, if modest, growth. Salinas's intelligence, political skills, and self-assurance inspired trust in the business community and in Washington. Investors and international financial agencies were impressed by his bold initiatives such as NAFTA, by his consistent and clear policies, and, perhaps most important, by his economic team's seeming ability always to make the right moves. Only after Salinas left office did his administration's serious policy errors emerge. It was those errors that imposed a major financial crisis on his successor, Ernesto Zedillo.

Getting Things Right.   By the start of the 1990s, Mexico had achieved a surprisingly broad consensus over the outlines of economic reform. Even PRD leader Cuauhtémoc Cárdenas had softened his opposition to NAFTA and accepted some aspects of the new order (though he has since reversed himself). There still remained, however, the difficult problem of how to implement the neoliberal policy package properly and how the burden of sacrifice should be shared. The components of economic restructuring are closely intertwined, yet often in conflict with each other. Consequently, the difficult task facing government planners since the early 1980s has been that of achieving the proper balance of economic objectives.

Government policies needed to address one problem (inflation, for example) often aggravate another (such as unemployment). Therefore, remedies must not be introduced too early or too late. They cannot be applied too narrowly or too broadly, nor sustained for too short a period of time or for too long. The huge budget deficits of the 1970s and early 1980s had contributed to mounting inflation. Together with large balance-of-trade deficits, they had weakened the peso and required substantial external borrowing.

As the rate of inflation passed 100 percent in 1983, and as the balance-of-payments deficit grew, the government was forced to introduce austerity measures: reduced spending, higher taxes, more comprehensive tax collection, higher interest rates, and devaluation of the peso. By their very nature these policies, designed to cool down the economy, inhibit economic growth and increase unemployment. Consequently governments must be careful not to deflate the economy too deeply or for too long. On the other hand, they also must be cautious not to restimulate the economy too quickly.

During the closing months of 1984, the de la Madrid government committed the last error. Convinced that inflation was under control after two consecutive years of declining GDP, it decided that the time had come to restimulate economic growth by boosting government spending. But that move was premature and overheated the economy. Rising international interest rates, declining petroleum prices, and the $4 to 5 billion cost of Mexico City's devastating 1985 earthquake exacerbated the problem. The economy resumed its nosedive with a 3.8 percent decline in GDP in 1986 and inflation of 132 percent in 1987.[55] De la Madrid's advisors considered declaring another moratorium on debt payments, but finally decided that the country needed to retain its new status as a "model debtor" committed to making payments regardless of the sacrifices that it might entail.[56] Consequently, severe austerity measures were reimposed.

Countries such as Mexico, facing serious balance-of-payments deficits, normally must devalue their currency. The purpose is to stimulate exports by lowering their cost in dollars, while also decreasing imports by raising their local cost. In time, an improved balance of trade decreases debt dependency. In the short term, however, devaluation is inflationary because it drives up the price of imported consumer goods and raises the cost of imported raw materials and capital equipment used by local industry.

There are other conflicts between long-term goals and immediate consequences. For example, because large budget deficits are inflationary, reducing inflation demands that governments reduce spending. In Latin America this inevitably includes cutting consumer subsidies. But in the short run those cuts contribute to inflation by driving up the price of fuel, food, and other basic necessities. Similarly, while removing trade barriers is designed to force national industries to become more competitive exporters eventually (thereby improving the balance of trade over time), in the short run it opens the door to a flood of imports that increases the trade deficit.

"Getting things right" is no easy task, and the job was made more difficult for Mexico by unanticipated and uncontrollable factors such as declines in the price of petroleum and the Mexico City earthquake. Like other Latin American countries, Mexico needed a decade to extricate itself from the debt crisis. By the time that Carlos Salinas took office, however, the economy had begun to turn the corner. As we have noted, growth exceeded 3 percent for three consecutive years (1989–91), a modest rate when compared with the petroleum boom era but better than at any time since 1979–81. By 1991 inflation had declined to 23 percent, down from 114 percent during de la Madrid's last year in office.[57]

The new administration stimulated growth, reduced protectionism, and intensified the privatization of state enterprise. So sweeping were Salinas's free market reforms that he was often compared to Margaret Thatcher, the patron saint of neoliberal economics. Others likened his assault on the state bureaucracy to Mikhail Gorbachev's program of perestroika in the Soviet Union. Thus, pundits wrote of Mexico's process of "Salinastroika."

Impressed by these reforms, many Mexican businessmen repatriated capital from abroad. Foreign investment also grew, encouraged by a more stable peso and by Mexico's preferred access to U.S. markets through NAFTA. From

1988 to 1991 foreign investment increased by more than $33 billion, most of it through the Mexican stock exchange. Lower trade barriers forced many Mexican firms to become more competitive as NAFTA was expanding opportunities for export. During Salinas's first year, manufactured exports grew by 32 percent, reducing the country's dependency on petroleum earnings.[58]

The Return to Economic Crisis.   Salinas's record won him considerable acclaim at home and abroad. Unlike any of his predecessors since the early 1960s, he left office with considerable public support and positive evaluations of his performance. International economic organizations such as the OECD and independent economic analysts issued favorable evaluations of the Mexican economy and its future. In fact, however, the economy at the close of Salinas's term was in more fragile shape than most experts realized or, perhaps, wished to admit. In the run-up to the 1994 presidential election the administration had enhanced the PRI's position by pumping up the economy through heavy government spending. Using creative bookkeeping methods, it had hidden the magnitude of the budget deficit. Excessive optimism about the economy had caused many Mexican consumers and businesses to overextend their credit lines. Rapidly growing imports created a serious balance-of-trade deficit.

Economists generally agreed that the peso was overvalued, and many members of Salinas's economic team (including Ernesto Zedillo) favored devaluation. But the president had no intention of announcing a politically unpopular devaluation shortly before the election (or, for that matter, at any time before he stepped down).[59] So it remained for Zedillo to devalue the currency soon after he took office in late 1994. The devaluation was designed to lower the value of the peso by about 14 percent (from 3.46 to 4.00 to the dollar).[60] Instead, as panicky private-sector investors rushed to unload pesos, the value of the peso declined by 40 percent within weeks (to about 5.50 to the dollar). Foreign investors that had bought stock in Mexico while counting on a stable peso rapidly withdrew their funds, causing the Mexican stock market to plunge and the peso to weaken further. The country entered into a new recession of unknown duration with extensive unemployment and a steep decline in living standards.

THE SOCIAL COSTS OF RESTRUCTURING

The fiscal reforms and structural changes that Mexico and other Latin American nations introduced during the 1980s were needed to lower inflation and reduce fiscal and balance-of-payments deficits. Like other harsh medicines, however, they were quite unpalatable, imposing enormous economic pain on the population, particularly the poor. Mexico's reforms were among the most far-reaching in the region and were consequently among the most painful.

One important element of the government's antiinflationary policies was to make wage hikes lag behind increases in the cost of living. Deflationary

Table 6-4. Economic Indicators: 1982–1995 (Percentage Change)

	1982	1983	1984	1988	1991	1994	1995[a]
GDP	− 0.6	− 4.2	3.6	1.3	3.6	3.1	− 7.0
Inflation	59	102	65	114	23	7.1	48.5
Real Wages	− 5.1	− 22.9	− 5.0	− 9.1	6.5	3.7	− 13.2

[a]Estimates.

Sources: Nora Lustig, Mexico: The Remaking of an Economy (Washington, D.C.: Brookings Institution, 1992), 40–41, 68–69; John Sheahan, Conflict and Change in Mexican Economic Strategy (La Jolla: University of California–San Diego, Center for U.S.-Mexican Studies, 1991), 13; Latin American Weekly Report, 12 January 1995, 8, 26 October 1995, 489; CEPAL, Notas sobre la economía y el desarrollo, no. 585/586 (December, 1995), 48–51.

wage policy had several effects: production costs for private firms were held down; lower real salaries for public-sector employees reduced the budget deficit;* and, as real wages fell, consumer demand declined, thereby reducing inflationary pressures.

To lower real wages, the government held down the income of public-sector employees; raised the legal minimum wage (earned by much of the Mexican population) at a lower rate than inflation;** and pressured PRI-affiliated labor unions to soften their wage demands (though this became increasingly difficult as time went on). By cooling down the economy, the government produced negative growth rates for several years as well as higher unemployment and under-employment. All of these factors exerted further downward pressure on wages.

From 1980 to 1989, per capita GDP declined by 9 percent.[61] Yet, it was not until the close of the 1980s that the government was finally to bring inflation under control (falling from 114 percent in 1988 to 20 percent in 1989). A 1983 government survey, early in the economic crisis, indicated that the average family was spending 63 percent of its total income on food and 20 percent on housing, leaving scant resources for anything else.[62] That picture worsened in succeeding years. From 1983 through 1988, real wages deteriorated every year, with a cumulative decline of 41.5 percent. For workers earning the minimum wage, the decline was 49.5 percent, one of the steepest drops in Latin America.[63] At the same time, unemployment doubled from 6.0 to 12.1 percent, while underemployment grew apace.[64]

To be sure, Mexico's real wage data somewhat overstate the deterioration in living standards among the poor, since a considerable share of their income is not earned in wages. Peasant cultivators, for example, raise subsistence crops for their own family consumption, an item not included in the wage data. Similarly, a large portion of the urban poor are employed at least part time in the "informal sector," working as street vendors, repair men, and the like. Much of that income also is not recorded. "This may explain, to some extent,"

* "Real" salaries and wages are measures of purchasing power. When wage increases do not match the rate of inflation, real wages go down.
** Indeed, as of 1980, some 40 percent of the Mexican population were actually earning less than the legal minimum wage (Lustig, Mexico: The Remaking of an Economy, 65).

writes Nora Lustig, "why consumption per capita fell much less than wages and why there was no widespread social protest."[65] But even when these adjustments are factored in, it is still true that the living standards of the poor, the working class, and much of the middle class fell sharply in the 1980s.

Government spending cuts were also painful, particularly when they involved consumer subsidies. Some changes were undoubtedly necessary. The state had been subsidizing the price of basic foods such as tortillas, rice, beans, cooking oil, bread, and eggs for all Mexican consumers regardless of their economic need. Since these extravagant subsidies for rich and poor alike could no longer be sustained in an era of austerity, they were replaced by targeted subsidies aimed at the needy (similar to food stamps in the United States). However, the new subsidies were less generous than the ones they replaced and failed to reach many of the poor, particularly in rural areas. Government expenditures for health and education also declined, malnutrition rose, and the school dropout rates increased as many children were obliged to enter the workforce in order to supplement their family income.[66]

THE NATIONAL SOLIDARITY PROGRAM (PRONASOL)

By 1988 Mexico's economy had bottomed out, and the country started a slow recovery. Inflation declined and unemployment gradually fell. Carlos Salinas, who had come to office with the lowest percentage of the vote of any PRI presidential candidate, understood how much the economic crisis had diminished support for the official party. One of his major initiatives aimed at restoring support for the government was the National Solidarity Program (PRONASOL).

Solidarity's most explicit objective was to restore some of the social spending that had been slashed in the 1980s and to address the many needs of the poor that had been so neglected during that "lost decade." The program built infrastructure, provided social services, and tried to reduce urban and rural poverty. In short, PRONASOL was intended

> to repair the tattered social safety net that it had inherited from the economic crisis and austerity measures of the 1982–1988 period . . . [and to show] that the technocrats presiding over Mexico's so-called neoliberal economic revolution were not insensitive and unresponsive to the social costs of the market-oriented policies that they espoused.[67]

Typical projects included "building and refurbishing of public schools, community electrification, street paving and feeder road construction, potable water, health care, nutrition, housing, [and] legal aid."[68] Between 1989 and 1993, the program's annual budget more than doubled, from $950 million to $2.5 billion. By the end of Salinas's term, its annual expenditure equaled nearly 2 percent of the country's GDP.[69]

At the same time, PRONASOL represented a new approach to formulating social development programs in low-income areas. Rather than having government planners design projects in a top-down manner, Solidarity, at least on paper, solicited input from organizations representing the aid recipients. Consequently, these projects were more likely to address problems of importance to the beneficiaries rather than what outside planners, however well-intentioned, thought was good for the poor. To accomplish this, the program incorporated into its decision-making process a broad range of grassroot organizations that represented peasants and the urban poor. At times PRONASOL even incorporated relatively militant or radical groups normally shunned by the government.

Solidarity embodied a fundamental departure from politics as usual in another respect. It was a massive program that linked the poor to the government outside of the PRI's corporatist structure. As a result, rather than having to work with conservative party bureaucrats, community groups had direct access to Solidarity officials who were generally "young, enthusiastic, and of diverse backgrounds. Some [PRONASOL officials] . . . had links to the 'new social movements' [independent grassroots groups] of the 1980s [and some] . . . were even associated with radical political groups."[70] Many of the grassroots leaders also come from a different mold: younger, more militant, and more often female than their predecessors.

Of course, beyond its manifest goal of alleviating poverty, PRONASOL, like any important government program, also had important political objectives. Cuauhtémoc Cárdenas's surprise performance in the 1988 presidential election and the opposition's strong showing in that year's congressional election demonstrated how severely the economic crisis had undermined the regime's legitimacy and reduced PRI support. Furthermore, since Salinas's victory had been deeply tainted by fraud, he had assumed the presidency without a clear popular mandate. Solidarity, then, was designed to restore support for the new president and his government. Its widely advertised projects provided a counterweight to the government's probusiness, neoliberal economic reforms.[71] Salinas frequently appeared on television in well-orchestrated PRONASOL events designed to foster a populist image reminiscent of Mexico's legendary president, Lázaro Cárdenas. Television coverage typically showed him walking, without bodyguards, through crowds of cheering beneficiaries.[72]

Which of Solidarity's two objectives—reducing poverty or advancing the administration's political agenda—took precedence? A study of PRONASOL expenditures by Juan Molinar Horcasitas and Jeffrey A. Weldon found that certain states received a disproportionate share. But these high-outlay states were not necessarily Mexico's poorest. Rather, funding was concentrated in states with impending elections, particularly ones such as Michoacán where the PRD had substantial support.[73]

Initially that political strategy seemed to work. The PRI easily won the 1991 state and congressional elections, performed reasonably well in the 1994 congressional elections (at least in terms of seats), and won the 1994 presidential race without the benefit of fraud. PRONASOL also contributed greatly to President Salinas's high personal approval ratings that only collapsed after he left office. More recently, however, heavy preelectoral expenditures for Solidarity projects have not produced dividends at the ballot box. In spite of substantial government investment in Chiapas following the Zapatista uprising, PRI support in that traditional party stronghold fell sharply in the 1994 state elections.[74] And in 1995, the government had to accept three PAN gubernatorial victories.

PRONASOL's most obvious accomplishment was to revive social spending for Mexico's poor. From 1988 to 1991, government outlays for social development—including Solidarity, public education, health and labor, and urban development—rose from 14.9 percent to 26.5 percent of the national budget.[75] Even if these funds were often used for political purposes, they still reached low-income Mexicans more effectively than previous antipoverty programs had.

Like all modern Mexican presidents, Ernesto Zedillo has phased out many of his predecessor's signature projects and replaced them with his own (though often the new projects are not substantially different from the ones they replace). He has announced plans to supplant PRONASOL with the Alliance for Well-Being, a program with similar goals. The economic crisis that Zedillo inherited may restrict available funding for any antipoverty program, but $1.6 billion was still budgeted in 1995 for the old Solidarity program.[76]

ZEDILLO AND THE CURRENT ECONOMIC CRISIS

Most economic analysts were relatively optimistic about the country's economic future as Carlos Salinas's term drew to an end. Neoliberal reforms seemed to have curbed inflation and improved Mexico's economic health. NAFTA seemed to offer new market opportunities for Mexican industry. Spurred by the seemingly favorable economic prospects, the Mexican stock market prospered in the closing years of the Salinas administration, with heavy foreign investment contributing substantially to that boom.

Three factors, however, threatened the recovery. First, the government had overextended its debt obligations by issuing nearly $30 billion worth of short-term treasury notes (*Tesobonos*) that would fall due in 1995. Second, as the economy expanded and free trade policies encouraged the inflow of foreign goods, imports grew at a much faster rate than exports, renewing the balance-of-payments problem. As the trade deficit grew, pressure mounted to devalue the peso. But as we have seen, Salinas refused to act, fearing that devaluation would remove some luster from his achievements and weaken the PRI in the 1994 election.* Furthermore, he hoped that the balance-of-payments problem would cure itself before becoming too serious. It didn't. Finally, Mexico's growing political tensions—the unresolved Zapatista uprising, the spate of political assassinations, and political intrigue and infighting within the PRI—made for-

---

* Salinas was the leading candidate to head the newly created World Trade Organization after his term ended.

eign investors jittery and ready to disinvest at the first signs of a weakened peso. Rising interest rates in the United States increased the prospects of capital flight.

The new Zedillo administration compounded Salinas's policy error by initially assuring investors that the peso would not be devalued. When the continuing trade deficit forced a devaluation, the president's credibility was undermined. Valued at 3.46 to the dollar in December 1994, the peso plummeted to 6.33 per dollar by mid-1995 and to 7.54 by the start of 1996. The devaluation accomplished its intended purpose of stimulating exports (now cheaper to buy with hard currencies). In 1995, the value of Mexican exports rose by 33 percent over the previous year, while imports fell slightly, moving the country from a sizable trade deficit in 1994 to a surplus.[77]

Otherwise, however, the country has suffered a severe economic setback. A $50 billion international rescue package organized early in 1995 required Mexico to implement a painful economic stabilization program (shock treatment) in order to bring its finances under control.[78] Inflation, which had seemingly been tamed in the early 1990s (dropping to 7.1 percent in 1994), jumped to about 50 percent in 1995.[79] Declining purchasing power created an economic slump and a shutdown of many firms. By year's end the nation's factories were operating only at about 40 percent of capacity, and more than one million persons had been thrown out of work.[80] The GDP declined by over 5 percent, a steeper fall than in any year of the 1980s crisis.

Analysts had generally understood that President Zedillo inherited a serious balance-of-payments problem and agreed that the new administration would have to devalue the peso. However, few expected the wholesale disinvestment by foreign investors at the end of 1994 after the devaluation was announced. The current economic decline seemed to be easing by 1996. But the second major recession in a dozen years, coming relatively soon after the country had emerged from the first, has badly shaken people's confidence in their political and economic systems.

CONCLUSIONS

As one of the Third World's major NICs, Mexico appeared poised to take off economically, just as the East Asian NICs have. It has a relatively well-educated and well-trained workforce, extensive natural resources, considerable entrepreneurial talent, and an enormous potential market in the United States. Yet it has been plagued for decades by serious government policy errors. Like most of Latin America, it followed an ISI model for too long and initially neglected opportunities for manufactured and other nontraditional exports. Its overly protected industries became inefficient and uncompetitive. Presidents Echeverría and López Portillo worsened the problem by spending and borrowing excessively.

Thus Carlos Salinas was hailed for opening up the economy to foreign trade and investment, privatizing parastatals, and slimming down the state while bringing the fiscal deficit and inflation under control. Ironically, Salinas's neoliberal revolution failed to live up to one of its alleged virtues. Under the new order, economic decisions were supposed to be guided by market forces rather than by political or social pressures. But the government allowed the trade deficit to get out of hand because it was politically inexpedient to devalue the peso.

While the new neoliberal model has some clear virtues, particularly in its greater efficiencies, it may worsen one of Mexico's most troublesome economic failings, its huge disparity in wealth and income. Mexico differs from South Korea, Taiwan, and other East Asian economic superstars in that its income and wealth are far more concentrated and education is less pervasive. Unless it can come to grips with these inequities, it may face future political difficulties even if it is able to resume sustained growth.

Notes

1. On Cárdenas's agrarian reform and its aftermath, see Nathaniel Weyl and Sylvia Weyl, *The Reconquest of Mexico: The Years of Lázaro Cárdenas* (London: Oxford University Press, 1939). On the subsequent modernization of agriculture and the growth of agribusiness, see Cynthia Hewitt de Alcántara, *Modernizing Mexican Agriculture: Socio-Economic Implications of Technological Change, 1940–1970* (Geneva: U.N. Research Institute for Social Development, 1976); Merilee S. Grindle, *Bureaucrats, Peasants, and Politicians in Mexico: A Case Study of Public Policy* (Berkeley: University of California Press, 1977); Steven E. Sanderson, *Agrarian Populism and the Mexican State* (Berkeley: University of California Press, 1981).

2. Antonio J. Bermúdez, *The Mexican National Petroleum Industry* (Stanford: Stanford University Press, 1963); Judith Teichman, *Policymaking in Mexico: From Boom to Crisis* (Boulder, Colo.: Westview Press, 1988); Lorenzo Meyer and Isidro Morales, *Petróleo y la nación (1910–1987)* (México: Fondo de Cultura Económica, 1989). Teichman's *Policymaking in Mexico,* chap. 2, and Miguel D. Ramírez, *Mexico's Economic Crisis: Its Origins and Consequences* (New York: Praeger, 1989), chaps. 2–3, offer excellent, concise discussions of the role of the state in Mexico's industrial takeoff.

3. On the process of ISI and the political consequences of "deepening" elsewhere in Latin America, see Guillermo A. O'Donnell, *Modernization and Bureaucratic-Authoritarianism: Studies in South American Politics* (Berkeley: Institute of International Studies, University of California, 1973).

4. Ramírez, *Mexico's Economic Crisis,* 44.

5. Roberto Newell and Luis Rubio, *Mexico's Dilemma: The Political Origins of Economic Crisis* (Boulder, Colo.: Westview Press, 1984), 80.

6. Calvin B. Blair, "*Nacional Financiera:* Entrepreneurship in a Mixed Economy," in *Public Policy and Private Enterprise in Mexico,* ed. Raymond Vernon (Cambridge, Mass.: Harvard University Press, 1964), 223–24.

7. Daniel C. Levy and Kathleen Bruhn, "Mexico: Sustained Civilian Rule without Democracy," in *Politics in Developing Countries: Comparing Experiences with Democracy,* ed. Larry Diamond, Juan J. Linz, and Seymour Martin Lipset (Boulder, Colo.: Lynne Rienner Publishers, 1995), 185.

8. Ramírez, *Mexico's Economic Crisis,* 47; Dale Story, *Industry, the State, and Public Policy* (Austin: University of Texas Press, 1986), 68.

9. Teichman, *Policymaking in Mexico,* 36; Roger Hansen, *The Politics of Mexican Development* (Baltimore: Johns Hopkins University Press, 1980), 210.

10. Teichman, *Policymaking in Mexico,* 34.

11. Howard Handelman, "The Politics of Labor Protest in Mexico: Two Case Studies," *Journal of Inter-American Studies and World Affairs* 18 (August 1976): 167–94.

12. Ricardo Carrillo Arronte, "The Role of the State and the Entrepreneurial Sector in Mexican Development," in *Government and Private Sector in Contemporary Mexico,* ed. Sylvia Maxfield and Ricardo Anzaldúa (La Jolla: University of California–San Diego Center for U.S.-Mexican Studies, 1987), 56.

13. Story, *Industry, the State and Public Policy,* 70. However, only five of the next seventy-five largest enterprises were parastatals.

14. Ramírez, *Mexico's Economic Crisis,* 46. Going back a decade earlier, Enrique Cárdenas notes that GDP growth averaged 5.7 percent annually (2.8 percent per capita) from 1930 to 1970. "Contemporary Economic Problems in Historical Perspective," in *Mexico's Search for a New Development Strategy,* ed. Dwight S. Brothers and Adele E. Wick (Boulder, Colo.: Westview Press, 1990), 10.

15. Rosario Enríquez, "The Rise and Collapse of Stabilizing Development," in *The Mexican Economy,* ed. George Philip (London: Routledge, 1989), 24.

16. On Mexico, see Carlos Tello, "Combatting Poverty in Mexico," in *Social Responses to Mexico's Economic Crisis of the 1980s,* ed. Mercedes González de la Rocha and Agustín Escobar Latapí (La Jolla: University of California–San Diego Center for U.S.-Mexican Studies, 1991), 57–58; Hanson, *Politics of Mexican Development,* 83.

17. Simon Kuznets, "Economic Growth and Income Inequality," *American Economic Review* 45, no. 1 (1955): 1–28. It should be noted that Kuznets's findings were based on historical data. Clearly income distribution has worsened in industrializing countries such as Mexico and Brazil. It is not yet certain, however, that they will become more equal in the future.

18. Teichman, *Policymaking in Mexico,* 36; data drawn from Hanson, *Politics of Mexican Development,* 83.

19. Judith Hellman, *Mexico in Crisis* (New York: Holmes and Meier, 1983).

20. Rosario Enríquez, "The Rise and Collapse of Stabilizing Development," 26.

21. Tello, "Combatting Poverty in Mexico," 58.

22. Jeff Botz, "El Salario obrero en el Distrito Federal, 1939–1975," *Investigación Económica,* no. 4 (1977); Ian Roxborough, "The Economic Crisis and Mexican Labour," in *Mexican Economy,* 111–12.

23. Tello, "Combatting Poverty in Mexico," 58. People living in "extreme poverty" were those receiving less than 60 percent of a subsistence standard of living.

24. Ibid. Overcrowding is defined as having more than two people per room.

25. Carrillo Arronte, "Role of the State and the Entrepreneurial Sector in Mexican Development," 56–58.

26. Peter M. Ward, "Social Welfare Policy and Political Opening in Mexico," in *Transforming State-Society Relations in Mexico,* ed. Wayne A. Cornelius, Ann L. Craig, and Jonathan Fox (La Jolla: University of California–San Diego Center for U.S.-Mexican Studies, 1994), 47–62.

27. Ramírez, *Mexico's Economic Crisis,* 77.

28. Donald Wyman, "The Mexican Economy: Problems and Prospects," in *Mexico's Economic Crisis: Challenges and Opportunities,* ed. Donald L. Wyman (La Jolla: University of California–San Diego Center for U.S.-Mexican Studies, 1983), 4.

29. Ibid., 2.

30. Nora Lustig, *Mexico: The Remaking of an Economy* (Washington, D.C.: Brookings Institution, 1992), 18.

31. Teichman, *Policymaking in Mexico,* 47.

32. Lustig, *Mexico: The Remaking of an Economy,* 17–18, 22.

33. Gary Gereffi, "Paths of Industrialization: An Overview," in *Manufacturing Miracles,* ed. Gary Gereffi and Donald L. Wyman (Princeton, N.J.: Princeton University Press, 1990), 8–9, 13, 15. Comparisons between the two countries are in dollar value.

34. John J. Bailey, *Governing Mexico: The Statecraft of Crisis Management* (New York: St. Martin's Press, 1988), 49–50.

35. Wyman, "Mexican Economy," 4.

36. Alan Riding, *Distant Neighbors* (New York: Vintage, 1984), 207.

37. Lustig, *Mexico: The Remaking of an Economy,* 32. Brazil is the Third World's largest debtor.

38. Armen Kouyoumdjian, "The Miguel de la Madrid *Sexenio:* Major Reforms or Foundation for Disaster?" in *Mexican Economy,* 87.

39. Lustig, *Mexico: The Remaking of an Economy,* 25.

40. Kouyoumdjian, "Miguel de la Madrid *Sexenio,*" 86.

41. Nora Lustig, "México, El 'Pacto de Solidaridad Económica': La heterodoxia puesta en marcha en México," in *Elecciones y política económica en América Latina,* ed. Guillermo Rozenwurcel (Buenos Aires: Grupo Editorial Norma, 1991).

42. Clark W. Reynolds, "Power, Value and Distribution in NAFTA," in *Political and Economic Liberalization in Mexico,* ed. Riordan Roett (Boulder, Colo.: Lynne Rienner, 1993), 80.

43. Lustig, *Mexico: The Remaking of an Economy,* 40–41.

44. M. Delal Baer, "Mexico's Second Revolution: Pathways to Liberalization," in *Political and Economic Liberalization,* 57.

45. Banco de México, *The Mexican Economy 1991: Economic and Financial Development in 1990, Policies for 1991* (México: May 1991), 119; on privatization, see Enrique Quintana, "Empresas privatizadas: divorcios y conflictos," *Este país,* no. 9 (December 1991): 12–13.

46. Banco de México, *Mexican Economy 1991,* 106–7.

47. Wayne A. Cornelius, "The Politics and Economics of Reforming the *Ejido* Sector in Mexico: An Overview and Research Agenda," *LASA Forum* 23, no. 3 (Fall 1992): 3. The analysis in this section draws from this article and from conversations with David Myhre, *ejido* reform project coordinator for the University of California–San Diego Center for U.S.-Mexican Studies Center, August 1994.

48. Billie R. DeWalt and Martha W. Rees, *The End of the Agrarian Reform in Mexico* (La Jolla: University of California–San Diego Center for U.S.-Mexican Studies, 1994), 4–6.

49. Marilyn Gates, *In Default: Peasants, the Debt Crisis, and the Agricultural Challenge in Mexico* (Boulder, Colo.: Westview Press, 1993), 12.

50. Cornelius, "Politics and Economics of Reforming the *Ejido* Sector," 4–5.

51. Ibid., 3.

52. Conversation with David Myhre, August 1994.

53. The data in this paragraph come from Wayne A. Cornelius, *The Political Economy of Mexico under de la Madrid: The Crisis Deepens, 1985–86* (La Jolla: University of California–San Diego Center for U.S.-Mexican Studies, 1986), 18–19.

54. Cornelius, *Political Economy of Mexico under de la Madrid,* 23.

55. On de la Madrid, ibid., esp. 1–18; data from Lustig, *Mexico: The Remaking of an Economy,* 40–41.

56. Armen Kouyoumdjian, "Miguel de la Madrid *Sexenio,*" 91–92.

57. Lustig, *Mexico: The Remaking of an Economy,* 40–41.

58. María de los Angeles Pozas, *Industrial Restructuring in Mexico* (La Jolla: University of California–San Diego Center for U.S.-Mexican Studies, 1993), 30.

59. Conversation with Professor George Philip of the London School of Economics, London, 6 April 1995.

60. Sidney Weintraub, "Honeymoon from Hell," *Hemisphile* (Institute of the Americas) 6, no. 1 (January–February 1995): 1–2.

61. John Sheahan, *Conflict and Change in Mexican Economic Strategy* (La Jolla: University of California–San Diego Center for U.S.-Mexican Studies, 1991), 10.

62. Study by the National Minimum Wage Commission cited in Alejandro Alvarez Béjar, "Economic Crisis and the Labor Movement in Mexico," in *Unions, Workers, and the State in Mexico,* ed. Kevin J. Middlebrook (La Jolla: University of California–San Diego Center for U.S.-Mexican Studies, 1991), 35.

63. Ibid.; Lustig, *Mexico: The Remaking of an Economy,* 69. Lustig's book is among the most clearly presented and insightful discussions of Mexico's economic crisis and the resulting economic reforms. This section relies heavily on her analysis.

64. Tello, "Combatting Poverty in Mexico," 59; Lustig, *Mexico: The Remaking of an Economy,* 75, offers lower figures for unemployment but notes that many people who were laid off from their jobs simply entered the informal sector.

65. Lustig, *Mexico: The Remaking of an Economy,* 73.

66. Ibid., 88.

67. Wayne A. Cornelius, Ann L. Craig, and Jonathan Fox, "Mexico's National Solidarity Program: An Overview," in *Transforming State-Society Relations in Mexico,* 3. This volume is the most comprehensive and useful study of PRONASOL available in English.

68. Ibid.

69. Ibid., 8; Nora Lustig, "Solidarity as a Strategy of Poverty Alleviation," in *Transforming State-Society Relations in Mexico,* 89.

70. Alan Knight, "Solidarity: Historical Continuities and Contemporary Implications," in *Transforming State-Society Relations in Mexico,* 39.

71. Denise Dresser, *Neopopulist Solutions to Neoliberal Problems* (La Jolla: University of California–San Diego Center for U.S.-Mexican Studies, 1991).

72. Alan Knight, "Solidarity: Historical Continuities and Contemporary Implications," in *Transforming State-Society Relations in Mexico,* 44.

73. Juan Molinar Horcasitas and Jeffrey A. Weldon, "Electoral Determinants and Consequences of National Solidarity," in *Transforming State-Society Relations in Mexico,* 123–41.

74. Two months after the EZLN uprising the government announced 2,600 new Solidarity projects for Chiapas with a combined budget of $235 million. *Excelsior,* 14 March 1994, 12.

75. Dresser, *Neopopulist Solutions to Neoliberal Problems,* 6.

76. *New York Times,* 3 July 1995, 5.

77. *Latin American Weekly Report,* 28 December 1995, 590–91; 18 January 1996, 23.

78. *LAWR,* 16 February 1995, 65.

79. *LAWR,* 18 January 1996, 21.

80. *LAWR,* 3 August 1995, 340; 21 September 1995, 422; 28 December 1995, 590.

7

Mexico and the United States

At times, the shadow of U.S. economic and military power has loomed over all of Latin America. Nowhere more so, however, than over Mexico, which shares a two-thousand-mile border and a long tradition of social, economic, and political interaction. To be sure, earlier in Mexican history other powerful nations were important actors on its stage. For example, in the mid-nineteenth century France supported an invasion designed to reassert European control over the former Spanish colony. Germany tried to establish a diplomatic beachhead during both world wars. More recently, Mexico has reached across its two ocean frontiers to forge closer economic and political links with Western Europe and East Asia. And in the 1970s and 1980s, Mexico helped mediate Central America's guerrilla conflicts. Yet today more than ever, bilateral relations with the United States are at the center of Mexico's foreign policy.

Mexicans have always viewed the "colossus of the North" with a mixture of envy, admiration, suspicion, and hostility. From the time of independence, they feared American designs on their territory, with good reason.[1] In the Mexican-American War (1846–48) the United States conquered over half the country's territory. Relations between the two nations remained strained until the last third of the nineteenth century and the Porfirian dictatorship. But Porfirio Díaz's very friendship with the United States—allowing American companies to penetrate deep into the Mexican economy—engendered public enmity and contributed to the outbreak of the 1910 Revolution. During the insurgency, relations between Mexico City and Washington sank to a new low and did not begin to recover until the Revolution had concluded its most radical phase at the end of the 1930s. With the onset of World War II, a rapprochement served the needs of both nations.

Relations between the two "distant neighbors" since that time have generally been cordial despite a number of ongoing irritants.[2] The North American Free Trade Agreement (NAFTA) intertwined the two economies, capping an era of rapidly growing commercial ties. Indeed, in some ways the NAFTA accord had as much symbolic as economic importance, signifying that an almost irrevocable bond had been forged between the two nations.

All of Mexico's major political parties—even the very nationalistic PRD—have conceded that the country's economic fate is inexorably tied to the United States, for better or for worse. The most important links are trade and investment, but other issues also create mutual bonds and continuing irritants.

Currently, the most dramatic of these are illegal immigration and narcotics trafficking.

This chapter will review the historical origins of Mexican-U.S. relations and then examine the most important contemporary issues involving the two countries. Finally, it will outline Mexico's political and economic relations with the rest of the world, most notably Central America and the Caribbean, Western Europe, and East Asia.

THE HISTORICAL TRAJECTORY OF MEXICAN-U.S. RELATIONS

In the years following Mexican independence, the economic gap separating the country from the United States widened considerably. Mexico's economy, which had been half as large as that of the United States at the start of the nineteenth century, was but one-eighth its size by 1867.[3] In the early decades of the twentieth century, the United States emerged as the world's leading economic and military power. The growing disparity between U.S. and Mexican economic, military, and diplomatic power inexorably drove a wedge between them. No other economically advanced democracy shares so long a border with a Third World country. The great disparities in wealth and power between the two would inevitably produce strains and tensions.

A Weakened Mexican Nation-State and U.S. Expansionism (1821–1868).   During their struggle for independence, some Mexicans hoped for U.S. support, while others remained apprehensive about American designs on their territory. After independence, the danger of Spanish reconquest or intervention by other European powers still remained. Responding to that threat, President James Monroe warned in 1823 that the United States would not tolerate European intervention in the hemisphere. Although Washington's capacity to enforce that policy was initially uncertain, the Monroe Doctrine eventually established the basis for U.S. hegemony in the Americas.

As the United States began its inexorable westward expansion, Mexico grew understandably concerned about American settlers moving into its lightly populated state of Coahuila and Texas. It had good reason to be concerned. Years earlier, Thomas Jefferson had declared to a fellow Virginian, "Our Confederacy must be viewed as the nest from which all America, North and South, must be peopled."[4] True to those words, thousands of proslavery Southerners poured into Texas in the early decades of the nineteenth century. When their attempts to have Texas separated from Coahuila into a separate Mexican state failed, the settlers declared the region's independence in 1836. With the aid of volunteers and arms from the United States, they defeated the government forces of General Antonio López de Santa Anna. The following year, President Andrew Jackson recognized Texas as a sovereign nation.

Conflicts between Mexico and Texas continued, punctuated by various military incursions into each other's territory. When the United States annexed

Texas in 1845 and sent troops to defend its frontier, Mexico and the United States went to war. By the time the conflict ended three years later, Mexico had not only lost its claim to Texas, but an area encompassing what is now California, New Mexico, and Arizona as well. In all, the country was stripped of half its territory (though only a small portion of its population) and a vast amount of yet unexploited natural resources. Reflecting on the extent of their nation's territorial, economic, and psychological losses, two contemporary Mexican historians have called the Treaty of Guadalupe Hidalgo, which ended the war, "among the harshest imposed by a winner upon a loser in the history of the world."[5]

The conflict was not the only serious blow to Mexican national unity and sovereignty in the mid-nineteenth century. Between the 1840s and the 1860s, the nation endured a civil war, a major uprising of Mayan Indians (the Caste War), a secessionist movement in the Yucatán peninsula, rebellions in Veracruz as well as the northern and central parts of the country, and a French-sponsored invasion.[6] Encouraged by Mexican monarchists, French emperor Napoleon III tried to take advantage of the country's internal disorder. He dispatched troops to conquer Mexico City and install Austrian Archduke Maximilian as emperor. Although Maximilian was able to accomplish that goal in 1864, he faced continued resistance from forces loyal to the ousted Liberal president, Benito Juárez. When the American Civil War drew to an end, U.S. secretary of state William H. Seward turned his attention to Mexico and pressed France to withdraw. Facing a challenge at home from Prussia, the French abandoned Maximilian, allowing Juárez to regain the presidency in 1867. His return ushered in the first extended period of Mexican-U.S. friendship since independence.

The Porfirian Dictatorship (1876–1911). While Manifest Destiny, America's expansionist march west, continued after the Civil War, it involved no further territorial acquisitions at Mexico's expense. Relations between the two nations improved when General Porfirio Díaz became president in 1876. Díaz created a strong state, capable of defending the nation's territorial sovereignty for the first time in its history. At the same time, however, his development program brought the country squarely into the American economic sphere of influence.

Díaz considered himself an antiimperialist (he had, after all, fought the French-sponsored invasion) and was initially wary of excessive U.S. influence in his country. But he also believed that Mexico's economic development required extensive foreign investment. Under his reign the construction of railroad lines linking Mexico City with Ciudad Juárez and Laredo, Texas, "seal[ed] the fate of the Mexican economy as complementary to that of the United States." Between 1870 and 1910, trade between the two countries rose thirteenfold.[7]

The *Porfiriato* coincided with the florescence of American capitalism and industrialization. Mexico became a favorite of U.S. investors as the territorial expansionism of Manifest Destiny was replaced by economic expansionism.

Meanwhile Díaz changed Mexican law to facilitate greater foreign investment, most notably in mining and railroads. By 1910, American holdings in Mexico nearly equaled total U.S. investment in the rest of Latin America.[8]

While such investment spurred economic growth, it also evoked a nationalist reaction. U.S. and other foreign enterprises owned substantial farm and cattle land, controlled the railroads, and dominated mining and petroleum. Not surprisingly, many Mexicans felt frozen out. In the words of one distinguished American historian, Mexico had become "the father of foreigners and the stepfather of Mexicans."[9] Porfirio Díaz, who would have preferred a greater balance between U.S. and European investment, admitted the problem himself. "Poor Mexico!" he allegedly said. "So far from God, so close to the United States!"

The Effect of the Revolution on Mexican-U.S. Relations (1910–1920). As Díaz prepared to seek his seventh term (1910–16), U.S. president William Taft met with the seventy-nine-year-old dictator. Remarkably, that was the first time there had ever been a meeting between the presidents of the two nations. Taft subsequently expressed trepidation privately over potential future instability if Díaz, long the bedrock of amicable Mexican-American relations, were to die. Little did he guess that the *Porfiriato* would soon end, not because of the Mexican president's death, but because of a mass insurrection.

The 1910 upheaval toppled the dictatorship with surprising ease. Only five months after the Revolution had begun, Díaz left office with most of his army still intact. Ironically, the man long seen by his opponents as a pawn of U.S. interests was eased out of power with some help from Washington. Shortly after the start of the insurrection, Taft had ordered U.S. military maneuvers along the Texas border and sent warships to several Mexican ports. This show of strength had helped convince Díaz to abdicate. In his resignation letter, the aged dictator indicated that one reason for his departure was to avoid "international conflicts."[10]

It was almost inevitable that the United States would be drawn into the Revolution, given Mexico's proximity, the extent of American economic investment there, and the involvement of many Mexican Americans and Mexicans living in the United States. Over time the American role became so substantial that a Mexican historian later called the insurrection an "intervened revolution."[11] In the bloody conflict that followed Díaz's resignation, rival military and political factions carefully watched the United States to see whom it was favoring.

Buffeted by conflicting pressures and motives, American policy was frequently inconsistent. For example, U.S. ambassador Henry Lane Wilson encouraged Victoriano Huerta, a former Díaz general, to oust reformist president Francisco Madero. He may even have subsequently given Huerta the go-ahead for Madero's execution. But American president Woodrow Wilson (no relation to the ambassador) opposed Huerta. As a committed democrat, the president strongly objected to the general's illegal seizure of power. Conflicting interest group pressures pushed American policy in different directions as well. Mexican Americans and U.S. labor unions generally sympathized with the revolutionaries. On the other hand, the Catholic Church (reacting to the insurrection's anticlerical flavor) and American oil companies (fearing expropriation of their property) were quite hostile.[12] Other business groups, most notably the banking industry, though unsympathetic to the Revolution, advocated compromise as the best way of reestablishing investment opportunities. In general, American public opinion was detached, except when national interests seemed threatened (such as when Pancho Villa raided several American border towns).[13] It is probably fair to say that the American public has responded similarly ever since, paying attention to its neighbor only when it feels threatened by troublesome issues such as illegal immigration and drug trafficking.

When General Huerta resisted U.S. pressure to resign in 1914 and held off Constitutionalist forces, President Wilson sent six thousand troops to the port city of Veracruz. This was the first of several American military incursions in the course of the Revolution. Like much subsequent U.S. intervention in the Third World, however, the action backfired. Huerta refused to step down, and even his principal opponents, Venustiano Carranza and Emiliano Zapata, denounced the invasion. The United States sent troops across the border twice more during the Revolution, those times in pursuit of Pancho Villa. Whatever their political orientation or view of the United States, most Mexicans look back at those encroachments with some bitterness.

The advent of World War I reduced American pressures on the Mexican government, then headed by General Carranza. The war forced Washington to filter all foreign policy decisions through the prism of the European conflict. As the United States edged toward entering the war, President Wilson grew concerned about a possible German diplomatic foothold in Mexico. That fear heightened when Britain passed on to the United States an intercepted telegram sent by the German Foreign Ministry to its embassy in Mexico City. The "Zimmermann telegram" proposed a German-Mexican alliance and discussed German support for a Mexican bid to reconquer territory previously lost to the United States. While President Carranza harbored some sympathy for Germany, he recognized the absurdity of the proposal and opted for continued Mexican neutrality.

Scholars dispute how much damage the Mexican Revolution and the American response did to relations between the two nations. Some historians minimize the problem, pointing out that trade between the two countries tripled in the course of the insurrection.[14] But most analysts believe that Mexico's nationalist resentments and American antagonism toward revolutionary change soured relations between the two for several decades.

Reform and the U.S. Reaction (1920–1940).   As World War I and the Mexican Revolution drew to a close, the United States emerged as the world's primary power. European nations, once anxious to influence Latin America, now accepted U.S. hegemony in the region. Mexico's leaders, however reluctantly, did the same.[15] Badly in need of financial support, Presidents Carranza and Obregón both favored a rapprochement with Washington. Toward that end, they tried to reassure U.S. firms, particularly oil companies, operating in Mexico.[16]

Initially these overtures elicited little response from Washington. Woodrow Wilson did remove the last U.S. troops from Mexican soil in 1919, but he was soon succeeded by Warren G. Harding, whose ties to big business made him more belligerent than Wilson toward the revolutionary regime. Meanwhile, Albert Fall, a powerful Republican senator, declared that unless Mexico repealed clauses in its constitution that threatened foreign investment, the United States should occupy the country and install a more sympathetic government. American oil firms remained suspicious of Mexico's claims to its subsoil deposits (petroleum and minerals). And other American companies with holdings in Mexico pressured Washington to oppose that country's social reforms in areas such as labor relations.[17]

But eventually, both governments recognized the value of normalizing relations. In 1923, negotiations between the two culminated in the Bucareli Agreement covering civil claims by citizens of both countries, American property claims, and matters of special concern to U.S. companies. The accord paved the way for U.S. recognition of the Obregón government and the reopening of diplomatic relations.

To be sure, there were still a variety of strains between the two countries. American oil companies continued their legal battles with the Mexican government. Washington took exception to Mexico's support for Augusto Sandino, a Nicaraguan guerrilla leader battling against American military occupation of his country. Ironically, that split was to be repeated some sixty years later when the Reagan administration resented Mexico's support for Nicaragua's Sandinista government, the revolutionary regime named after Sandino.

It was Lázaro Cárdenas's (1934–40) far-reaching reforms that particularly infuriated American corporations. After strengthening the oil workers' unions, Cárdenas intervened in the industry's labor-management disputes by expropriating seventeen American and European petroleum companies.[18] Cárdenas's seizure of the country's most valued natural resource was enormously popular at home. The government oil company he created, PEMEX (Petróleos Mexicanos), subsequently, developed into the largest corporation in Latin America. It became the centerpiece of the powerful state sector and a symbol of Mexican nationalism. While the petroleum nationalization played very well at home, it was a major irritant in Mexican relations with the United States. Of course, Washington also objected to the nationalization of foreign railroads and the expropriation of American-owned property under the agrarian reform law.

Fortunately for the Cárdenas administration, however, the Franklin Roosevelt administration was less hostile to Mexico's social welfare reforms than its Republican predecessors had been. Furthermore, Roosevelt had initiated a "Good Neighbor Policy" toward Latin America, designed to improve relations with the region following years of heavy-handed American interventionism and gunboat diplomacy. Compared with the three Republican administrations that preceded it, the Roosevelt administration was not as certain to side automatically with American firms lodging complaints against Mexico. U.S. ambassador Josephus Daniels enjoyed a particularly warm relationship with Mexico's leaders and was instrumental in soothing tensions between the two countries.[19] For example, when American landowners portrayed the Mexican agrarian reform program as dangerously radical, Daniels compared it to Franklin Roosevelt's New Deal.

The outbreak of World War II gave Washington further incentive to improve relations. Anxious to exclude German influence from the hemisphere, the United States was quite pleased with President Cárdenas's firm antifascist policy. Consequently, as soon as the first American oil company reached a compensation settlement with the Mexican government for its property, the State Department ceased pressing Mexico City on that issue.[20] Thus, a major irritant was removed from relations between the two countries.

World War II and Postwar Economic Expansion: A New Era of Mexican-U.S. Friendship (1940–1970). The year 1940 was a turning point in Mexican-U.S. relations. The election of Manuel Avila Camacho, a centrist president, marked the end of the most radical phase of the Mexican Revolution. Within two years virtually all outstanding claims against the Mexican government by nationalized American firms were settled. Thereafter, aside from some constitutional restraints on foreign operations, Mexico encouraged American investment and trade.

After a brief period of neutrality during World War II, Mexico entered the battle against the Axis powers in 1942. This marked the first time that the two neighbors had ever joined in a military alliance. While Mexico was not a significant actor in the war, its involvement brought it closer to the American orbit. Later, during the Cold War, Washington wished to build an anticommunist alliance in the Americas. Consequently it was pleased with the Mexican government's increasing use of anticommunist rhetoric and applauded the decline of the left (Cardenista) wing of the PRI.[21]

Of course, occasional policy differences still divided the two countries. In the 1950s and 1960s, these disputes usually related to hemispheric relations. With its revolutionary tradition of strong nationalism and its suspicion of any outside intervention, Mexico was naturally wary of Washington's intentions in Central America and the Caribbean. Hence, it was the only nation in Latin America that failed to sign the 1952 Inter-American Reciprocal Aid Treaty, a military assistance pact between the United States and Latin America.[22] Two years later it opposed the CIA-sponsored overthrow of Guatemala's leftist president Jacobo Arbenz. Following the Cuban Revolution, Mexico was also one of the only Latin American countries to maintain diplomatic and economic ties with Havana in the face of strong U.S. pressure. And it was one of only five Latin American countries in the Organization of American States (OAS) that refused to endorse the U.S. invasion of the Dominican Republic in 1965.

The Echeverría and López Portillo Administrations: Relations Sour (1970–1982). Following some thirty years of relative harmony, relations between Mexico City and Washington deteriorated during the presidency of Luis Echeverría (1970–76). One of Echeverría's major priorities was rebuilding his government's legitimacy in the wake of the Tlatelolco massacre. To do so he pursued a populist and nationalist course at home and abroad. In his attempts to become a leader of the Third World, Echeverría distanced Mexico from the United States and sometimes took positions that offended American public opinion. Thus when Mexico backed an Arab-sponsored United Nations resolution that equated Zionism with racism, the American Jewish community initiated a tourist boycott.[23] To the chagrin of the Nixon administration, Echeverría also supported Salvador Allende's socialist government in Chile.

Mexico's petroleum boom enhanced its role as a Third World leader in the late 1970s. Although Presidents López Portillo (1976–82) and de la Madrid (1982–88) were more middle of the road than Echeverría, their independent foreign policies still sometimes alienated the United States. For example, Mexico extended economic help to the beleaguered Sandinista regime in Nicaragua and opposed the U.S.-sponsored Contra (counterrevolutionary) war aimed at toppling the Nicaraguan government.[24] Similarly, during El Salvador's civil war, Mexico recognized the marxist FMLN guerrillas and their allied political party (the FDR) as legitimate political actors that should be included in peace negotiations.[25] Although endorsed by many Western European nations, Mexico's Central American policy and its continued diplomatic and commercial ties to Cuba angered the Reagan administration.[26]

The de la Madrid and Salinas Administrations: Economic Integration with the United States (1982–1994). Over the years, there has often been a correlation between Mexico's domestic and foreign policies. In "radical" periods such as the Revolution or the Cárdenas era and under reformist leaders such as Echeverría, foreign policy has been more nationalistic and more independent of the United States. Conversely, in more conservative times such as the *Porfiriato*, Mexico has established closer diplomatic and economic ties to the United States. Not surprisingly, Washington has increased tensions between the two countries by reacting hostilely to Mexico's more radical administrations.

In the 1980s, Mexico's new neoliberal development policy mandated a change in foreign policy. As we have seen, Presidents de la Madrid and Salinas abandoned the country's import-substituting industrialization model (ISI) and thrust the country more deeply into the international economy, emphasizing its ties to the United States. Declining oil prices and the debt crisis forced Mexico to develop new sources of export revenue. Lower import barriers were introduced to force manufacturers to become more efficient and, hence, more competitive in the world market. While intensifying trade, Mexico also opened its doors to the highest level of foreign investment since the *Porfiriato*.

Internationalization of the economy has especially affected the lifestyles of Mexico's middle-class and upper-class consumers. Even before NAFTA took effect, American products had penetrated middle-class culture. Shopping clubs such as Wal-Mart have made major inroads into the urban retail market. In Coyoacán and other middle-class neighborhoods in Mexico City, billboards now advertise Jenny Craig's weight-loss clinics and cellular phones by Roving Internacional. For many Mexicans these are signs of progress, the first steps toward a more affluent consumer society. For others, they are an affront to Mexican nationalism and a sign of growing dependency.

For better or for worse, Carlos Salinas tightened the links between the Mexican and American economies and established more intimate political ties to Washington than at any time in Mexican history. Still, some tensions and policy disagreements persist, and others will surely arise in the future. Let us now turn our attention to several important contemporary issues that both bind and divide the two nations at this time.

THE NORTH AMERICAN FREE TRADE AGREEMENT (NAFTA)

No connection between Mexico and the United States has received greater attention of late than the North American Free Trade Agreement (NAFTA). The agreement was first initialed by Canada, Mexico, and the United States on 7 October 1992. Thirteen months later, the U.S. House of Representatives ratified it by a narrow margin after extended and heated debate. Senate ratification followed shortly thereafter. In the succeeding weeks, Mexico and Canada approved the treaty with far less contentiousness.* When the agreement finally took effect on 1 January 1994, it established an economic union whose combined GNP exceeded the European Union's.[27]

The extensive American resistance to NAFTA contrasted sharply with the treaty's relatively smooth acceptance in Mexico. Passage by the PRI-dominated Senate was never in doubt, and the accord was also backed by the PAN. Even the PRD, while demanding significant revisions of the treaty, did not oppose the principle of a free trade zone. Opinion polls suggested that most Mexicans also backed the accord, though the level of enthusiasm dropped when Ross Perot and other American critics of NAFTA resorted to bashing Mexico.

The broad public support for NAFTA in Mexico was particularly remarkable considering the treaty's substantial impact on the country. With an economy less than one-twentieth that of the United States, Mexico will be affected far more intensely by the advent of free trade, and the costs of transition will surely be greater. NAFTA symbolizes Mexico's embrace of the world market, closing the door on protectionism and ISI. Deeply ingrained nationalist sensibilities and understandable fears of American economic domination were firmly set aside. To understand more fully the nature of that transformation,

---

* Canada and the United States had already signed a bilateral free trade accord in 1989. Although that treaty met considerable opposition from Canadians who feared American economic domination, NAFTA itself has not been controversial in Canada since that country has relatively little trade with Mexico.

we will first examine the factors that led President Salinas to pursue the North American free trade area.

The Origins of NAFTA.   Since World War II one of the most important developments in the international economy has been the enormous growth of world trade and economic interdependence. Seeking to revive their economies after the war, the twenty-two founding members of the General Agreement on Tariffs and Trade (GATT) began to lower their trade barriers in 1948.[28] Today, the GATT, along with its recently created companion, the World Trade Organization, is the preeminent vehicle for facilitating international commerce. At last count 127 nations, accounting for over 90 percent of world trade, were members, with 23 more countries applying for affiliation.[29] Regional common markets such as the European Union and informal trading zones in East Asia and elsewhere have also greatly augmented international trade and investment.

While the effects of free trade are still intensely debated, most mainstream economists feel that it has benefited participating nations by promoting competition, encouraging specialization of function, and raising efficiency. At the same time, however, trade liberalization is vigorously opposed by the economic sectors that fear they will be unable to compete in the new environment. Indeed, even free trade advocates admit that the transition from a protected economy can be very painful. Less efficient firms that cannot adjust to foreign competition and cannot export will fail, leaving unemployed workers in their wake. But the hope is that more competitive firms will compensate by expanding their exports and employing additional workers.

NAFTA's short- and long-term effects on Mexico and the United States were especially difficult to predict, and hence more controversial, because the agreement links countries with such disparate levels of economic development. Many American producers feared that they would not be able to compete with cheaper-labor Mexican exports, while Mexican firms and farmers were concerned about the United States' substantial lead in technology.

For many years, Mexico's ISI had limited its entry into the global economy. Of course, it was a major petroleum exporter and traded extensively with the United States for many years. But until the 1980s Mexico was slow to develop industrial exports, while industries producing for the home market were shielded from foreign competition by permit requirements, import quotas, and tariffs that sometimes surpassed 100 percent.[30]

The first explosion in manufactured exports came from the *maquiladoras*, plants along the U.S. border that assemble American-made parts (most notably for garments, electronic goods, and toys) and export them back to the United States. By the start of the 1980s, Mexico had become America's third largest trading partner, behind Canada and Japan. And while falling petroleum prices and the debt crisis soon forced it to reduce imports for a while, trade with the United States rebounded to record levels by the close of the decade.[31] So before President Salinas had even proposed NAFTA, Mexico was already the largest exporter of color televisions, computer keyboards, and refrigerators to the United States.[32]

Protectionist pressures from industry and labor had kept Mexico from joining the GATT for decades. In 1986, however, it joined the agreement, capping Miguel de la Madrid's efforts to open up the economy. By the end of the '80s average tariff rates had been lowered 9–10 percent, a small fraction of their former level. Consumers could purchase a wide range of foreign imports at lower prices. At the same time, increasingly efficient Mexican manufacturers, stimulated by greater foreign competition, expanded their exports substantially. In the first years after joining the GATT, Mexico's trade with the United States rose at an annual rate of 25 percent.[33] Capital that previously had fled abroad returned home, and foreign investment surged. Still there were the predictable transition costs, as less competitive firms folded and laid off their workers.

In 1990 President Salinas decided to take export-oriented industrialization one step further through the creation of a North American free trade area. Citing the Western European and East Asian trading blocs, Salinas argued that Mexico could expand its economy substantially only by gaining greater access to the U.S. market. The following year, the United States Congress granted President Bush authority to negotiate an agreement.

Mexican and American Reactions.   Years ago the United States had first broached the idea of establishing a free trade area with Mexico. But the Mexican government had not been receptive, constrained as it was by nationalism at home and fears of American economic domination.[34] By 1990, however, each country's position had changed somewhat. Carlos Salinas was now the most vigorous proponent of free trade, while George Bush and then Bill Clinton first reacted cautiously in the face of well-organized domestic resistance.

The most intense U.S. opposition to a free trade area came from organized labor. Unions feared that many American firms would be unable to compete with low-cost Mexican exports while other companies might relocate to Mexico in search of cheap labor. Many environmental organizations also opposed the accord, afraid that American companies would move to Mexico in order to evade U.S. environmental regulations. Since both labor and environmentalists are important Democratic Party constituencies, their concerns translated into congressional opposition (Democrats then controlled Congress). The business community generally endorsed NAFTA, but some industries, such as sugar growers and manufacturers of glass products, were apprehensive about Mexican competition. As NAFTA moved toward a congressional vote, former presidential candidate Ross Perot galvanized public opposition through television appearances that played on these fears.*

All too often, advocates on both sides of the NAFTA debate exaggerated its positive or negative effects. Prior to the congressional vote on the treaty, American tariffs on Mexican imports already averaged less than 4 percent.

---

* When finally forced to defend his position in a nationally televised debate with Vice President Al Gore, Perot did very poorly. His weak performance took some of the steam out of the anti-NAFTA movement.

Thus, further reduction would scarcely lead to "the sound of jobs being sucked into Mexico" that Perot warned of. Actually free trade reduced trade protection more in Mexico than in the United States. Though reduced sharply in the 1980s, Mexican tariffs still averaged 10 percent, two and one-half times higher than the American level. Yet public reaction to the treaty in Mexico was strangely muted. To be sure, PRD leader Cuauhtémoc Cárdenas criticized NAFTA for inadequately protecting Mexican living standards. In its stead, he proposed a "Continental Initiative on Development and Commerce" that would protect workers' rights and the environment more vigorously.[35] Yet even Cárdenas, the leading spokesperson for Mexican nationalism, accepted the underlying argument for a free trade zone.*

It is difficult to gauge accurately the Mexican public's reaction to NAFTA or to measure precisely the feelings of affected interest groups. Because Mexico remains a semiauthoritarian political system, it did not carry out the kind of open foreign policy debate that took place in the United States.[36] For example, whatever qualms Mexico's unions may have felt about free trade, they would be reluctant to voice their criticisms publicly because of their close association with the government and the PRI. Since television and other mass media usually present only the government's position, the public had little access to dissenting points of view. Thus, when the accord was first proposed in 1990, opinion polls indicated that over 60 percent of all Mexicans favored North American free trade, a higher level of support than in either Canada or the United States.[37] While public enthusiasm declined somewhat as the ratification process continued, substantial opposition to NAFTA never developed. With the PRI holding 61 of 64 Senate seats, easy confirmation was never in doubt. Ultimately, the treaty passed by a margin of 56 to 2.[38]

The Terms of the NAFTA Accord.   NAFTA substantially reduces Mexico's trade barriers with the United States and Canada. Most tariffs were either eliminated when the agreement took effect on 1 January 1994 or will be removed within five years of that date.[39] Other barriers such as quotas and import licenses also will be abolished. Signatories are permitted to impose special trade restrictions when they are needed to protect life and the environment. But the standards used must apply equally to domestic and imported goods. Thus the United States cannot set more stringent safety standards for imported Mexican toys than for American products.

NAFTA was strongly supported by American banks, financial service firms, and insurance companies because it opened up Mexico's previously inaccessible financial service industry. By the end of this century, Mexico will eliminate most of its current constraints on foreign investment in those areas. Agricultural imports, a particularly difficult subject in most trade negotiations,

---

* In January 1994, the PRD's head of international relations, Ricardo Pascoe, told me that the integration of the Mexican and American economies was already a fait accompli prior to NAFTA. Consequently, he said, the party's main objective was to provide a safety net for Mexican workers adversely affected by the accord and to make the treaty more socially responsible. Subsequent to NAFTA's passage Cuauhtémoc Cárdenas has become more critical of it.

have received special treatment. All agricultural quotas and quantitative re-strictions as well as 50 percent of existing tariffs were eliminated as soon as NAFTA took effect. The remaining agricultural tariffs will be phased out over a five-to-fifteen-year period. As the NAFTA votes in the U.S. Congress ap-proached, the Clinton administration gained additional support by negotiat-ing several last-minute side agreements giving special protection to specific crops. While these agreements violated NAFTA's spirit, Mexican negotiators agreed to them in order to insure treaty passage.

NAFTA's Effects.   It is still too early to adequately evaluate NAFTA's eco-nomic effects. But there are already some short-term indicators. In the treaty's first year, each country's bilateral exports rose by about 25 percent. U.S. ex-ports to Mexico grew from $40.1 billion in 1993 to $49.1 billion, while Mex-ican exports to the United States increased from $38.4 billion to $48.5 bil-lion.[40] There is no way of knowing whether that kind of growth can be sustained, how much of it was caused by NAFTA, or whether the relative par-ity in trade between the two countries will continue. The sharp drop in the value of the peso has substantially augmented Mexico's exports while influ-encing imports far less.

Contrary to Ross Perot's strident rhetoric, the dire forecasts by many American labor unions, and the extravagant promises of some NAFTA propo-nents, most economists believe that the number of jobs gained or lost because of the agreement will have a relatively small impact on the U.S. labor market. American environmental groups have been somewhat divided on the treaty. Some feel that the side agreements that were added to the accord as a result of their pressures offer reasonable environmental safeguards. Others, however, remain strongly opposed to the agreement.[41]

NAFTA will have a greater effect on Mexico's economy than on that of the United States because it is so much smaller. Still, for Mexico the treaty is not so much a dramatic change of course as a continuation of trends begun in the early 1980s. The volume of manufactured exports, trade with the United States, and foreign investment all had been on the rise before NAFTA. Almost two-thirds of Mexico's trade already was with the United States.[42] Trade bar-riers on both sides of the border had been coming down. Thus even before NAFTA took effect, tariffs on approximately 80 percent of Mexican exports to the United States had been lowered to less than 5 percent, with half of that total entering duty-free.[43] At the same time, Mexico's middle-class and upper-class markets were already saturated with American products.

Why then did Carlos Salinas consider the trade accord so crucial and why did he stake his prestige on it? The agreement was profoundly important to Mexico because it offered U.S. and Canadian legitimation of Mexico's transi-tion to an outwardly oriented economy. Similarly, it greatly reduces the likeli-hood that the process can be reversed.

Most trade experts believe that in the long run NAFTA will benefit both the Mexican and American economies somewhat.[44] In addition to its effect on trade, the accord also may enhance Mexico's investment potential. Western European and Japanese manufacturers are likely to build plants in Mexico to expedite exports to the U.S. market. At the same time, we have noted that NAFTA facilitates greater American investment in Mexican banking and financial services. Treaty proponents hope this will attract needed capital, while Mexican nationalists fear a U.S. takeover of their financial nerve centers.

CROSSING THE BORDER: THE DEBATE ON IMMIGRATION

A Volatile Issue.   Despite the impassioned debate in the United States over NAFTA, the furor dissipated rather quickly after congressional ratification. Instead, the most emotional issue in Mexican-U.S. relations today, at least from the American perspective, is immigration. Since World War I, millions of Mexicans have crossed the border in search of employment and a better way of life. Many have come legally, while others have not. Often undocumented (illegal) workers live in the United States for only a few years, returning home when they have accumulated sufficient savings. But others remain permanently.

Prior to the 1950s, Mexicans constituted a relatively small percentage of the legal immigrants to the United States. Since 1960, however, they have been the largest national group, with 2.75 million arriving between 1960 and 1990—nearly 20 percent of all legal immigration. Indeed, Mexicans currently represent over one-fifth of all legal and illegal immigrants residing in the United States, more than three times the proportion coming from any other country.[45]

Of course, data on *illegal* immigrants are inherently controversial and imprecise. In recent years, estimates of the total number of illegal aliens residing in the United States have varied tremendously, ranging from four to twelve million, with most experts supporting a figure toward the lower end of that range. Whatever their total numbers may be, some 60 percent of all illegal aliens are believed to be Mexicans.[46]

Many Americans have come to feel threatened by immigration from Mexico and other parts of Latin America. There is a common misperception that both legal and illegal immigrants draw heavily on welfare services and are a serious drain on the taxpayer. In a widely watched California referendum, voters recently endorsed a state proposition denying most social services to illegal immigrants. Some U.S. senators and congressmen have advocated legislation terminating welfare payments for *all* immigrants, legal or illegal.

Reducing or eliminating immigration has become a "hot button" issue in many parts of the United States, sure to appeal to voters. But popular attitudes have frequently been shaped by ill-informed stereotypes. For example, research by the University of California–San Diego's Center for U.S.-Mexican Studies indicates that, for the most part, the taxes paid by undocumented workers actually exceed the value of the government services that they draw upon. Other studies reject the assumption that illegal aliens are taking away a substantial number of jobs from American workers.

Several factors have added to public apprehensions about this issue. Like many Western democracies, the United States has experienced a surge of immigration from less-developed countries in recent decades. Higher educational levels and greater media access among Third World peoples have increased popular awareness of Western consumer societies and made that lifestyle seem especially attractive. More affordable international transportation also has contributed to the surge of immigrants. Consequently many developed Western nations, including the United States, have begun to feel that they are losing control of their borders.*

In the 1980s, a wave of illegal immigrants from Central America arrived in the United States, fleeing their war-torn homelands. As Salvadorian, Nicaraguan, and Guatemalan refugees joined the ranks of Mexicans illegally entering the United States, support for sealing the border grew. In the early 1990s, antiimmigrant sentiment in California was bolstered by high unemployment (primarily related to defense industry cutbacks, not immigration).

A Reciprocal Labor Market.   Many experts argue that, contrary to popular belief, Mexican emigration to the United States provides important benefits to both countries (though it obviously also creates some problems). On the one hand, it has reduced Mexico's labor surplus, as emigrant workers receive better wages in the United States and provide income for their families back home. At the same time, it often has also served the American economy, as immigrants have filled important gaps in the U.S. labor market.[47] For example, during World War I, when substantial emigration from Mexico began, the United States recruited Mexican agricultural workers over the objections of the Mexican government.[48] During both world wars, Mexico contributed badly needed workers to America's defense industries.

Since that time, immigrants have worked the fields of California, Texas, and Arizona, usually taking backbreaking farmwork that Americans did not want to do. For several decades, under the *bracero* program, Washington and Mexico City annually negotiated a quota that allowed agribusiness in California and the Southwest to employ seasonal farmworkers from Mexico. At times, U.S. policy makers have even helped employers skirt the immigration laws. Thus, when Congress debated the McCarran-Walters Act in 1952, the Texas delegation feared that the bill's restrictions on immigration would hurt powerful growers in their state. Consequently, they inserted a proviso allowing farmers to hire undocumented workers under certain conditions. Until that provision was eliminated by the 1986 Immigration Reform and Control Act, the United States was perhaps the only nation in the world whose immigration laws explicitly allowed certain employers to hire illegal aliens.[49]

In recent years, the need for migrant labor has shifted from farming to other sectors of the economy. Currently, less than one-sixth of the Mexican workers in California, Texas, and Arizona are employed in agriculture. The

---

* The proportion of immigrants in the total population is actually lower in the United States than in France and several other Western European nations.

greatest U.S. labor shortages are currently in service industries, such as restaurants, and in low-wage manufacturing, such as the apparel industry.[50] These industries would be in serious difficulty if they could not hire legal immigrants or undocumented workers.

Interestingly, Mexico's emigration rate has generally corresponded more closely to the U.S. demand for labor than to Mexico's unemployment levels.[51] And although undocumented Mexicans are accused of taking jobs from American workers, more often than not they have been employed in positions that few Americans want. Even in times of high unemployment, laid-off aerospace engineers and defense workers in California or Texas are not inclined to accept work as hospital orderlies, busboys, restaurant dishwashers, farm laborers, or maids.

Undocumented workers also are willing to accept less dependable employment and changing work schedules. Many of them work for firms that

> are under intense . . . competitive pressure and that suffer from sharp fluctuations in demand for the goods or services they produce. For such companies, the principal advantage of undocumented immigrant labor is not its cheapness, but its *flexibility* (or *disposability*). . . . The immigrant work force is more willing than U.S.-born workers to accept high variability in working hours, working days per week, and per month, and low job security.[52]

Obviously undocumented workers do replace or undercut some American workers. They may compete with unskilled workers for low-wage jobs, particularly threatening members of minority groups. But at the same time, employing illegal aliens actually saves American jobs in certain situations. For example, many American garment factories would move abroad were they unable to hire low-wage, undocumented workers for their less-skilled positions. By hiring illegal aliens those firms can remain in the United States and offer higher-end jobs to American workers. In short, the complex, reciprocal relationship between the American and Mexican job markets defies the easy generalizations and quick solutions that too often characterize public debate on the issue.[53]

U.S. Immigration Policy. Washington has been under mounting pressure of late to limit the flow of illegal (or even legal) immigration to the United States. At their worst, immigration opponents appeal to racial fears and misleading cultural stereotypes. But a broad consensus in favor of some limitation has developed, encompassing many groups that can scarcely be accused of harboring prejudice. For example, opinion surveys in the early 1990s revealed that 75 percent of Mexican Americans and 84 percent of *legal*, resident aliens believe that current levels of Mexican emigration are too high.[54] Those proportions are fairly similar to the range of opinions within the American population as a whole.

Until recently, U.S. policy makers have been wary of imposing extremely restrictive measures. Their desire to regulate immigration has been tempered by their reluctance to impose draconian solutions such as building a "Berlin Wall" along the border or requiring all Americans to carry national identity cards. Elected officials and many interest groups also recognize the numerous contributions that immigrants have made to the United States. That degree of understanding may be vanishing, however, as politicians such as California's governor, Pete Wilson, have made immigrants a major campaign issue. U.S. border patrols have become more vigorous in their enforcement methods, and a variety of restrictive laws have been enacted or are under consideration at the state and federal levels.

After years of heated debate, the U.S. Congress passed the Immigration Reform and Control Act (IRCA) of 1986, the most important piece of immigration legislation in decades. Like previous policy in this area, the act tried to balance the need for greater immigration control with the American economy's labor requirements. It also sought to balance restrictions on future immigration with fair and politically viable treatment of illegal immigrants already residing in the United States. Thus the bill allowed undocumented aliens who had migrated to the United States prior to 1982 to apply for an amnesty giving them legal resident status. Recognizing the special need of western and southwestern agricultural interests for immigrant labor, it also offered amnesty to farmworkers who had entered the country after the 1982 deadline, providing that they had been employed in the United States for ninety days between May 1985 and May 1986. Concurrently, however, the IRCA tried to limit further illegal immigration by intensifying border patrols and imposing sanctions on employers hiring any undocumented worker who had entered the country since the start of 1982.

Despite its sweeping provisions and the high hopes attached to it, the IRCA's record has been disappointing. For one thing, fewer people applied for amnesty than had been anticipated. Only 1.5 to 1.8 million eligible immigrants (70 to 75 percent of whom were Mexicans) applied under the principal terms of the law, while an additional one million agricultural workers (mostly Mexican) petitioned under their special provisions.[55] While their exact numbers are unknowable, it is certain that millions of eligible illegal residents failed to apply, out of either fear or ignorance.

At the same time, the law has failed to achieve its primary goal, curtailing further illegal immigration. Initial indications of a drop in the rate of border crossings proved to be ephemeral. One of the most technically sophisticated migration studies, charting movement through the Zapata Canyon near Tijuana (a major route for illegal border crossings), showed no appreciable decline in traffic from 1986 to 1988.[56] Indeed, most estimates of the number of undocumented workers currently entering the United States suggest that the rate is as high as ever.

Congress passed new legislation in 1990 that raised the level of legal immigration from all parts of the world by 40 percent. But any future congressional action on this issue is likely to involve tougher restrictions on immigration and on the rights of resident aliens.

The Mexican Perspective.   Like Washington, Mexico's government also has been ambivalent about illegal emigration to the United States. On the one hand, it recognizes that emigration functions as an important pressure valve, relieving unemployment and defusing potential political discontent at home. Because the areas along the border are so economically interdependent, and because so many people from both countries cross the border legally every day, Mexico opposes burdensome controls on cross-border traffic or massive border fences to prevent illegal crossings. The most extreme proposals for limiting immigration now being discussed in the United States have offended many Mexicans, who perceive them as expressions of prejudice. At the same time, however, the magnitude of Mexican emigration is an embarrassment to many of that nation's political leaders, a poignant reminder that their economy has failed to provide sufficient employment at a satisfactory wage.

In short, Mexican authorities view proposals for a sealed border or for other drastic limitations on immigration as unrealistic or even racist. Instead, they argue that the reciprocal relationship between the Mexican and U.S. labor markets requires finely calibrated, joint solutions. But political realities constrain what the Mexican government can do. It has neither the resources nor the political will to control the outflow of illegal emigrants from its own territory. Its task is made yet more difficult because Mexican "border authorities . . . have since time immemorial been among the most corrupt in Mexico."[57]

Prospects for the Future.   The IRCA's failure to stem the tide of illegal immigration to the United States suggests that neither employer sanctions nor intensified border patrols will appreciably reduce that flow. With a two-thousand-mile frontier that is legally crossed daily by over 750,000 people, it is almost impossible to shut off the illegal traffic.[58] While some prior attempts to crack down have been successful for a while, they have been ineffective in the long run.

If the Mexican economy can begin growing once again, and if the benefits of that growth can be more equitably distributed throughout society, the population exodus may be reduced. But it is unlikely that economic development alone will have a major impact. Even in the most optimistic scenario, there still will be a wide gap between the Mexican and American standards of living. Moreover, as Mexican economic modernization creates a more urbanized and educated population, the lure of America's consumer society is likely to increase. At the same time, more Mexicans will have the education and skills to compete in the U.S. labor market.

If Americans increasingly believe that illegal immigration pulls down U.S. wages and imposes a financial burden on taxpayers, demands for a crackdown will intensify. But, as we have noted, undocumented workers are more likely to take low-end jobs that most Americans do not want or quickly leave. As the United States enters the twenty-first century, its low birthrate may cause greater labor shortages for a number of occupations.[59] One possible solution would be to establish a category of foreign "guest workers," as Germany has. Legally registered guest workers would be allowed to enter the United States for a specific period of time in order to fill openings where there is a need. Bilateral solutions such as that, however, will require increased government cooperation and a cooling of political rhetoric on both sides of the border.

CONTROLLING NARCOTICS TRAFFIC

In 1985, Enrique Camarena, a United States Drug Enforcement Agency (DEA) undercover agent working in Mexico, was kidnapped by drug dealers, brutally tortured, and then murdered. Americans were outraged when subsequent investigations revealed that the men who killed him had ties to agents of the Mexican Federal Security Bureau. Five years later, hired bounty hunters kidnapped Dr. Humberto Alvarez-Machain, a Mexican physician whom the DEA accused of being involved in Camarena's torture and death. The doctor was smuggled across the border and turned over to American law officials. Incensed at the DEA-directed abduction of a Mexican citizen, the Mexican government threatened to curtail its joint drug operations with the United States.[60]

Enrique Camarena's assassination and Alvarez-Machain's abduction were emblematic of the strains between Mexico and the United States growing out of their differing perceptions of the narcotics trade. Americans tended to see Camarena's brutal murder as the worst manifestation of the corruption pervading the Mexican law enforcement system. Many Mexicans, on the other hand, believed that the DEA's decision to have Alvarez-Machain kidnapped, rather than seek extradition, demonstrated Washington's disregard for Mexican sovereignty. Mexican indignation intensified when the U.S. Supreme Court later ruled that it was constitutional for American authorities to kidnap foreign criminal suspects from their own country in order to bring them before a U.S. court. Mexico responded by suspending the activities of all DEA agents in the country, interrupting several years of close cooperation. Finally, hoping to defuse the tension, Washington announced that it would not kidnap suspects from foreign soil in the future.*[61]

As drug consumption has spiraled in the United States, narcotics trafficking has become a sensitive binational issue. Mexico is currently the leading source of heroin and marijuana for the American market as well as the transshipment route for over one-third of all South American cocaine bound for the United States. Drug revenues currently are believed to represent over 1 percent of Mexico's GNP.[62]

Some of the U.S. news media and American politicians such as Jesse Helms, chairman of the Senate Foreign Relations Committee, have criticized Mexico for failing to pursue the war on drugs adequately. Unquestionably, corruption within the Mexican law enforcement system is a serious problem. At the same time, however, several important U.S. studies of the narcotics trade credit Mexico with making a serious effort to control that traffic. For example, a recent inquiry commissioned by the U.S. Department of Defense lauded the level of Mexican-U.S. cooperation and concluded that "for the past twenty years, Mexico has taken aggressive actions against drug production."[63] It notes

---

* Ironically, a U.S. federal judge subsequently dismissed all charges against Alvarez-Machain, ruling that there was insufficient evidence to send the case to a jury. Shortly thereafter, the doctor returned to Mexico.

that Mexico was one of the first countries in the world to involve its armed forces extensively in the war on drugs and one of the first to attack narcotics cultivation through aerial spraying.

Not surprisingly, then, Mexican authorities feel that they are criticized unfairly. Like governments elsewhere in Latin America, they believe that the finger of blame has too often pointed in the wrong direction. The source of the narcotics problem, they insist, is America's unquenchable thirst for drugs. Hence, the only effective solution is to reduce U.S. consumption levels. They note that per capita use of cocaine, heroin, and marijuana in the United States is two to six times as high as in Mexico (depending on the drug).[64] Because the American narcotics market is so enormously lucrative, experts generally agree that even the strictest Mexican interdiction efforts could never cut off more than a small percentage of the trade.

During the early stages of the war on drugs, Mexican authorities considered narcotics largely an American problem. Their cooperation in drug interdiction merely reflected their desire to maintain good relations with Washington. Since the early 1980s, however, Mexico's leaders have grown more concerned about the drug cartels' potential for destabilizing Mexican society and politics. Although its own rate of drug use remains relatively low, Mexico has been sobered by events in Colombia and Bolivia, where powerful narcotics operations have infiltrated the highest echelons of the political system. In early 1996, for example, Colombia was shaken by revelations that its president had apparently solicited and received campaign contributions from the country's drug cartels. Drug lords also have been responsible for the deaths of thousands of innocent Colombian citizens, including several presidential candidates.

The political influence of Mexico's narcotics traffickers to date is not nearly as great. But they have already destabilized the politics of several states with extensive drug cultivation, most notably Chihuahua, Durango, and Sinaloa. More ominously, drug rings are believed to be responsible (though likely unintentionally) for the murder of Cardinal Juan Jesús Posadas Ocampo. They are rumored to have been involved in Luis Donaldo Colosio's assassination and, possibly, the death of José Francisco Ruiz Massieu.

Miguel de la Madrid was the first Mexican president to label narcotics trafficking as a national security issue and "an affair of state." Those purposefully chosen words indicated the great importance his administration attached to the problem. For the remainder of his term the government accelerated its attacks on drug-smuggling operations and its confiscation of narcotics. Several powerful drug lords were also incarcerated.

President Carlos Salinas promised that he would further intensify the war on drugs "for the health of Mexicans, for national security, and for international cooperation."[65] Salinas, of course, was committed to forging closer ties with the United States (and the creation of NAFTA) and realized how important it was to convince Washington that his administration was taking the war on drugs very seriously. His administration increased funding for antinarcotics activities and increased the penalties for drug-related crimes. Authorities confiscated one hundred times as much cocaine in one month of 1989 as they had in all of 1982–83.[66] Major drug dealers such as Felix Gallardo and Rafael Caro Quintero were captured and sentenced to long prison terms. In all, American analysts credited the Salinas government with implementing one of Mexico's most forceful antidrug campaigns.

The Zedillo administration was forced to concentrate its energies on the nation's economic crisis during its first year in office. In early 1996, however, it earned Washington's approval by capturing one of the country's most powerful drug traffickers, Juan García Abrego, and extraditing him to the United States (García Abrego was born in the United States and is an American citizen).

Despite such progress, officials on both sides of the border continue to harbor mutual suspicions and to nurse mutual grievances. For its part, Mexico complains that no matter how many American requests it honors, Washington always wants it to do more. Eventually, every Mexican administration must decide how extensively it can cooperate with America's war on drugs without sacrificing its own national sovereignty. Because of past U.S. incursions into their country, Mexicans are understandably sensitive about the presence of DEA agents or, potentially, American military personnel on their soil. The kidnapping of Dr. Humberto Alvarez-Machain further inflamed the sovereignty issue. While repulsed by Enrique Camarena's brutal murder, Mexicans felt that the DEA had no right to arrange the abduction, any more than Mexican police would have the right to sweep an American fugitive from Mexican justice off the streets of Chicago.

At the same time, the United States has its own grievances. While crediting the Salinas and Zedillo administrations with reducing drug-related government corruption, Washington is still frustrated by the problem's widespread persistence. After Carlos Salinas left office, both his brother Raúl and a former, high-ranking government prosecutor, Mario Ruiz Massieu, were found to hold millions of dollars in questionable funds, money widely believed to come from drug traffickers.

Narcotics profits are so immense that dealers throughout the world have ample resources to corrupt politicians and law enforcement officials in both developed and developing nations. In the United States, for example, local police and DEA officials have been tainted. In the Third World, where government salaries are far lower, the temptation to accept bribes is enhanced. The pervasive corruption within Mexican politics well before the rise of the drug cartels offered traffickers a receptive environment. A variety of local and national law enforcement officials have been linked to narcotics dealers. For example, the former director of Mexico's Interpol operations was arrested and charged with aiding a major cartel.[67] Imprisoned drug kingpins often receive special treatment, including license to carry on business from their jail cells. And during some drug raids, the authorities have actually encountered armed resistance from corrupt police units (sometimes led by high-level officers) working for the dealers.

Mexican citizens, who must routinely pay small bribes to the police and other local officials, are keenly aware of their government's corruption problem. Most are also concerned about the growing influence of drug cartels. Writing in *La Opinión,* Carlos Ramírez noted that "the crux of the [Enrique] Camarena case is . . . the revelations of intricate ties relating drug trafficking with police and political power in Mexico."[68]

But even if Mexico could reduce police corruption sharply, the country would still be an attractive base for narcotics traffickers. Its long frontier with the United States, the world's largest narcotics consumer, makes Mexico an obvious conduit for the drug trade just as nearby Caribbean and Central American nations also serve as transshipment points for South American cocaine. Within Mexico itself, cultivation of marijuana or heroin offers poor farmers far higher incomes than they could hope to earn from legitimate crops.

Moreover, successful Mexican efforts to reduce the flow of drugs to the United States—most notably in the 1970s—merely caused the dealers to develop alternative supply routes. Indeed, Mexico's tougher enforcement policies in recent years have caused some drug traffickers to shift their operations to Guatemala or other transshipment points. Ultimately, then, only a decline in American drug consumption will substantially reduce the flow of narcotics from Latin America.

LOOKING SOUTH, WEST, AND EAST

Having examined the most important aspect of Mexico's foreign relations, its ties to the United States, we will now turn briefly to its links to the rest of the world. In particular, we will examine three areas: Mexico's role in Central America and the Caribbean; its economic and cultural ties to Western Europe; and its growing economic bonds with East Asia.

Central America and the Caribbean.   With the second biggest population and second largest GNP in Latin America, Mexico ranks as one of the hemisphere's most important diplomatic actors. It has been particularly influential in its neighboring areas of Central America and the Caribbean. Mexico has long insisted on the principles of national sovereignty and nonintervention in the region, a stance that has sometimes brought it into conflict with the United States. During much of the 1980s, the two countries had very different perspectives on Central America's revolutionary struggles. As those conflicts wound down, however, Presidents de la Madrid and Salinas reestablished a warm relationship with the United States, perhaps the closest that Mexico had enjoyed in decades.

The Cuban Revolution and the subsequent outbreak of marxist insurgencies in Nicaragua and El Salvador were perceived quite differently in Washington and Mexico City. American presidents from John Kennedy's time through the end of the Cold War considered Cuba a wedge for Soviet influence in the hemisphere and a breeding ground for revolutionary unrest. Even now, Washington continues to isolate Havana. On the other hand, Mexico's government, though hostile to marxist movements on its own soil, has usually been more tolerant of revolutionary struggles abroad. For decades Mexican foreign policy has had a more radical tone than its domestic policy, allowing the government to use foreign relations as an olive branch to radical intellectuals and the PRI's left wing. At the same time, Mexico's leaders, drawing on their own historical experience, also have been concerned about excessive U.S. intervention in the internal affairs of revolutionary Latin American states.

Following Fidel Castro's victory in 1959, Mexico resisted American pressure to break diplomatic and commercial ties with Havana and for years was one of the only Latin American countries not to do so. Castro's occasional high-profile meetings with several Mexican presidents irritated Washington considerably. In the 1980s, tensions between Mexico City and Washington intensified when Mexico rejected the Reagan administration's hard-line policy toward Central American revolutionary movements.

There was considerable sympathy in Mexico for Nicaragua's Sandinista revolutionaries (the FSLN) when they toppled the corrupt and brutal dictatorship that the Somoza clan had maintained for decades. In the spring of 1979, as the FSLN was on the verge of seizing power, the Carter administration had hoped to avert a full Sandinista triumph by replacing Somoza with a reformist coalition government. But Mexico and other Latin American nations opposed that plan when it was raised at the Organization of American States (OAS), and the way was cleared for the FSLN victory.[69] When the Reagan administration cut off trade and aid to Nicaragua, both Mexico and Venezuela supported the struggling marxist regime by offering it cheap petroleum at subsidized prices. Through the 1980s, Mexico extended over $1 billion in petroleum credits to the Sandinista regime (though most of that came before 1986).[70]

The battle against the FMLN guerrillas in El Salvador, like the American-sponsored Contra war against the Sandinista government, was a major obsession of the Reagan administration's foreign policy. But Mexico, though not sympathetic to the FMLN, rejected Washington's attempts to win militarily in El Salvador. Instead it favored a negotiated settlement. Soon after Ronald Reagan took office, Presidents López Portillo and François Mitterand of France recognized the FMLN as a "representative political force" that deserved a place at the bargaining table. It took nearly a decade of war before the United States and the Salvadoran government accepted that position and negotiated a peace accord.

Eventually Mexico became more critical of the Sandinista regime as President de la Madrid sought a closer relationship with the United States. But Washington and Mexico City continued to see Central America differently. Assistant Secretary of State for Inter-American Affairs Elliot Abrams (an architect of the Contra war in Nicaragua) called Mexico a "vocal left-wing element" undercutting U.S. policy in the region. And at a Mexican-U.S. summit conference, Ronald Reagan asked President de la Madrid to explain "why [Mexico] hasn't backed the United States during U.N. votes on Central America."[71]

Following the 1982 debt crisis, however, Mexico was forced to modify its position. Now heavily dependent on U.S. economic support, it tempered its criticism of American policy and favored a multilateral approach to the Central American crisis. It joined with Colombia, Panama, and Venezuela in 1983 to form the Contadora Group. In the next three years that Group offered a series of proposals for reducing conflict in Central America: curtailing foreign intervention, limiting armaments and the size of the region's armed forces, securing national borders, and negotiating a peaceful settlement to the civil wars in El Salvador, Guatemala, and Nicaragua.

The Contadora initiative was undercut by Washington's indifference (or hostility) and by the disinclination of Central America's governments to make concessions at that time. The Reagan administration continued to arm the Nicaraguan Contra guerrillas and the Salvadoran military in hopes of achieving military victories in those countries. Still, even though it failed to bring peace, Contadora created the foundation for successful negotiations subsequently. In 1986, Central America's presidents launched a new, joint peace offensive known as the Esquipulas process. Eventually, a plan fathered by Costa Rican president Oscar Arias brought about the Nicaraguan and Salvadoran peace accords.* Thus, after many difficult turns, Mexico could take credit for having helped to start Central America down the difficult road to peace.

By the end of the decade, the Bush administration reduced American involvement in the region substantially, ending U.S. support for the Contra rebels and supporting a negotiated accord in El Salvador. With the settlement of those conflicts (and the defeat of the Sandinistas at the polls), Central American policy ceased being an irritant in Mexican-U.S. relations.

Western Europe.   Mexico has always felt a cultural bond with Europe, particularly Spain. Today, with the countries of the European Union (EU) making up one of the world's major economic powers, Mexico also looks to Western Europe for trade, investment, and technology. To be sure, Europe's *share* of world trade with Mexico has declined in recent years and will probably continue to fall as NAFTA strengthens Mexico's trade links to the United States. In the first half of the 1980s, about 20 percent of Mexico's exports went to Western Europe. Since then that proportion has dropped to approximately 15 percent. But even if Mexico's economic and political ties to Europe are far weaker than those to the United States, they still provide a useful counterweight to American influence. Within Europe, Spain has been Mexico's largest export market, followed by France and Germany.[72] While Mexico has diversified its exports to the United States (with manufactured products now accounting for the largest share), petroleum still accounts for most sales to Europe.

With the collapse of communism in Eastern Europe, the EU—particularly Germany, its leading member—has turned its attention eastward. Indeed, Carlos Salinas's understanding that the fall of the Berlin Wall and German reuni-

---

* For his critical role in the process, President Arias later received the Nobel Peace Prize.

fication would limit future German investment in Mexico helped convince him to launch his NAFTA initiative. While the United States currently contributes 60 percent of Mexico's foreign investment, the European Union accounts for less than 20 percent. Still, Europe is an important source of capital and technology and will grow in importance if EU manufacturers use Mexican plants as an entryway to the American market. Among the nations of Europe, Britain and Germany are the largest foreign investors.[73]

During the 1980s, several European countries, particularly France and Spain, backed Mexico's diplomatic efforts for peace in Central America. The European Community (the predecessor to the EU) endorsed the Contadora Group's activities and coordinated European policy with Latin America's Rio Group (composed of the four Contadora nations plus Argentina, Brazil, Peru, and Uruguay). European diplomatic support can be very valuable to Mexico in the future if it pursues a foreign policy more independent of the United States.

East Asia.   Mexico's ties to East Asia have developed relatively recently. The phenomenal economic growth of the region's newly industrializing countries (NICs)—Hong Kong, Singapore, Taiwan, South Korea, and, more recently, Thailand, Malaysia, and Indonesia—has greatly impressed Mexico's leaders as it has governments throughout Latin America. Carlos Salinas, who sent his children to Mexico City's Japanese school, took note of that country's work ethic and its potential as an investor in Mexico.[74] As he helped build NAFTA, Salinas reached out to Asia for investment as well. After all, as Mexican government officials like to point out, Mexico is "a Pacific nation," interested in forming bonds with the booming economies of East Asia.

Japan currently accounts for a mere 5 percent of total foreign investment in Mexico, considerably less than the United States or the EU. Since the late 1960s, however, its investment has grown at a faster rate than that of any other source.[75] For example, it is already the second largest investor in the *maquiladoras* (assembly plants) along the U.S. border.[76] Corporate giants such as Hitachi, Sony, Matsushita, and Sanyo all have invested there.[77] Japan is already Mexico's second-largest trading partner. The creation of NAFTA will likely stimulate further investment by East Asian nations seeking easier access to the American market.

Like the European Union, East Asia offers Mexico an opportunity to diversify its economic and diplomatic relations and thereby reduce its dependency on the United States. The region can also provide unique technology transfers that are unavailable from the United States or Europe. In but a few decades, several East Asian nations developed astonishingly from very poor countries to industrial powers. Now that Mexico has begun to emulate the East Asian export-oriented development model, Taiwanese and Korean investment could help transfer management techniques and technology that are particularly appropriate for a developing NIC.

There are also broader aspects of the East Asian economic miracle that could provide useful lessons for Mexico. These include the development of widespread secondary education; equitable land tenure distribution in rural areas; and more equitable national income distribution including improvement in rural living standards. All of those features have contributed to East Asian economic development but are sorely lacking in Mexico and much of Latin America.

CONCLUSIONS

For better or for worse, Mexico's destiny is intertwined with that of the United States. Their physical proximity and interdependence make this inevitable. Many Mexican nationalists and American scholars have surely exaggerated the perils that such interdependence presents for Mexico. Many contemporary political leaders and journalists on both sides of the border exaggerate its potential benefits. Mexico's challenge will be to maximize the relationship's advantages and minimize its inescapable problems and tensions.

To date, NAFTA has obviously not been the panacea for the Mexican economy that the Salinas administration had hoped for. At the same time, it is not the cause of the current economic crisis, whose origins lie in the Mexican government's failure to devalue the peso in a timely fashion. If the country is to avoid constant economic shocks, future administrations will have to base their policy decisions on realistic economic indicators rather than on electoral politics or unrealistic optimism. That will be a particular challenge if the country continues to progress toward a more competitive electoral system.

As American anxieties over immigration grow, particularly in the Southwest and California, the issue threatens to damage Mexican-U.S. relations and to promote cultural prejudices. The Mexican government has little control over illegal emigration to the United States, and the current economic crisis intensifies that flow. Consequently, Washington and various state governments are taking increasingly draconian steps to curtail immigration. While the United States clearly needs to control its borders and cannot throw open its doors to all comers, many experts believe that current fears are greatly exaggerated. As we have seen, they argue that undocumented Mexican workers often fill gaps in the American labor market, taking jobs most Americans do not want. Civil libertarians also raise questions about much of the legislation currently being proposed.

In the past, bursts of antiimmigrant sentiment have risen and subsided. And this wave may do so as well. For now, however, the United States needs to take care that a legitimate policy concern does not lead to measures that alienate Mexico and threaten the civil liberties of legal immigrants and native-born Hispanics.

The narcotics trade will also continue to be a hot-button issue despite evidence that American consumption of cocaine and other hard drugs is declining. Increasingly, drug traffickers are using Mexico as a transshipment point for South American cocaine and as a base for laundering funds. For Mexico, the problem far transcends its relations with the United States. The growing influence of drug kingpins is corrupting its political system and threatening the process of democratization.

Despite its past record of support for authoritarian regimes throughout Latin America, the United States is currently better positioned to support a democratic transition in Mexico. With the Cold War over, Washington views democracy as a stronger foundation than authoritarianism for political and economic stability. Hence, future American administrations are likely to support Mexican democratization. American campaign experts, human rights specialists, pollsters, journalists, and other professional advisors can contribute marginally to the process. But unlike many developing nations, Mexico has considerable expertise in these areas. Ultimately, then, Mexicans themselves will determine the course of democratization.

Notes

1. Josefina Zoraida Vázquez and Lorenzo Meyer, *The United States and Mexico* (Chicago: University of Chicago Press, 1985), chap. 3.

2. The striking improvement in Mexican-U.S. relations during that period is discussed in Laurence Whitehead, "Mexico and the 'Hegemony' of the United States: Past, Present and Future" in *Mexico's External Relations in the 1990s*, ed. Riordan Roett (Boulder, Colo.: Lynne Rienner Publishers, 1991), 243–62; the term "distant neighbors" is taken from Alan Riding, *Distant Neighbors* (New York: Vintage, 1984).

3. John Coatsworth, "The Decline of the Mexican Economy, 1800–1860," paper for the Symposium on the Formation of Latin American National Economies, Berlin, 1983, 7 and 9.

4. Quoted in Zoraida Vázquez and Meyer, *United States and Mexico*, 21.

5. Ibid., 49. That claim is probably overstated, but reflects an ongoing feeling of bitterness.

6. W. Dirk Raat, *Mexico and the United States: Ambivalent Vistas* (Athens: University of Georgia Press, 1992), 75; Jan Bazant, *A Concise History of Mexico* (New York: Cambridge University Press, 1977), 58–61.

7. Zoraida Vázquez and Meyer, *United States and Mexico*, 84 and 91.

8. Ibid., 92; Luis Nicolau d'Olwer, "Las inversiones extranjeras," in *Historia moderna de México—El Porfiriato: La vida política exterior*, ed. Daniel Cosío Villegas (México: Hermes, 1963).

9. Frank Brandenburg, *The Making of Modern Mexico* (Englewood Cliffs, N.J.: Prentice Hall, 1964), 40.

10. Zoraida Vázquez and Meyer, *United States and Mexico*, 101–2.

11. Berta Ulloa, *La revolución intervenida: relaciones diplomáticas entre México y Estados Unidos, 1910–1940* (México: El Colegio de México, 1976).

12. John Womack, Jr., "The Mexican Revolution, 1910–1920," in *Mexico since Independence*, ed. Leslie Bethell (New York: Cambridge University Press, 1991), 140–41. Huerta was more conservative than Madero, but American oil companies disliked him because they felt he was too sympathetic to competing British firms.

13. Alan Knight, *U.S.-Mexican Relations, 1910–1940* (La Jolla: University of California–San Diego Center for U.S.-Mexican Studies, 1987), 91–95.

14. Womack, "Mexican Revolution," 135. Alan Knight, *U.S.-Mexican Relations*, argues that relations between the two countries were actually not that antagonistic (chap. 9).

15. Zoraida Vázquez and Meyer, *United States and Mexico*, 125.

16. Lester D. Langley, *Mexico and the United States: The Fragile Relationship* (Boston: Twayne Publishers, 1991), 16.

17. George Grayson, *The United States and Mexico: Patterns of Influence* (New York: Praeger Publishers, 1984), 23.

18. Ibid., 24.

19. Zoraida Vázquez and Meyer, *United States and Mexico,* 146–47.

20. Alan Knight, "The Rise and Fall of Cardenismo," in *Mexico since Independence,* 286.

21. Peter Smith, "Mexico since 1946," in *Mexico since Independence,* 342.

22. Raat, *Mexico and the United States,* 158.

23. Samuel Schmidt, *The Deterioration of the Mexican Presidency: The Years of Luis Echeverría* (Tucson: University of Arizona Press, 1991).

24. George Grayson, *Oil and Mexican Foreign Policy* (Pittsburgh: University of Pittsburgh Press, 1988), 140–54. By 1983, however, relations between the two countries had soured, and Mexico held up oil deliveries.

25. Smith, "Mexico since 1946," 379.

26. H. Rodrigo Jauberth et al., *The Difficult Triangle: Mexico, Central America and the United States* (Boulder, Colo.: Westview Press and PACCA, 1992).

27. Barry Bosworth, Robert Lawrence, and Nora Lustig, Introduction, in *North American Free Trade,* ed. Lustig, Bosworth, and Lawrence (Washington, D.C.: Brookings Institution, 1992), 4–5.

28. Jack Finlayson and Mark Zacher, "The GATT and the Regulation of Trade Barriers: Regime Dynamics and Functions," *International Organization* (Autumn 1981): 561–602.

29. United States Trade Representative, *1995 Trade Policy Agenda and 1994 Annual Report* (Washington, D.C., 1995), 35.

30. Juan José Morena Sada, "Mexican Trade Policy and the North American Free Trade Agreement," in *North America without Borders?* ed. Stephen J. Randall (Calgary, Alberta: University of Calgary Press, 1992), 105.

31. Robert Pastor, *Integration with Mexico* (New York: Twentieth Century Fund Press, 1993), 14–15.

32. Gabriel Székely, "Forging a North American Economy: Issues for Mexico in the 1990s," in *Mexico's External Relations,* 217.

33. Sally Shelton-Colby, "Mexico and the United States: A New Convergence of Interests," in *Mexico's External Relations,* 235.

34. Pastor, *Integration with Mexico,* 20.

35. Cuauhtémoc Cárdenas, "TLC: Una propuesta alternativa," *Nexos* (June 1991); Denise Dresser, "Mr. Salinas Goes to Washington: Mexican Lobbying in the United States," conference paper no. 62, Columbia University–New York University Center for Latin American and Caribbean Studies, 1991, 19.

36. Adolfo Aguilar Zinser, "Authoritarianism and North American Free Trade: The Debate in Mexico," in *The Political Economy of North American Free Trade,* ed. Ricardo Grinspun and Maxwell A. Cameron (New York: St. Martin's Press, 1993), 205–16.

37. Judith Adler Hellman, "Mexican Perspectives on Free Trade: Support and Opposition to NAFTA," in *Political Economy of North American Free Trade,* 195.

38. *New York Times,* 23 November 1993.

39. See Pastor, *Integration with Mexico,* 42–51, for a clear, nontechnical discussion of NAFTA's general terms and impact.

40. International Economic Review, *Chartbook: Composition of U.S. Merchandise Trade, 1994* (Washington, D.C.: U.S. International Trade Commission), 33, and 1995 edition, 33.

41. The *Journal of Environment and Development* devoted its Winter 1993 issue (vol. 2, no. 1) to various articles on NAFTA and the environment.

42. Gabriel Székely, "Forging a North American Economy: Issues for Mexico in the 1990s," in *Mexico's External Relations,* 217.

43. Shelton-Colby, "Mexico and the United States: A New Convergence of Interests," 235.

44. Sidney Weintraub, "U.S.-Mexico Free Trade: Implications for the United States," in *As-*

sessments of the North American Free Trade Agreement, ed. Ambler H. Moss, Jr. (Miami, Fla.: University of Miami, North-South Center, 1993), 87–105.

45. Data cited in Pastor, *Integration with Mexico,* 11.

46. David S. North, "The Migration Issue in U.S.-Mexican Relations," in *United States Relations with Mexico,* ed. Richard D. Erb and Stanley R. Ross (Washington, D.C.: American Enterprise Institute, 1981), 126; *New York Times,* 4 June 1994.

47. Wayne Cornelius, "Mexican Migration to the United States: An Introduction," in *Mexican Migration to the United States,* ed. Wayne A. Cornelius and Jorge A. Bustamante (La Jolla: University of California–San Diego Center for U.S.-Mexican Studies, 1989).

48. Manuel García y Griego and James W. Wilkie, "Mexican Migration to the United States and the Possibilities of Bilateral Cooperation," in *Mexico and the United States,* ed. Daniel G. Aldrich, Jr., and Lorenzo Meyer (San Bernardino, Calif.: Borgo Press, 1993), 84.

49. Jorge A. Bustamante, "U.S. Immigration Reforms: A Mexican Perspective," in *Mexico in Transition,* ed. Susan Kaufman Purcell (New York: Council on Foreign Relations, 1988), 70.

50. Cornelius, "Mexican Migration to the United States," 5.

51. Ibid., 3.

52. Ibid., 4.

53. U.S. Council of Economic Advisors, *Economic Report to the President* (Washington, D.C., 1986), 233; Thomas Muller and Thomas J. Espenshade, *The Fourth Wave: California's Newest Immigrants* (Washington, D.C.: Urban Institute Press, 1985).

54. Rodolfo O. de la Garza et al., *Latino Voices* (Boulder, Colo.: Westview Press, 1992); *New York Times,* 15 December 1992.

55. Kitty Calavita, "The Immigration Policy Debate," in *Mexican Migration,* 163. For slightly different data, see Diego Ascencio, "Long Range Perspectives on the Immigration Reform and Control Act," in *Mexico and the United States: Leadership Transition and the Unfinished Agenda,* ed. M. Delal Baer (Washington, D.C.: Center for Strategic and International Studies, 1988), 35–36; Jorge Castañeda, "The Fear of Americanization," in *Limits to Friendship,* ed. Robert Pastor and Jorge Castañeda (New York: Alfred A. Knopf, 1988), 318.

56. Jorge A. Bustamante, "Measuring the Flow of Undocumented Immigrants," in *Mexican Migration.* The study used both interview surveys and photographic surveillance.

57. Jorge Castañeda, "The Border: A Mexican View," in *Limits to Friendship,* 309.

58. Pastor, *Integration with Mexico,* 11.

59. Wayne A. Cornelius, "The U.S. Demand for Mexican Labor," in *Mexican Migration,* 25–47; Michael Piore, "The New Immigration," *New Republic,* 22 February 1975.

60. *New York Times,* 20 April 1990; Ellen Lutz, "State Sponsored Abductions: The Human Rights Implications," *World Policy Journal* 9, no. 4 (Fall 1992).

61. *New York Times,* 16 June 1992; 21 June 1992; 14 December 1992; 16 December 1992; *Washington Post,* 16 December 1992; 17 December 1992).

62. Peter Reuter and David Ronfelt, *Quest for Integrity: The Mexican-U.S. Drug Issue in the 1980s* (Santa Monica, Calif.: RAND, 1992), v and 3; Langley, *Mexico and the United States,* 99; Francis A. Keating, "A U.S. Executive Branch View of U.S.-Mexican Narcotics Policy," in *Mexico and the United States: Leadership Transition and the Unfinished Agenda,* 26–33. Much of the discussion that follows is drawn from Reuter and Ronfelt.

63. Reuter and Ronfelt, *Quest for Integrity,* v; see also Miguel Ruiz-Cabañas I., "Mexico's Permanent Campaign," in *Drug Policy in the Americas,* ed. Peter H. Smith (Boulder, Colo.: Westview Press, 1992).

64. María Celia Toro, "Drug Trafficking from a National Security Perspective," in *Mexico: In Search of Security,* ed. Bruce Michael Bagley and Sergio Aguayo Quezada (New Brunswick, N.J.: Transaction Publishers, 1993), 320.

65. Ruiz-Cabañas I., "Mexico's Permanent Campaign," 160.

66. Toro, "Drug Trafficking from a National Security Perspective," 324–25 and 329.

67. Reuter and Ronfelt, *Quest for Integrity,* 9.

68. Carlos Ramírez, "El caso Camarena y las relaciones bilaterales," *La Opinión,* 25 May 1990, 5.

69. Laurence Whitehead, "Mexico and the 'Hegemony' of the United States," in *Mexico's External Relations*, 253–54; Robert Pastor, *Condemned to Repetition: The United States and Nicaragua* (Princeton, N.J.: Princeton University Press, 1987).

70. Cheryl L. Eschbach, "Mexico's Relations with Central America: Changing Priorities, Persisting Interest," in *Mexico's External Relations*, 183.

71. Jesús Hernández, "Mexican and U.S. Policy toward Central America," in *Difficult Triangle*, 33 and 48 n. 62.

72. Roberta Lajous, "Mexico's European Policy Agenda: Perspectives on the Past, Proposals for the Future," in *Mexico's External Relations*, 77–78.

73. Riordan Roett, "Mexico's Strategic Alternatives in the Changing World System: Four Options, Four Ironies," in *Mexico's External Relations*, 13.

74. Bruce Babbit, "Reviving Mexico," *World Monitor* 2 (March 1989): 32–34, 36–41.

75. Gabriel Székely and Donald Wyman, "Japón: Relaciones con México y Estados Unidos," in *México-Estados Unidos, 1985*, ed. Gabriel Székely (México: El Colegio de México, 1986), 205–6.

76. Roett, "Mexico's Strategic Alternatives," 9.

77. "The Magnet of Growth in Mexico's North," *Business Week*, 23 November 1989, 63–67.

8

Prospects for the Future

Political scientists note that there is a correlation between socioeconomic and political development.[1] Increased education, higher literacy rates, urbanization, industrialization, rising income levels, and the growth of the middle and working classes often are associated with the emergence of modern political parties, more effective government bureaucracies, a better-informed citizenry, and other manifestations of political modernization.

Over the years, however, there has been considerable debate regarding the precise relationship between modernization and democracy. Guillermo O'Donnell, in his influential theory of bureaucratic authoritarianism, argued that, unlike Western Europe, Latin America's most industrialized and economically advanced nations were particularly likely to develop highly repressive, authoritarian regimes as the interests of workers and industrialists clashed.[2] O'Donnell pointed to the rise of bureaucratic-authoritarian (BA) regimes during the 1960s and 1970s in four of Latin America's most economically developed countries: Argentina, Brazil, Chile, and Uruguay. Their experiences seemed to challenge the widely held assumption that economic and social modernization strengthened the forces of democracy.

But subsequently each of those countries has restored democracy, suggesting that their authoritarian regimes may have been a transitional interlude. If we also look at political systems beyond Latin America, we find that countries with higher social and economic indicators are more likely to have democratic governments.[3]

We will define a democratic government here as one that has the following components: fair and competitive elections for important political posts; universal or near-universal suffrage; a real possibility of alternating power between political parties or party coalitions; government officials that are accountable to the public; freedom of expression especially in the mass media; and protection of minority rights.[4]

To be sure, there are established democracies like Japan and Sweden where one political party has controlled the government almost permanently for decades, much like the PRI. However, the dominant party in those countries has stood ready to relinquish power to the opposition, precisely as the Swedish Socialists and Japanese Liberal Democrats recently did for a period of time. Only now is that becoming a conceivable scenario in Mexico.

Of course socioeconomic development is no guarantee of democracy, nor is it an absolute prerequisite. In fact, there are some notable exceptions to the pattern. For example, India, an extremely poor country which did not reach 50 percent literacy until the 1990s, has been governed democratically for most of its half-century of independence. Conversely, Singapore, one of the Third World's most affluent nations with a literacy rate of approximately 90 percent, is ruled by a fairly authoritarian regime. But such exceptions aside, it remains true that as countries become more urban, more educated, more literate, and more affluent, their chances of establishing and maintaining democratic government improve.[5]

Mitchell Seligson has observed that "there appears to be a lower threshold of economic and sociocultural development beneath which stable democratic rule is unlikely to emerge."[6] He notes that the two key thresholds seem to be an annual per capita income of at least $250 in 1957 dollars (roughly $1,500 in current dollars) and a 50 percent literacy rate. Few countries below those two levels have established stable democracies, while nations above them are fairly likely to be democratic.

MEXICO: MODERNIZATION WITHOUT DEMOCRACY

As we have seen, from the 1940s through the early 1980s Mexico had an enviable record of industrialization and economic growth. With that growth came rising literacy rates (surpassing 90 percent by the 1990s), increased urbanization, and the expansion of the middle and working classes. Thus, Mexico has become an "upper-middle-class" nation with one of the Third World's higher levels of modernization. Its Human Development Index (a composite measure of real GDP per capita, life expectancy, literacy, and education) ranks fifty-second among the world's 173 nations and seventeenth of 127 developing countries. A real GDP per capita of some $6,000 places Mexico fifteenth in the Third World. Moreover, all but three of the developing countries that are wealthier are in some way atypical—either small, petroleum-producing nations (such as Kuwait, Bahrain, and the United Arab Emirates) or tiny island countries (including Trinidad-Tobago, Singapore, and Cyprus).[7]

But while Mexico surpassed both socioeconomic thresholds for achieving democracy many years ago (having achieved 50 percent literacy shortly after World War II), it still does not meet several important criteria for democratic government, most notably fair elections and a real possibility of alternating political power. That does not mean that economic development has left the political system unaffected. To the contrary, we will see that modernization has moved the country toward a more competitive political party system. However, it has not yet democratized the country or diminished the pervasive corruption that corrodes the political order.

THE STRUGGLE FOR ECONOMIC JUSTICE

The Zapatista rebellion in Chiapas refocused attention on Mexico's political and economic deficiencies. Until recently Chiapas has suffered from some of the country's most authoritarian political practices: overwhelming PRI domination, extensive corruption, far-reaching voting fraud, and serious human rights violations. Chiapas's severe poverty also highlights major contradictions in the nation's economy. While Mexico's per capita income is among the highest in the Third World, much of its rural population remains impoverished, particularly in poorer states such as Chiapas, Oaxaca, Guerrero, and Hidalgo.

A recent study by the United Nations and the Mexican government determined that one-sixth of the country's population, some 13.6 million people, are mired in "extreme poverty."[8] The rural sector, with only 20 percent of the nation's population, encompasses about two-thirds of the very poor. Although the study found that the proportion of Mexicans living in extreme poverty had dropped somewhat in the 1970s and 1980s (a finding that many social scientists dispute), poverty had still grown in rural areas. Many experts believe that the government's current efforts to privatize *ejido* land will further impoverish the countryside. Jonathan Fox, an authority on rural Mexico, recently warned that

> while national economic growth is likely to have significant spillover effects within urban areas, reaching at least some of those near the poverty line, there is no reason at all to assume that [general] economic growth will reduce extreme poverty in rural areas [unless there is a targeted government antipoverty program].[9]

Throughout Mexico, as we have noted, income and wealth remain very unequally distributed, with the poorest half of the population earning less than one-fifth (18.4 percent) of the national income. Income is more highly concentrated in Mexico than in a number of considerably poorer countries such as Pakistan, India, Indonesia, and Peru. Indeed Mexico has the ninth most concentrated income pattern among the twenty-nine developing countries for which the United Nations has data.[10]

MEXICO'S POLITICAL AND ECONOMIC ROLLER COASTER

Following decades of political and economic stability, Mexico has experienced a series of dramatic changes of course since the late 1960s. Apparent progress toward a more competitive electoral system one year has seemingly come to a halt in the following election and then resumed a few years later. Periods of rapid economic growth have been followed by sharp downswings that have reduced or wiped out prior gains. Political leaders have sometimes achieved great popularity only to be later discredited. These constant changes in direction make it difficult to predict the nation's future.

After more than thirty years of healthy economic growth, Mexico experienced a serious financial crisis and recession in the mid-1970s brought on by President Echeverría's overly ambitious economic policies and his estrangement of the private sector. Toward the end of the decade, however, the discovery of huge petroleum reserves once again fueled rapid economic growth. Overestimating the country's new oil wealth, the López Portillo administration borrowed and spent excessively. By 1982, Mexico's inability to pay its external debt ushered in Latin America's worst economic crisis since the Great Depression.

At the start of the 1990s, Carlos Salinas seemed to have resolved the debt crisis, brought inflation under control, and begun a modest economic recovery. But like several of his predecessors, Salinas undercut his economic accomplishments with questionable policy decisions at the end of his term. Just as López Portillo had overestimated the government's future petroleum income, Salinas underestimated the seriousness of the country's large balance-of-payments deficits. He refused to devalue the peso lest it damage his reputation and the PRI's election chances. Soon after Ernesto Zedillo took office the value of the national currency plunged, foreign capital fled, the stock market took a nosedive, and Mexico once again fell victim to a deep recession.

Political change has been equally unpredictable. The 1968 Tlatelolco massacre seriously undermined the government's legitimacy. At the same time, rank-and-file insurgencies against labor union bosses threatened an important pillar of PRI/state control. President Echeverría's populist policies initially gained new support for the government from students and workers. However, his mismanagement of the economy and his heavy-handed political tactics eventually undermined his popularity. Under his successor, José López Portillo, political reform and the petroleum boom temporarily increased the government's legitimacy, but the painful economic decline in the 1980s produced the most serious challenge yet to PRI domination.

Cuauhtémoc Cárdenas's surprisingly strong performance in the 1988 presidential election raised hopes that Mexico might finally be moving toward a competitive party system. Once Carlos Salinas took office, however, his strong leadership and popular programs restored support for the government. At the same time the Cardenistas proved to be divided and poorly organized. Only three years after Salinas's tainted presidential victory, the PRI won the 1991 congressional elections convincingly.

By the last year of Salinas's term, the political pendulum had swung back yet again. The Zapatista uprising and the unsolved assassination of Luis Donaldo Colosio renewed popular doubts about the government and contributed to a strong PAN showing in the 1994 presidential election. Since then, the Zedillo administration has been undermined by the latest economic crisis and by revelations of corruption in the Salinas family. These factors undoubtedly contributed to several impressive PAN victories in the 1995 state elections.

Carlos Salinas's personal rise and fall also demonstrate the uncertain course of contemporary Mexican politics. He was elected president with the lowest percentage of the vote ever received by a PRI candidate. A seemingly colorless technocrat, Salinas took office with little credibility. Yet his impressive presidential performance made him the most popular and admired of recent Mexican chief executives.

Only months after finishing his term, however, Salinas fell into total disgrace. Most Mexicans quite appropriately have blamed him for the economic crisis that followed his administration. Indeed when a respected citizens' group held an unofficial national referendum, 97 percent of the 612,000 participants endorsed the suggestion that Salinas should be "put on trial" for ruining the country's economy.[11] Worse yet, investigating authorities charged his brother, Raúl, with ordering the assassination of PRI secretary general José Francisco Ruiz Massieu. When Carlos Salinas violated protocol by publicly criticizing President Zedillo, he was told to leave the country.

Subsequently he disappeared into seclusion, reportedly somewhere in Canada and then in Cuba. Eventually he turned up in Ireland. Further evidence of extensive corruption in his administration surfaced when Swiss police arrested Raúl Salinas's wife after she tried to withdraw $84 million from a secret bank account in that country. That money, possibly linked to the drug trade, may be part of $100 million or more that Raúl is believed to have accumulated during his brother's administration. Most Mexicans believe, with good reason, that corruption on that scale could not have existed without the president's knowledge.

PROSPECTS FOR THE FUTURE

Securing Competitive Elections.   These repeated reversals of fortune obscure the short-term course of Mexican politics. But beyond these changes several important trends can be discerned that are likely to continue into the future. The PRI's electoral dominance is clearly less pronounced than it once was. Over the past thirty years, its share of the vote in national elections has declined at an average annual rate of 1 percent. In state races PRI support has dropped by a yearly average of 1.5 percent over the past twenty years. About half of those votes have gone to the PAN, with various other parties dividing the rest.

Between 1958 and 1970, the PRI presidential candidate's share of the valid vote varied from 84.13 percent to 90.43 percent. In the three most recent elections, however, that portion has ranged from only 50.74 percent to 71.0 percent.[12] Similarly, the PRI's vote ranged from 69.3 percent to 85.2 percent in the three Chamber of Deputies elections held between 1976 and 1982. But in the three most recent elections, its share was only between 50.3 percent and 61.4 percent (table 4-2). And while it had been impossible for an opposition party candidate to win a single gubernatorial race until the late 1980s, the PAN won three statehouses in 1995 alone. President Zedillo has been far more willing than any of his predecessors to accept opposition victories of that magnitude.

Analysis of the vote at the level of electoral districts indicates how socioeconomic modernization has contributed to a more competitive electoral system. Since the 1960s, opposition parties have performed better in districts that are more urban, more industrialized, and more highly educated. Conversely, the PRI draws its strongest vote in poor, uneducated, and rural areas.[13] Thus, as Mexico's population becomes more educated and urban, and as the middle class swells, support for opposition parties will likely grow, enhancing the possibility that one of them will eventually wrest power from the PRI.

Urbanization and higher educational levels have also enhanced civil society. That is to say that Mexico has developed a more extensive and coherent network of politically active organizations—ranging from labor unions to human rights groups—that are independent of state and PRI control. The government's poor response to the massive Mexico City earthquake of 1985 (and public disgust over revelations that deficient building construction had been passed over by corrupt government inspectors) unleashed a wave of self-help organizations, many of which later developed into enduring political groups.

In the years that followed, the nation's capital and other Mexican cities saw a blossoming of new "social movements"—politically active, grassroots organizations independent of the government, the PRI, and even opposition political parties.[14] Many of them have effectively represented formerly excluded or underrepresented segments of the population such as women and the urban poor. They have filled some of the open political space as the PRI's corporatist structures can no longer maintain their iron grip on society. Officially-sanctioned labor unions and peasant associations have exerted diminishing control over their members, while at the same time a number of independent unions and peasant groups have emerged (chapter 5).

Finally, civic organizations, largely representing middle-class constituencies, have developed an important political presence. One of the most respected and influential of these is the Civic Alliance. In recent elections it has produced thousands of independent poll observers and contributed greatly to securing honest election tallies. Other public monitoring groups have pressured the government on issues such as human rights and the environment. Thus, Mexico's more educated and better-informed population is less willing to accept government malfeasance today than prior generations were. There has been a growing outcry against government corruption, the growing influence of drug lords on the political process, and the reemergence of political assassinations.

While socioeconomic development has been an important long-term force for democratization, the country's severe economic decline in the 1980s was also an immediate catalyst for change. The electoral success and the base of political support for the PRI/government had been closely linked to the state's ability to dispense patronage and economic subsidies. The regime had subsidized basic foods, medical care, gasoline, energy, housing, and other items for consumers and businesses alike, while also distributing jobs through the state bureaucracy and parastatals. After 1982, however, the country's economic crisis and the neoliberal reforms undertaken to restore its economic health deprived the PRI machine of the benefits it needed to dispense in order to maintain the corporatist system.

If the anticipated 1996 electoral reform law (or any additional reform) succeeds in reducing media bias and diminishing the PRI's enormous financial advantage in campaigns, then Mexico will have finally achieved reasonably fair and competitive national elections. Indeed, experts on Mexican politics now generally believe that the day may not be far off when the PRI is beaten in a presidential election.[15]

Achieving a Democratic Society.   Merely achieving open and competitive presidential elections, though a major accomplishment in and of itself, will not be sufficient to transform Mexico into a fully democratic society. More extensive reform of government and social institutions will be needed.

For one thing, the Mexican government has long been overly centralized: the national government has excessive control over state and local government; within the national government itself, power is highly concentrated in the president's hands. During the past three administrations there have been a number of legislative and administrative efforts to decentralize public administration and policy making.[16] While some progress has been made, there is still far to go.

President Zedillo has been especially committed to reducing "presidentialism." More than any other modern president he has opened a dialogue with congressional leaders and tried to raise the profile and status of the nation's legislature. He not only has consulted on policy with the PAN leadership, as had Salinas, but has conferred with PRD leader Porfirio Muñoz Ledo as well. In an unprecedented move, Zedillo appointed someone from outside the PRI to the post of attorney general. He gave Antonio Lozano, a respected PAN lawyer, the politically sensitive task of investigating government corruption and continuing the probe of the Colosio and Ruiz Massieu assassinations.

Perhaps most important, Zedillo has begun to reduce presidential control over the PRI and thereby separate the official party from the Mexican state, much as Mikhail Gorbachev separated the Soviet state and the Communist Party. Whereas previous presidents personally selected, or at least approved, all of the official party's gubernatorial nominees, Zedillo has allowed the PRI's state organizations to select those candidates. And he has pledged to have the party organization name the next PRI presidential candidate as called for in the party's 1990 reforms. If Zedillo fulfills his pledge he will bring to an end Mexico's long-established practice of incumbent presidents naming the next official party presidential candidate.

The PRI itself is badly in need of democratization. Since the mid-1960s there have been several attempts at party reform to make it more responsive to its own members and to involve the party's rank and file in the selection of party candidates.[17] To date, however, these efforts have not been very successful. Presidents de la Madrid, Salinas, and Zedillo have promoted to the upper echelons of the party many technocrats and intellectuals who are committed to modernizing and liberalizing Mexican politics. But at the state and local level, *caciques* (political strongmen or bosses) remain equally committed to corrupt and undemocratic politics as usual.

Several attempts to hold state party primaries were not very successful, as hard-line political bosses terminated them or manipulated the vote. In the mid-1980s the party rejected demands for internal democratization by the Democratic Current led by Cuauhtémoc Cárdenas and Porfirio Muñoz Ledo. In response to Cárdenas's electoral scare in the 1988 national elections, however, the PRI's 1990 convention adopted reforms that are designed to eventually transfer the selection of PRI candidates from the president and party leaders to conventions or party primaries. But the provisions have major loopholes, and so far the new selection methods have been introduced in only a small number of areas. Even in those cases, the conventions and primaries have been controlled by local *caciques*.[18]

Ernesto Zedillo's efforts to rein in presidential power and strengthen the other branches of government are long overdue. Similarly, decentralizing Mexico's overly centralized political system is a necessary component of democratization. Unfortunately, however desirable these long-term objectives may be, changes currently under way may have undesirable short-term consequences. The immediate effect of decentralization is to shift power from the president to political bosses at the state and local level who are far less responsive to the electorate than he is and who continue to manipulate the electoral process. Ultimately, then, real democratization will require changes in state and local politics that parallel national-level reforms.

Moreover, the challenge of democratization extends beyond the political arena. Mexican culture and social institutions themselves have authoritarian aspects that must be addressed if a stable democracy is to develop.* Juan Molinar, a leading authority on Mexican politics, has suggested that many of his countrymen are fearful of democracy.[19] In part, that anxiety has a historical basis. The nation's two most democratically elected administrations until Zedillo—Juárez's and Madero's—were identified with civil war or revolution. "Anarchy is particularly frightening to many Mexicans, perhaps because of the nation's history, and many have felt they could little afford democracy."[20] As we have noted, the PRI has played on that fear in the past by suggesting that an opposition party victory would lead to either anarchy or extremist dictatorship.[21] Thus, a substantial number of those who voted for the PRI in the past two presidential elections did so because they were fearful of change and hes-

---

* It is risky to generalize about a nation's political culture. In fact, scholars have reached very different conclusions about Mexico's. There appear to be both authoritarian and democratic subcultures in Mexican society, with individual attitudes varying according to educational level and degree of political experience.

itant to give the opposition a chance to govern. As the violence of the Revolution and its aftermath has receded further into the past, however, and as the public's political sophistication has increased, that kind of negative appeal has become less effective.

Another problem lies in the political socialization process. Until recently, Mexico's schools often have failed to instill democratic values in their charges. Even today schoolchildren in poor neighborhoods and villages frequently are taught deferential political attitudes.[22] But like so much of Mexican culture, these attitudes are changing. For example, contemporary survey research suggests that most urban Mexicans, particularly those who are more educated and middle class, support democratic values.[23] Furthermore, we may expect democratic norms to spread as the nation's educational level rises.

A number of politically important institutions will also need to change. Mexico's trade unions are among the nation's most authoritarian organizations. Even if the country were to develop a democratic political system, its labor unions would not necessarily be affected. There is considerable evidence from both industrial democracies and developing nations that unions help shape their rank and file's political attitudes and behavior. Hence, democratizing the country's unions would likely increase working-class political participation and raise support for democratic political institutions. In the nation's *ejidos* and other peasant communities, the problem of boss control is even more severe, and authoritarian or deferential values are more deeply rooted. Democratizing urban labor unions and village government in the countryside will require considerable grassroots mobilization. It will also require government and PRI officials to withdraw their support for union and village *caciques*.

During the remaining years of this century Mexico's leaders must discover how to restore sustained economic growth without excessive inflation or foreign indebtedness. At the same time, the nation's political stability will depend on its ability to achieve greater democracy and social justice. These challenges are tremendous. More than most Third World nations Mexico has the trained personnel and skilled political leadership to confront the task. But they will need to overcome the entrenched forces of conservatism that still exercise considerable power in the PRI and the state bureaucracy.

Notes

1. For discussion of modernization theory, see Myron Weiner and Samuel Huntington, eds., *Understanding Political Development* (Boston: Little Brown, 1987); Howard J. Wiarda, ed., *New Directions in Comparative Politics* (Boulder, Colo.: Westview Press, 1985).

2. David Collier, ed., *The New Authoritarianism in Latin America* (Princeton, N.J.: Princeton University Press, 1979).

3. Dietrich Rueschemeyer, Evelyne Huber Stephens, and John Stephens, *Capitalist Development and Democracy* (Chicago: University of Chicago Press, 1992), reviews the research on this issue. It should be noted, however, that among Latin American nations alone the correlation between socioeconomic development and democracy has not been as strong.

4. This definition draws upon Robert Dahl, *Polyarchy* (New Haven, Conn.: Yale University Press, 1971), and Scott Mainwaring, "Transitions to Democracy and Democratic Consolidation," in *Issues in Democratic Consolidation,* ed. Mainwaring, Guillermo O'Donnell, and J. Samuel Valenzuela (Notre Dame, Ind.: Notre Dame University Press, 1992), 296–98. See also Philippe C. Schmitter and Terry Lynn Karl, "What Democracy Is. . .and Is Not," in *The Global Resurgence of Democracy,* ed. Larry Diamond and Marc F. Plattner (Baltimore: Johns Hopkins University Press, 1993), 39–60.

5. Axel Hadenius, *Democracy and Development* (Cambridge: Cambridge University Press, 1992), found that democracy was especially strongly linked to literacy levels.

6. Mitchell A. Seligson, "Democratization in Latin America: The Current Cycle," in *Authoritarians and Democrats,* ed. James M. Malloy and Mitchell A. Seligson (Pittsburgh: University of Pittsburgh Press, 1987), 7.

7. United Nations Development Programme (UNDP), *Human Development Report, 1994* (New York: Oxford University Press, 1994), 130–33, 164–65 (tables 1, 2, and 18).

8. Cited in Wayne A. Cornelius, "Designing Social Policy for Mexico's Liberalized Economy," in *The Challenge of Institutional Reform in Mexico,* ed. Riordan Roett (Boulder, Colo.: Lynne Rienner Publishers, 1995), 142.

9. Correspondence by Jonathan Fox cited in ibid., 143.

10. UNDP, *Human Development Report, 1993* (New York: Oxford University Press, 1993), 170–71. I calculated these rankings based on each nation's Gini coefficient (a measure of distribution inequality).

11. *Washington Post,* 28 February 1995.

12. See table 4-1 (chapter 4) of this text. The 1976 election was atypical in that a PAN boycott left López Portillo with no real opposition and over 92 percent of the vote.

13. Joseph L. Klesner, "Realignment or Dealignment?" in *The Politics of Economic Restructuring: State-Society Relations and Regime Change in Mexico,* ed. Maria Lorena Cook, Kevin J. Middlebrook, and Juan Molinar Horcasitas (La Jolla: University of California–San Diego Center for U.S.-Mexican Studies, 1994), 169–72.

14. Joe Foweraker, *Popular Mobilization in the Mexican Teachers Movement, 1977–87* (New York: Cambridge University Press, 1993); Arturo Escobar and Sonia E. Alvarez, eds., *The Making of Social Movements in Latin America: Identity, Strategy and Democracy* (Boulder, Colo.: Westview Press, 1992).

15. See, for example, Sergio Aguayo Quezada, "The Inevitability of Democracy in Mexico," in *Political and Economic Liberalization in Mexico,* ed. Riordan Roett (Boulder, Colo.: Lynne Rienner Publishers, 1993), 117–26.

16. Miguel de la Madrid et al., *La descentralización de los servicios de salud: el caso de México* (México: Porrúa, 1986), deals with the decentralization of health services.

17. On earlier party reform efforts, see John J. Bailey, *Governing Mexico* (New York: St. Martin's Press, 1988), 106–20.

18. Ann L. Craig and Wayne A. Cornelius, "Houses Divided: Parties and Political Reform in Mexico," in *Building Democratic Institutions: Party Systems in Latin America,* ed. Scott Mainwaring and Timothy R. Scully (Stanford, Calif.: Stanford University Press, 1995), 283.

19. Juan Molinar, presentation at the XVIII International Congress of the Latin American Studies Association, Atlanta, March 1994. For a discussion of the conflicting research on Mexican political culture, see Daniel C. Levy and Kathleen Bruhn, "Mexico: Sustained Civilian Rule without Democracy," in *Politics in Developing Countries: Comparing Experiences with Democracy,* ed. Larry Diamond, Juan J. Linz, and Seymour Martin Lipset (Boulder, Colo.: Lynne Rienner Publishers, 1995), 196–98.

20. Levy and Bruhn, "Mexico: Sustained Civilian Rule without Democracy," 209.

21. Carlos Monsiváis, "La ofensiva ideológica de la derecha," in *México, hoy,* ed. Pablo González Casanova and Enrique Florescano, 5th ed. (México: Siglo XXI, 1981), 315.

22. Rafael Segovia, *La politicización del niño mexicano,* 2d ed. (México: El Colegio de México, 1982).

23. John Booth and Mitchell Seligson, "The Political Culture of Authoritarianism in Mexico: A Reexamination," *Latin American Research Review* 19, no. 1 (1984): 110–13.

Acronyms

AMIS Mexican Association of Insurance Institutions
BANRURAL Rural Bank
CANACINTRA National Chamber of Manufacturers
CAP Permanent Agrarian Congress
CCE Entrepreneurial Coordinating Council
CEN National Executive Council (of the PRI)
CMHN Mexican Council of Businessmen
CNC National Peasant Confederation
CNDH National Commission for Human Rights
CNOP National Confederation of Popular Organizations (a wing of the PRI)
CNPC National Confederation of Chambers of Small Commerce
CNPP National Confederation of Small Property Owners
CONASUPO National Commission of Popular Subsistence
CONCAMIN National Confederation of Chambers of Industry
CONCANACO Confederation of National Chambers of Commerce
COPARMEX Mexican Employers' Confederation
CROC Revolutionary Confederation of Workers and Peasants
CROM Regional Confederation of Mexican Workers
CT Congress of Labor
CTM Confederation of Mexican Workers
EZLN Zapatista Army of National Liberation
FDN National Democratic Front
FSTSE Confederation of Government Workers Unions at the Service of the State
GATT General Agreement on Tariffs and Trade
IFE Federal Electoral Institute
INI National Indigenous Institute
IRCA Immigration Reform and Control Act
ISI Import-substituting industrialization
MSR Revolutionary Union Movement
NAFTA North American Free Trade Agreement

NIC   Newly Industrializing Country
PAN   National Action Party
PARM   Authentic Party of the Mexican Revolution
PECE   Pact for Stability and Economic Growth
PEMEX   Petróleos Mexicanos
PFCRN   Party of the Cardenista Front for National Reconstruction
PMS   Mexican Socialist Party
PNR   National Revolutionary Party
PPS   Popular Socialist Party
PRD   Party of the Democratic Revolution
PRI   Institutional Revolutionary Party
PRM   Party of the Mexican Revolution
PRONASOL   National Solidarity Program
PRT   Revolutionary Workers Party
PST   Socialist Workers Party
PT   Labor Party
STFRM   Union of Railroad Workers of the Republic of Mexico
STRPRM   Union of Revolutionary Petroleum Workers of the Mexican
   Republic
UNAM   National Autonomous University
UNORCA   National Union of Autonomous Regional Peasant
   Organizations

Bibliography

Aguilar Camin, Hector, and Lorenzo Meyer. *In the Shadow of the Mexican Revolution*. Austin: University of Texas Press, 1993.

Aguilar Mora, Manuel, and Mauricio Schoijet, eds. *La revolución Mexicana contra el PRI*. México: Fontmara, 1991.

Alcocer, Jorge, and Rolando Cordero, eds. *México: presente y futuro*. México: Ediciones de Cultura Popular, 1988.

Aldrich, Daniel G., Jr., and Lorenzo Meyer, eds. *Mexico and the United States*. San Bernardino, Calif.: Borgo Press, 1993.

Alonso, Jorge, Alberto Aziz, and Jaime Tamayo, eds. *El nuevo estado Mexicano*. Vol. 2, *Estado y política*. México: Nueva Imagen, 1992.

———. *El nuevo estado Mexicano*. Vol. 3, *Estado, actores y movimientos sociales*. México: Nueva Imagen, 1992.

———. *El nuevo estado Mexicano*. Vol. 4, *Estado y sociedad*. México: Nueva Imagen, 1992.

Alvarado Mendoza, Arturo, ed. *Electoral Patterns and Perspectives in Mexico*. La Jolla: University of California–San Diego Center for U.S.-Mexican Studies, 1987.

Aziz Nassif, Alberto. *El estado Mexicano y la CTM*. México: La Casa Chata, 1989.

Aziz Nassif, Alberto, and Jacqueline Peschard, eds. *Las elecciones federales de 1991*. México: Centro de Investigaciones Interdiciplinarias en Humanidades—UNAM, 1992.

Baer, M. Delal, and Sidney Weintraub, eds. *The NAFTA Debate: Grappling with Unconventional Trade Issues*. Boulder, Colo.: Lynne Rienner Publishers, 1994.

Bagley, Bruce Michael, and Sergio Aguayo Qezada, eds. *Mexico: In Search of Security*. New Brunswick, N.J.: Transaction Publishers, 1993.

Bailey, John J. *Governing Mexico: The Statecraft of Crisis Management*. New York: St. Martin's Press, 1988.

Bailey, Norman, and Richard Cohen. *The Mexican Time Bomb*. Winchester, Mass.: Allen and Unwin, 1987.

Basáñez, Miguel. *La lucha por la hegamonia en México, 1968–1980*. México: Siglo XXI, 1982.

———. *El pulso de los sexenios: 20 años de crisis en México*. México: Siglo XXI, 1990.

Bethell, Leslie, ed. *Mexico since Independence*. New York: Cambridge University Press, 1991.

Bracher-Márquez, Viviene. *The Dynamics of Domination.* Pittsburgh: University of Pittsburgh Press, 1994.

Brothers, Dwight, and Adele Wick, eds. *Mexico's Search for a New Development Strategy.* Boulder, Colo.: Westview Press, 1990.

Bustamante, Jorge, Clark Reynolds, and Raúl Hinojosa Ojeda, eds. *U.S.-Mexican Relations: Labor Market Interdependence.* Stanford, Calif.: Stanford University Press, 1992.

Butler, Edgar W., and Jorge A. Bustamante, eds. *Sucesión Presidencial: The 1988 Presidential Election.* Boulder, Colo.: Westview Press, 1991.

Camp, Roderic A. "Family Relations in Mexican Politics." *Journal of Politics* 44 (August 1982): 848–62.

———. *Entrepreneurs and Politics in Twentieth-Century Mexico.* New York: Oxford University Press, 1989.

———. "Camarillas in Mexican Politics: The Case of the Salinas Cabinet." *Mexican Studies* 6, no. 1 (Winter 1990): 85–107.

———. *Generals in the Palacio: The Military in Modern Mexico.* New York: Oxford University Press, 1992.

———. *Politics in Mexico.* New York: Oxford University Press, 1993.

———. *Who's Who in Mexico Today.* 2d ed. Boulder, Colo.: Westview Press, 1993.

———. *Mexico's Political Stability: The Next Five Years.* Boulder, Colo.: Westview Press, 1986.

Cárdenas, Cuauhtémoc. "Misunderstanding Mexico." *Foreign Policy* (Winter 1989–90).

Casar, María Amparo. *The 1994 Mexican Presidential Elections.* London: Institute of Latin American Studies, 1995.

Centeno, Miguel Angel. *Mexico in the 1990s: Government and Opposition Speak Out.* La Jolla: University of California–San Diego Center for U.S.-Mexican Studies, 1991.

———. *Salinastroika or Gorbymania.* New York: Graduate School of the CUNY, 1992.

———. *Democracy within Reason: The Technocratic Revolution in Mexico.* University Park: Pennsylvania State University Press, 1994.

Cleaves, Peter S. *Professionals and the State: The Mexican Case.* Tucson: University of Arizona Press, 1987.

Collier, Ruth Berins. *The Contradictory Alliance: State-Labor Relations and Regime Change in Mexico.* Berkeley: IAS-University of California–Berkeley, 1992.

Cook, Maria Lorena, Kevin J. Middlebrook, and Juan Molinar Horcasitas, eds. *The Politics of Economic Restructuring.* La Jolla: University of California–San Diego Center for U.S.-Mexican Studies, 1994.

Cordera Campos, Rolando, Raúl Trejo Delarbre, and Juan Enrique Vega, eds. *México: El reclamo democrático.* México: Siglo XXI, 1988.

Cornelius, Wayne A., *Politics and the Migrant Poor in Mexico City.* Stanford, Calif.: Stanford University Press, 1975.

———. *The Political Economy of Mexico under de la Madrid.* La Jolla: University of California–San Diego Center for U.S.-Mexican Studies, 1986.

———. "Political Liberalization and the 1985 Elections in Mexico." In *Elections and Democratization in Latin America, 1980–1985,* ed. Paul W. Drake and Eduardo Silva. La Jolla: University of California–San Diego Center for Iberian and Latin American Studies, 1986.

Cornelius, Wayne A., and Jorge A. Bustamante, eds. *Mexican Migration to the United States.* La Jolla: University of California–San Diego Center for U.S.-Mexican Studies, 1989.

Cornelius, Wayne A., and Ann L. Craig. *The Mexican Political System in Transition.* La Jolla: University of California–San Diego Center for U.S.-Mexican Studies, 1991.

Cornelius, Wayne A., Judith Gentleman, and Peter H. Smith, eds. *Mexico's Alternative Political Futures.* La Jolla: University of California–San Diego Center for U.S.-Mexican Studies, 1989.

Cosio Villegas, Daniel. *El sistema político mexicano: las posibilidades de cambio.* México: Cuadernos de Joaquín Mortiz, 1972.

———, ed. *Historia moderna de México.* México: Hermes, 1963.

Cotner, Thomas E., and Carlos E. Castañeda, eds. *Essays in Mexican History.* Westport, Conn.: Greenwood Press, 1972.

Craig, Ann, and Wayne Cornelius, "Houses Divided: Parties and Political Reform in Mexico." In *Building Democratic Institutions: Party Systems in Latin America,* ed. Scott Mainwaring and Timothy Scully. Stanford, Calif.: Stanford University Press, 1995. 249–97.

Cumberland, Charles C. *Mexico: The Struggle for Modernity.* New York: Oxford University Press, 1968.

———, ed. *The Meaning of the Mexican Revolution.* Boston: D. C. Heath, 1967.

Cypher, James. *State and Capital in Mexico: Development Policy since 1940.* Boulder, Colo.: Westview Press, 1990.

Dresser, Denise. *Neopopulist Solutions to Neoliberal Problems: Mexico's National Solidarity Program.* La Jolla: University of California–San Diego Center for U.S.-Mexican Studies, 1991.

———. *Mr. Salinas Goes to Washington: Mexican Lobbying in Congress.* New York: Columbia-NYU Consortium, 1991.

Eckstein, Susan. *The Poverty of Revolution: The State and the Urban Poor in Mexico.* Princeton, N.J.: Princeton University Press, 1988.

Erb, Richard D., and Stanley R. Ross, eds. *United States Relations with Mexico.* Washington, D.C.: American Enterprise Institute, 1981.

Fagen, Richard R., and William S. Tuohy. *Politics and Privilege in a Mexican City.* Stanford, Calif.: Stanford University Press, 1972.

El Financiero. *Sucesión pactada: La ingeniera política del Salinismo.* México: Plaza y Valdes, 1993.

Foweraker, Joe. *Popular Mobilization in the Mexican Teachers Movement, 1977–87.* New York: Cambridge University Press, 1993.

Foweraker, Joe, and Ann L. Craig, eds. *Popular Movements and Political Change in Mexico.* Boulder, Colo.: Lynne Rienner Publishers, 1990.

Flores Lúa, Graciela, Luisa Paré, and Sergio Sarmiento Silva. *Las voces del campo: movimiento campesino y política agraria, 1976–1984.* México: Siglo XXI, 1988.

Gentleman, Judith, ed. *Mexican Politics in Transition.* Boulder, Colo.: Westview Press, 1987.

Gil, Carlos B., ed. *Hope and Frustration: Interviews with Leaders of Mexico's Political Opposition.* Wilmington, Del.: Scholarly Resources, 1992.

Glade, William, ed. *Privatization of Public Enterprises in Latin America.* La Jolla: ICS Press/University of California–San Diego Center for U.S.-Mexican Studies, 1991.

Globerman, Steven, and Michael Walker, eds. *Assessing NAFTA: A Trinational Analysis.* Vancouver, B.C.: Fraser Institute, 1993.

González Casanova, Pablo. *Democracy in Mexico.* New York: Oxford University Press, 1970.

──────. *La clase obrera en la historia de México.* México: Siglo XXI, 1985.

──────. *Elecciones en México.* México: Siglo XXI, 1985.

──────. *El estado y los partidos políticos en México.* 3d ed. México: Ediciones Era, 1986.

──────, ed. *Segundo informe sobre la democracia: México el 6 de Julio de 1988.* México: Siglo XXI, 1990.

González Graf, Jaime, ed. *Las elecciones de 1988 y la crisis del sistema político.* México: Editorial Diana, 1989.

Grayson, George. *Oil and Mexican Foreign Policy.* Pittsburgh: University of Pittsburgh Press, 1988.

──────. *Foreign Policy in U.S.-Mexican Relations.* La Jolla: University of California–San Diego Center for U.S.-Mexican Studies, 1989.

──────. *Prospects for Democracy in Mexico.* New Brunswick, N.J.: Transaction Publishers, 1990.

──────, ed. *The United States and Mexico: Patterns of Influence.* New York: Praeger Publishers, 1984.

Grindle, Merilee S. *Bureaucrats, Peasants, and Politicians in Mexico: A Case Study of Public Policy.* Berkeley: University of California Press, 1977.

──────. *Searching for Rural Development: Labor Migration and Employment in Mexico.* Ithaca, N.Y.: Cornell University Press 1988.

Grinspun, Ricardo, and Maxwell A. Cameron, eds. *The Political Economy of North American Free Trade.* New York: St. Martin's Press, 1993.

Haber, Stephen. *Industry and Underdevelopment: The Industrialization of Mexico, 1890–1940.* Stanford, Calif.: Stanford University Press, 1988.

Hamilton, Nora. *The Limits of State Autonomy: Post Revolutionary Mexico.* Princeton, N.J.: Princeton University Press, 1982.

Hamilton, Nora, and Timothy Harding, eds. *Modern Mexico: State, Economy, and Social Conflict.* Beverly Hills, Calif.: Sage Publications, 1986.

Harvey, Neil. *The New Agrarian Movement in Mexico.* London: Institute of Latin American Studies, 1990.

──────. *Mexico: Dilemmas of Transition.* London: University of London, Institute of Latin American Studies, 1993.

Hellman, Judith Adler. *Mexico in Crisis.* 2d ed. New York: Holmes and Meier, 1983.

Jauberth, H. Rodrigo, Gilberto Castañeda, Jesús Hernández, and Pedro Vuskovic. *The Difficult Triangle: Mexico, Central America, and the United States.* Boulder, Colo.: Westview Press, 1992.

Johnson, Kenneth F. *Mexican Democracy: A Critical View.* Rev. ed. New York: Praeger Publishers, 1978.

La Betz, Dan. *Mask of Democracy: Labor Suppression in Mexico Today.* Boston: South End Press, 1992.

Langley, Lester D. *Mexico and the United States: The Fragile Relationship.* Boston: Twayne Publishers, 1991.

Levy, Daniel C., and Kathleen Bruhn. "Mexico: Sustained Civilian Rule without Democracy." In *Politics in Developing Countries: Comparing Experiences with*

Democracy, ed. Larry Diamond, Juan J. Linz, and Seymour Martin Lipset. Boulder, Colo.: Lynne Rienner Publishers, 1995. 171–217.

Levy, Daniel, and Gabriel Székely. *Mexico: Paradoxes of Stability and Change*. 2d ed. Boulder, Colo.: Westview Press, 1987.

Loaeza, Soledad, and Rafael Segovia, eds. *La vida Mexicana política en crísis*. México: El Colegio de México, 1987.

Loaeza, Soledad, and Claudio Sterns, eds. *Las classes media en la conyuntura actual*. México: El Colegio de México, Cuadernos del CES, 1990.

Lomnitz, Larissa Adler. *Networks of Marginality*. New York: Academic Press, 1977.

———. *A Mexican Elite Family, 1820–1980*. Princeton, N.J.: Princeton University Press, 1987.

———. "El fondo de la forma: La campaña presidencial del PRI en 1988." *Nueva Antropología* 11, no. 38 (1990).

Lomnitz, Larissa Adler, Claudio Lomnitz-Adler, and Illya Adler. *El fondo de la forma: actos públicos de la campaña presidencial del Partido Revolucionario Institucional, México 1988*. Notre Dame, Ind.: Helen Kellogg Institute of International Studies, 1990.

Looney, Robert. *Economic Policymaking in Mexico*. Durham, N.C.: Duke University Press, 1985.

Lustig, Nora. *Mexico: The Remaking of an Economy*. Washington, D.C.: Brookings Institution, 1992.

———. *Poverty in Mexico*. Notre Dame, Ind.: Helen Kellogg Institute of International Studies, 1992.

Lustig, Nora, Barry P. Bosworth, and Robert Z. Lawrence, eds. *North American Free Trade: Assessing the Impact*. Washington, D.C.: Brookings Institution, 1992.

Mabry, Donald J. *Mexico's Acción Nacional: A Catholic Alternative to Revolution*. Syracuse, N.Y.: Syracuse University Press, 1973.

Maxfield, Sylvia. *Governing Capital: International Finance and Mexican Politics*. Ithaca, N.Y.: Cornell University Press, 1990.

Maxfield, Sylvia, and Ricardo Anzaldúa Montoya, eds. *Government and Private Sector in Contemporary Mexico*. La Jolla: University of California–San Diego Center for U.S.-Mexican Studies, 1987.

Maxfield, Sylvia, and Miguel Angel Centeno. *The Marriage of Finance and Order: . . . Change in the Mexican Elite*. New York: Columbia University Press, 1989.

Meyer, Lorenzo. *México frente a los Estados Unidos (1776–1988): un ensayo*. México: Fondo de Cultura Económica, 1989.

———. *La segunda muerte de la Revolución Mexicana*. México: Cal y Arena, 1992.

Meyer, Lorenzo, and Hector Auilar Camín. *In the Shadow of the Mexican Revolution (1910–1989)*. Austin: University of Texas Press, 1993.

Meyer, Lorenzo, and Isidro Morales. *Petróleo y la nación (1910–1987)*. México: Fondo de Cultura Económica, 1989.

Meyer, Michael, and William Sherman. *The Course of Mexican History*. 5th ed. New York: Oxford University Press, 1995.

Middlebrook, Kevin J. "Political Liberalization in an Authoritarian Regime: The Case of Mexico." In *Transitions from Authoritarian Rule: Latin America*, ed. Guillermo O'Donnell, Philippe C. Schmitter, and Laurence Whitehead. Baltimore, Md.: Johns Hopkins University Press, 1986.

————. "Union Democratization in the Mexican Automobile Industry." *Latin American Research Review* 24, no. 2 (1989): 69–93.

————, ed. *Unions, Workers and the State in Mexico*. La Jolla: University of California–San Diego Center for U.S.-Mexican Studies, 1991.

Miller, Robert Ryal. *Mexico: A History*. Norman: University of Oklahoma Press, 1985.

Molinar Horcasitas, Juan. "The Mexican Electoral System: Continuity in Change." In *Elections and Democratization in Latin America, 1980–1985*, ed. Paul W. Drake and Eduardo Silva. La Jolla: University of California–San Diego, 1986.

————. *El tiempo de la legitimidad: elecciones, autoritarismo y democracia en México*. México: Cal y Arena, 1991.

Moss, Ambler H., Jr., ed. *Assessments of the North American Free Trade Agreement*. New Brunswick, N.J.: Transaction Press, 1993.

Needler, Martin C., *Mexican Politics: The Containment of Conflict*. New York: Praeger Publishers, 1990.

Nuncio, Abrahám, ed. *La sucesión presidencial en 1988*. México: Grijalbo, 1988.

Parkes, Henry Bamford. *A History of Mexico*. 3d ed. Boston: Houghton Mifflin, 1960.

Pastor, Robert A. *Integration with Mexico: Options for U.S. Policy*. New York: Twentieth Century Fund Press, 1993.

Pastor, Robert A., and Jorge G. Castañeda. *Limits to Friendship: The United States and Mexico*. New York: Alfred A. Knopf, 1988.

Paz, Octavio. *The Labyrinth of Solitude: Life and Thought in Mexico*. New York: Grove Press, 1961.

Pérez Fernández del Castillo, Germán, et al., eds. *La voz de los votos: Un análisis crítico de las elecciones de 1994*. México: FLACSO, 1995.

Philip, George. *The Presidency in Mexican Politics*. New York: St. Martin's Press, 1991.

————, ed. *Politics in Mexico*. London: Croom Helm, 1985.

————, ed. *The Mexican Economy*. New York: Routledge, 1989.

Pozas, María de los Angeles. *Industrial Restructuring in Mexico*. La Jolla: University of California–San Diego Center for U.S.-Mexican Studies, 1993.

Purcell, Susan Kaufman, ed. *Mexico in Transition: Implications for U.S. Policy*. New York: Council on Foreign Relations, 1988.

Quirk, Robert E. *Mexico*. Englewood Cliffs, N.J.: Prentice-Hall, 1971.

Raat, W. Dirk. *Mexico and the United States: Ambivalent Vistas*. Athens: University of Georgia Press, 1992.

Ramírez, Miguel. *Mexico's Economic Crisis: Its Origins and Consequences*. New York: Praeger Publishers, 1989.

Randall, Stephen J., ed. *North America without Borders?* Calgary, Alberta: University of Calgary Press, 1992.

Reyna, José Luis, and Richard S. Weinert, eds. *Authoritarianism in Mexico*. Philadelphia: ISHI, 1977.

Riding, Alan. *Distant Neighbors*. New York: Vintage, 1984.

Rodríguez, Jaime E., ed. *The Revolutionary Process in Mexico: Essays on Political and Social Change, 1880–1940*. Los Angeles: UCLA Latin American Center, 1990.

Roett, Riordan. *Mexico and the United States*. Boulder, Colo.: Westview Press,

Roett, Riordan, ed. *Mexico's External Relations in the 1990s*. Boulder, Colo.: Lynne Rienner Publishers, 1991.

———, ed. *Political and Economic Liberalization in Mexico: At a Critical Juncture*. Boulder, Colo.: Lynne Rienner Publishers, 1993.

Ronfeldt, David, ed. *The Modern Mexican Military: A Reassessment*. La Jolla: University of California–San Diego Center for U.S.-Mexican Studies, 1984.

Roniger, Luis. *Hierarchy and Trust in Modern Mexico and Brazil*. New York: Praeger, 1990.

Roxborough, Ian. *Unions and Politics in Mexico: The Case of the Automobile Industry*. New York: Cambridge University Press, 1984.

Russell, Philip L., *Mexico under Salinas*. Austin, Tex.: Mexico Resource Center, 1994.

———. *The Chiapas Rebellion*. Austin, Tex.: Mexico Resource Center, 1995.

Sánchez Guttiérez, Arturo, ed. *Las elecciones de Salinas: un balance crítico a 1991*. México: FLACSO and Plaza y Valdes, 1992.

Saragoza, Alex M. *The Monterrey Elite and the Mexican State, 1880–1940*. Austin: University of Texas Press, 1988.

Schmidt, Samuel. *The Deterioration of the Mexican Presidency: The Years of Luis Echeverría*. Tucson: University of Arizona Press, 1991.

Semo, Ilán, et al. *La transición interrumpida: México 1968–1988*. México: Nueva Imagen, 1993.

Sheahan, John. *Conflict and Change in Mexican Economic Strategy*. La Jolla: University of California–San Diego Center for U.S.-Mexican Studies, 1991.

Smith, Peter H. *Labyrinths of Power: Political Recruitment in Twentieth-Century Mexico*. Princeton, N.J.: Princeton University Press, 1979.

———. *Mexico: Neighbors in Transition*. New York: Foreign Policy Association Headline Series, 1984.

———, ed. *Drug Policy in the Americas*. Boulder, Colo.: Westview Press, 1992.

Story, Dale. *Industry, the State, and Public Policy*. Austin: University of Texas Press, 1986.

———. *The Mexican Ruling Party*. New York: Praeger, 1986.

Székely, Gabriel. *Mexico and the United States*. México: Colegio de México, 1986.

———. "Dilemmas of Export Diversification in a Developing Economy." *World Development* 17, no. 11 (1989): 1777–97.

Tannenbaum, Frank. *The Struggle for Peace and Bread*. New York: Alfred A. Knopf, 1960.

———. *Peace by Revolution: Mexico after 1910*. 2d ed. New York: Columbia University Press, 1966.

Teichman, Judith. *Policymaking in Mexico: From Boom to Crisis*. Boulder, Colo.: Westview Press, 1988.

Thorup, Cathryn L., ed. *The United States and Mexico: Face to Face with New Technology*. New Brunswick, N.J.: Transaction Books, 1987.

Trejo Delarbre, Raul. *El espacio de silencio: la televisión Mexicana*. México: Edición Nuestro Tiempo, 1988.

———. *Así se calló el sistema: comunicaciones y elecciones en 1988*. Guadalajara: University of Guadalajara, 1991.

———. *La sociedad ausente*. México: Cal y Arena, 1992.

Villa Aguilera, Manuel. *La institución presidencial*. México: UNAM, 1987.

———. *A quién le interesa? La democracia en México.* México: Miguel Angel Porrúa, 1988.

Ward, Peter. *Welfare Politics in Mexico: Papering Over the Cracks.* Winchester, Mass.: Allen and Unwin, 1986.

———. *Mexico City: The Production and Reproduction of an Urban Environment.* London: Belhaven Press, 1990.

Weintraub, Sidney. *A Marriage of Convenience: Relations between Mexico and the United States: A Twentieth Century Fund Report.* New York: Oxford University Press, 1990.

———. *NAFTA: What Comes Next?* Westport, Conn.: Praeger, 1994.

———, ed. *Industrial Strategy and Planning in Mexico and the United States.* Boulder, Colo.: Westview Press, 1986.

Weintraub, Sidney, Luis Rubio F, and Alan Jones, eds. *U.S.-Mexican Industrial Integration.* Boulder, Colo.: Westview Press, 1991.

Wilkie, James W., Michael C. Meyer, and Edna Monzón de Wilkie, eds. *Contemporary Mexico: IV International Congress of Mexican History.* Berkeley: University of California Press, 1976.

Zoraida Vázquez, Josefina, and Lorenzo Meyer. *The United States and Mexico* Chicago: University of Chicago Press, 1985.

VALUABLE JOURNALS AND PERIODICALS

El Financiero. An excellent Mexican newspaper.

La Jornada. Perhaps the most informative Mexican newspaper.

Latin American Weekly Report. A weekly publication covering all of Latin America. Along with the various Regional Reports, it is one of the most respected and valuable sources of information on Mexico and the rest of Latin America.

Mexican Studies/Estudios Mexicanos. A scholarly journal published by the University of California Press.

Mexico and NAFTA Report (Latin American Regional Report). One of a series of British publications that cover all Latin American regions on a rotating basis.

Nexos. A respected Mexican scholarly journal.

Proceso. The most authoritative Mexican newsmagazine.

Index